Legislative Effectiveness in the United States Congress
The Lawmakers

This book explores why some members of Congress are more effective than others at navigating the legislative process and what such differences imply for how Congress is organized and what policies it produces. Craig Volden and Alan E. Wiseman develop a new metric of individual lawmaker effectiveness (the Legislative Effectiveness Score) that will be of interest to scholars, voters, and politicians alike. They use these scores to study party influence, the successes or failures of women and African Americans in Congress, policy gridlock, and the specific strategies that lawmakers employ to advance their agendas.

Craig Volden is Professor of Public Policy and Politics, with appointments in the Frank Batten School of Leadership and Public Policy and the Woodrow Wilson Department of Politics at the University of Virginia. He has published numerous articles in such journals as the *American Political Science Review, American Journal of Political Science, Journal of Politics, Legislative Studies Quarterly, Journal of Law, Economics & Organization,* and *Publius: The Journal of Federalism.* Volden is a coauthor (with David W. Brady) of *Revolving Gridlock: Politics and Policy from Jimmy Carter to George W. Bush* (2006).

Alan E. Wiseman is Associate Professor of Political Science, with a secondary appointment in Law at Vanderbilt University. He has published numerous articles in peer-reviewed journals such as the *American Political Science Review, American Journal of Political Science, Journal of Politics, Legislative Studies Quarterly,* and *Journal of Theoretical Politics.* He is the author of *The Internet Economy: Access, Taxes, and Market Structure* (2000).

Legislative Effectiveness in the United States Congress

The Lawmakers

CRAIG VOLDEN
University of Virginia

ALAN E. WISEMAN
Vanderbilt University

CAMBRIDGE
UNIVERSITY PRESS

CAMBRIDGE
UNIVERSITY PRESS

32 Avenue of the Americas, New York NY 10013-2473, USA

Cambridge University Press is part of the University of Cambridge.

It furthers the University's mission by disseminating knowledge in the pursuit of education, learning and research at the highest international levels of excellence.

www.cambridge.org
Information on this title: www.cambridge.org/9780521152266

First published 2014

A catalogue record for this publication is available from the British Library

Library of Congress Cataloguing in Publication data
Volden, Craig.
Legislative effectiveness in the United States Congress : the lawmakers / Craig Volden, Alan E. Wiseman.
    pages   cm
ISBN 978-0-521-76152-9 (Hardback)
1. United States. Congress.   2. United States – Politics and government.   3. Coalition governments – United States.   I. Wiseman, Alan E.   II. Title.
JK1021.V65   2014
328.73–dc23   2014011962

ISBN 978-0-521-76152-9 Hardback
ISBN 978-0-521-15226-6 Paperback

For more on the Legislative Effectiveness Project, and to browse the Legislative Effectiveness Scores for all Representatives in Congress, see www.thelawmakers.org. Check back often for updates.

Contents

Tables and Figures

FIGURES

Acknowledgments

As detailed in the pages of our book, effective lawmaking requires both perseverance and collaboration. To the extent that we ourselves have been effective in undertaking this scholarly endeavor, the same two traits have been essential.

In terms of perseverance, the origins of this project date back to October 2006 when we were both members of the political science faculty at The Ohio State University. Our offices were around the corner from each other on the second floor of Derby Hall, and we had lunch together nearly every day to discuss research, classes, politics, and far less important matters. Having come from the same graduate program in the Stanford University Graduate School of Business, we often saw political science research through similar lenses, and had each built early careers by entering into scholarly debates and attempting to advance them with new theoretical models and empirical investigations.

What had mostly escaped us, however, was the degree to which the political science field had fallen largely silent on many important issues of the day. Our discussions eventually came to the topic of overcoming policy gridlock, with the question of which specific lawmakers can "get things done" in Congress. The topic was both sufficiently ignored within political science and sufficiently intriguing to us, such that we began to dive into in-depth conversations about how we could systematically detect the most effective members of Congress and use those measures to better understand the workings of Congress itself and the nature of the public policies it produces.

That is when the need for perseverance began. Developing a series of computer programs to collect all the information on bill sponsorship in the House of Representatives and convert such raw data into easily interpretable and useful measures was itself a multi-year project. Analysis and writing followed, albeit with happy interruptions for the births and infancy of children (one for Alan and two for Craig) and with relocations (Alan to Vanderbilt and Craig to Virginia). While each such event delayed the move to completion, they also served to improve the final product. Sleep-deprived nights lead not only to crazy ideas that are nonsensical but also to crazy ideas that turn out to be valuable. Meeting new colleagues and teaching new classes not only takes time but also opens up different and valuable perspectives on how best to present new ideas to diverse audiences.

Along the journey, we built up numerous debts to colleagues, research assistants, students, friends, and family, which we can only partially repay by finally acknowledging them here. It is here that the collaborative nature of lawmaking is mimicked by the collaborative work needed for our scholarly endeavor.

As we were writing, we distributed chapters widely, as soon as we felt that they were sufficiently polished, to a collection of scholars who we hoped would provide us with some feedback regarding our approach, our characterizations of the extant literatures, and (what they deemed to be) our major findings. It is always a bit of a gamble circulating draft chapters to as many as thirty people, as one never knows how many, if any, will have a sufficiently flexible schedule (and find the topic of sufficient interest) to take the time to read and offer genuinely constructive feedback on the materials they have received. On this point, however, we were not disappointed. We think that it is fair to say that the legislative studies community sets a pretty high bar for its general collegiality and willingness to offer constructive criticism of their colleagues' work. (In fact, one of our colleagues has, in the past, compared the annual legislative studies section at the APSA meetings to "a family reunion … but one where the family members actually like one another.") If the scope and depth of responses that we received from our colleagues are any indication, the tradition of collegiality and constructive feedback is definitely alive and well among contemporary scholars of legislative politics.

Over the past several years, we have received particularly constructive written and oral feedback on various aspects of the project from numerous colleagues including Claire Abernathy, Scott Adler, John Aldrich, Mike Bailey, Larry Bartels, Jim Battista, Larry Baum, Paul Beck, Bill Bendix, Ken Benoit, Chris Berry, Janet Boles, Jan Box-Steffensmeier, David Brady, Barry Burden, Dan Butler, Greg Caldeira, David Canon, Cliff Carrubba, Jamie Carson, Josh Clinton, Joshua Cohen, Gerry Connolly, Kimberly Beth Cowell-Meyers, Gary Cox, Kathy Dolan, Jamie Druckman, Diana Evans, Mo Fiorina, Juanita Firestone, Gerald Gamm, John Geer, John Griffin, Jacob Hacker, Rick Hall, Kerry Haynie, Alex Hirsch, Matt Hitt, John Hudak, Molly Jackman, Jeff Jenkins, Bill Keech, Luke Keele, Keith Krehbiel, Chris Kypriotis, Dave Lewis, Tony Madonna, Lauren Mattioli, Nolan McCarty, Sid Milkis, William Minozzi, Mike Neblo, Eric Patashnik, John Patty, Kathryn Pearson, Carl Pinkele, Keith Poole, Beth Reingold, Rip Ripley, Jason Roberts, Dave Rohde, Kira Sanbonmatsu, Lynn Sanders, Wendy Schiller, Ken Shepsle, Chuck Shipan, Ken Shotts, Barbara Sinclair, Betsy Sinclair, Theda Skocpol, Steve Smith, Jed Stiglitz, Tracy Sulkin, Michele Swers, Andrew Taylor, Sean Theriault, Sophie Trawalter, Rick Valelly, Georg Vanberg, Denise Walsh, Gerry Warburg, Greg Wawro, John Wilkerson, and Jack Wright. In addition to these colleagues who offered valuable feedback, Sarah Binder, Laurel Harbridge, and Eric Schickler deserve special thanks for offering insightful feedback on almost every draft chapter of the manuscript; and Bruce Oppenheimer deserves particular praise for his willingness to read, and offer timely feedback on, nearly every page of the manuscript. This book is unambiguously stronger because of the collective feedback we received from these colleagues, and we are grateful for their time and support.

In addition to the insights of these colleagues, the book has benefited immensely from feedback we received at numerous research workshops and conference presentations including seminars at the Batten School at the University of Virginia, the Center for the Study of Democratic Institutions at Vanderbilt University, the College of William and Mary, Columbia University, Duke University, the Emory Conference on Institutions and Lawmaking, Georgetown University, the Harris School at the University of Chicago, the London School of Economics and Political Science, Northwestern University, The Ohio State University Research in American Politics Workshop, Stanford University, the University of Georgia, the University of Michigan, the University of North Carolina–Chapel Hill, the University of Pittsburgh, the University of Wisconsin–Madison (on two separate occasions), and Vanderbilt University Law School. These seminars were extremely helpful as we strived to refine our arguments, identify which points resonated with different audiences, and (similar to the written feedback that we received from our colleagues) ensure that we were engaging the relevant literatures in the appropriate manners. We are grateful for the invitations that we received to present our work in these forums.

Along the way, we published initial findings from the Legislative Effectiveness Project in a variety of venues. Portions of Chapter 2 were originally published in an essay entitled "Legislative Effectiveness and Representation" in the 10th edition of *Congress Reconsidered* (eds. Larry Dodd and Bruce Oppenheimer, 2012), and we appreciate CQ Press's willingness to let us incorporate materials from that essay into this book. Chapter 4 draws on material from an article entitled "When Are Women More Effective Lawmakers Than Men?" which was coauthored with Dana E. Wittmer and published in the *American Journal of Political Science* (2013), and we appreciate Wiley Press's willingness to let us incorporate materials from that article into this book. Additionally, some of the material in Chapter 5 is drawn from an earlier essay entitled "Breaking Gridlock: The Determinants of Health Policy Change in Congress" that was published in 2011 in the *Journal of Health Politics, Policy and Law*, and we appreciate Duke University Press's willingness to allow us to incorporate materials from that essay into this book.

We also thank James Austrow, Maddie Bergner, Zach Blackburn, Tracy Burdett, Ken Gillette, Matt Hitt, Chris Kypriotis, Katy Lai, Lauren Mattioli, Brian Pokosh, Rachel Schneider, and Nicholas Zeppos, Jr., for outstanding research assistance at various stages of the project. Moreover, Claire Abernathy deserves special praise, as her enthusiastic research support was instrumental in collecting much of the material that served as the foundation for the narratives in Chapter 6, as well as providing help on other aspects of the project; and Dana Wittmer's efforts are also highly appreciated, as they contributed greatly to some of the arguments that we make in Chapter 4 (which led to the aforementioned collaboration).

We appreciate the collaboration and perseverance offered by our publisher, Cambridge University Press. From our early interactions with Ed Parsons (and his unflagging enthusiasm and support) through the recent efforts of Lew Bateman, Shaun Vigil, Sumitha Nithyanandan, and Mark Fox, as well as all of the Cambridge team, we greatly value the time and direction they have offered to improve the manuscript at every stage of its development.

Beyond the appreciation that we extend to those who provided guidance and formal assistance with the book, both of us enjoyed immense support of many others who offered less direct feedback on the manuscript but whose contributions were greatly felt nonetheless. Craig thanks the numerous colleagues who offered him kindness and support at The Ohio State University. The research that led to this book could not have been accomplished without the financial and logistical support given by the OSU Political Science Department. Craig is blessed in the continued friendship he receives from many of his former OSU colleagues. In moving to the University of Virginia, he is grateful to the faculty, staff, and students of the Frank Batten School of Leadership and Public Policy, who taught him to better understand the leadership roles played by effective lawmakers in Congress. He especially thanks Eric Patashnik and Harry Harding, who were instrumental in bringing about his move to Virginia, and also those in the Politics Department who offered a second home at UVa, including the support and friendship of Jeff Jenkins and David Leblang.

Alan also greatly appreciates the help and support he received from his colleagues at The Ohio State University, where this project began, and the constant encouragement, feedback, and prodding from Jack Wright, in particular, who challenged, and continues to challenge, him in his various research pursuits. Moving away from Ohio State, he is grateful to the Vanderbilt community, and especially thankful to Josh Clinton, Carolyn Dever, John Geer, David Lewis, Bruce Oppenheimer, and Chancellor Nick Zeppos for helping bring him to Vanderbilt University; and he appreciates the professional and personal support he has received at Vanderbilt, including in the Center for the Study of Democratic Institutions, which helped make this work notably stronger than what might have been obtained if he hadn't joined the Vanderbilt family. Since arriving at Vanderbilt, he has also benefited from the friendship of Cindy Kam and Robert Mikos (and Charlotte and Henry), who have gone out of their way to welcome him and the rest of his family to Nashville; and he greatly appreciates the feedback and support from Tracey George, whose enthusiasm for this project has proved to be infectious at times.

David Brady is thanked for providing both Alan and Craig with the resources to spend time in residence at the Hoover Institution, which led to several constructive conversations with various scholars-in-residence at Stanford University. David Baron is thanked for being an incredibly conscientious and patient teacher to Alan during his graduate school days, helping provide him with the tools necessary to develop and analyze theoretical models of politics. Keith Krehbiel is thanked for encouraging both Alan and Craig in their interest in Congress, for being instrumental in helping them learn how to think like political scientists as graduate students, and for continuing to be an outstanding teacher, colleague, and friend for nearly twenty years.

Moving beyond professional colleagues, we thank our parents, Cec and Dave Lambeth, Ron and Diane Volden, and Israel and Trudy Wiseman, and our brothers and sisters-in-law, Rob and Robin Volden, Tom and Kristen Volden, and David and Jennifer Wiseman, who have been constant sources of support and inspiration. Craig is thankful each and every day for the unconditional love and boundless joy offered by Andrea, Isabel, and Gabriel. Alan is most appreciative of Kelly Wang and Madeleine Wiseman for always being a source of inspiration, humor, and joyful times in his life. Though neither of them truthfully has a clue as to what much of his job is about, they both continue to be supportive of him in all of his professional endeavors, and to show him all of the reasons that he has so much to be grateful for.

We wrote this book for four main audiences with four overlapping goals. First, for academic scholars of the U.S. Congress, we hope that this work will draw their attention to new and intriguing findings regarding the lawmaking process, which will stimulate further empirical and theoretical scholarship on the ways in which individual lawmakers, when faced with various institutional constraints, create policy. Second, for students of American politics, both graduate and undergraduate, we're hopeful that the findings in this book pique their interest about the workings of the U.S. Congress (and especially the effectiveness of congressional lawmakers), such that they pursue these topics in further scholarly inquiries, becoming the next generation of legislative scholars. Third, for journalists, political commentators, and readers interested broadly in American politics, we hope that the findings in this book complement and extend their understandings of the contemporary lawmaking process.

Finally, for American voters and citizens at large, we hope that a renewed focus on the effectiveness of our representatives helps turn our politics away from polarized and partisan deadlock and toward demands to confront the major problems faced by our nation, and that citizens will increasingly support those leaders who are willing and able to overcome those differences and actually get things done in Washington once again. We hope to stimulate a broad discussion about what it means to be an effective lawmaker and to facilitate a greater appreciation for those whose perseverance and collaborative efforts do not merely pass policy problems off to future generations. In this respect, we wrote this book for our own children, who are themselves just learning to read, in the hopes that our own peculiar efforts will in some small way help leave them a better world. It is to them that we dedicate this book.

I

Introduction

Participation in Congress is seldom universal. It is never equal.
                    – Richard L. Hall. *Participation in Congress* (1996, p. 2)

As the lawmakers left their hometowns and cities scattered across the mountains, prairies, and shores of the United States, they carried with them the goals and concerns of the American people who voted them into office. Arriving in Washington to start the 110th Congress, excitement and ambition were particularly high among Democrats. They had just recaptured the House of Representatives after twelve years of Republican control. They had an opportunity to oppose President George W. Bush in the final years of his second term, and to advance their own agendas in hopes of setting the stage for Democratic control of the presidency in the 2008 elections. Between early 2007 and the fall of 2008, these men and women could confront the president on the unpopular Iraq War and on his tax cuts for big corporations and wealthy Americans. They could also attempt to take the country in new directions, with minimum wage increases, green energy policies, and health policy reforms.

Yet, beyond their collective concerns, each lawmaker was keenly aware of the many local needs of constituents back home. Experienced Democrats knew that this was an opportunity they should not take for granted. Those senior members who had entered Congress under Democratic control prior to the 1994 Republican Revolution had seen the difference in what they could accomplish in the majority party or the minority party. Would they make the most of the situation to help their constituents back home? How effective would they be in advancing their own policy agendas?

Four such senior Democrats each entered Congress with policy goals for themselves, their districts, and all Americans. Earl Pomeroy represented the entire state of North Dakota, with its vast rural landscape. Would he be able to help the agricultural sector, address concerns of Native Americans, or direct federal funds toward renewable energy given the great potential for wind power in the state? Next door, Jim Oberstar represented Minnesota's 8th district, including the city of Duluth on Lake Superior. Would he be able to address needs in the Great Lakes area, or to provide support for the railroad industry given the confluence of rail traffic through his district from the upper Midwest and southern Canada? Would he be able to advance even more localized concerns, such as the need for a hospital in rural Cass County?

Further east, Dale Kildee represented Michigan's 5th District. Like Pomeroy, Kildee was interested in policies to address the needs of Native Americans, and particularly the Saginaw Chippewa Tribe in his district. Like Oberstar, Kildee was interested in Great Lakes policy, with parts of his district nestled on the shores of Lake Huron. But, with the city of Flint playing a central role in his district, Kildee was also deeply concerned about the auto industry and international trade. And, for a variety of reasons, he was also personally concerned about advancing educational opportunities for children. Finally, in New York's 21st District, Mike McNulty was sent to Congress to represent Albany, Schenectady, and much of the Mohawk River Valley. How effective would he be at advancing policies to help the region's hydroelectric power plants and its textile industry?

Although each had different goals and agendas, these four lawmakers all looked relatively similar to one another. They were all white, male members of the majority party. They had all served in Congress for many terms; in fact, the least senior of the four was starting his ninth term, having served for sixteen years. They were all coming from relatively safe districts, with their previous vote margins ranging from 64 percent to 74 percent. None of the four members held formal positions of party leadership, and none of the four had previously served as committee chairs in the House. How would these otherwise quite similar lawmakers use their institutional positions and legislative skills to advance their policy agendas?

The first and most fundamental tool every member of Congress has at his or her disposal is the ability to sponsor a piece of legislation, in an attempt to change the laws of the land and make policy perhaps a bit better for the people whom they represent. Yet members differ in how much they take advantage of their sponsorship opportunities. Of our four lawmakers, Pomeroy and Oberstar introduced the most legislation in the 110th Congress by far, with thirty-six and thirty-nine bills, respectively. In contrast, Kildee introduced eleven bills, whereas McNulty introduced only five bills. In thinking about these numbers, it seems that the differences in the sizes of legislative portfolios cannot be easily explained by such factors as committee assignments. McNulty and Pomeroy were both members of the House Committee on Ways and Means (a traditional "power" committee), yet they had starkly different policy agendas. Likewise, while not sitting on power committees, Oberstar and Kildee both sat on major substantive committees (as Chair of Transportation and Infrastructure for Oberstar, and on Natural Resources and on Education and Labor for Kildee); yet they, too, introduced notably different amounts of legislation.

Moving beyond simple introductions, however, there is also a question regarding the policy focus of the different bills. While Oberstar and Pomeroy both introduced almost forty bills, the majority of their introductions came from one issue area, with Oberstar introducing twenty transportation-related measures, and Pomeroy introducing nineteen bills that engaged taxation and revenue issues. Such introduction patterns seem quite sensible given their respective committee assignments. In contrast to the focus of these portfolios, however, Kildee and McNulty not only introduced much less legislation, but their respective policy portfolios were also relatively more diffuse.

Yet each lawmaker sought in no small measure to address his constituents' needs. Pomeroy focused much of his agenda on issues of importance to North Dakota, such as farming, rural education, and energy. Oberstar introduced bills dealing with the Great Lakes and railroads, as well as one for the Cass County hospital. Kildee spent his efforts on trade in the automotive industry, Native Americans, and college access and Head Start for kids. And McNulty's legislation dealt with the Mohawk River Hydroelectric Projects and with textiles. Additionally, each advocated for agenda items that may not have been obvious given their districts, such as Pomeroy's beer-tax reduction bill, Oberstar's Appalachian regional development bill, or McNulty's identity theft prevention bill. Were such agenda items being introduced to further the interests of other legislators, perhaps because Pomeroy, Oberstar, and McNulty held institutional positions of influence that others lacked?

The sum of these sponsored bills offers a glimpse into the needs and aspirations of constituents from back home. These legislative suggestions are the instruments by which American democracy is designed to translate good ideas into public policy. Yet by the end of the legislative term, two of these four legislators would not have succeeded in passing a single piece of their sponsored legislation; one would shepherd more than half of his agenda into law; and one would be considered among the most effective lawmakers in the 110th Congress. Who would succeed and who would fail? Why are some members able to translate their policy proposals into public law, while others are routinely ignored and dismissed? And what is it about these four members in particular that might explain their relative levels of legislative effectiveness?

Regardless of profession, from salespeople to journalists to major league sluggers, some individuals simply outperform their peers. Lawmakers are no different. It takes a certain set of political skills (and the right political circumstances) to formulate a viable solution to a major public policy problem, to construct a coalition in support of that solution, and to shepherd the related legislation through committee, across the floor, and into law. Uncovering the personal and institutional characteristics that lead some members of Congress to be more effective legislators than others is crucial to understanding the American system of political representation and public policy formation. At a time when public satisfaction with Congress is at historic lows, assessing the opportunities for effective lawmaking is particularly important.[1]

The problems faced by the modern American society are immense, ranging from the threat of terrorism to the new challenges of the information age, from concerns about the national debt to fears about climate change. The nation needs leaders who can help address these problems. It needs effective lawmakers who can move ideas into policy. Some of these new policies will help solve the country's problems. Others will be ineffective, needing to be revised or abandoned later. Still others will create altogether new problems to be overcome. Indeed, the public policy process is uncertain and prone to error. One thing is clear, however. Absent effective leaders to address societal problems, our system of representative democracy cannot thrive.[2] With such leaders, it may or may not thrive, depending on the choices that they make.

The need for effective leadership was expressed in more colorful terms by Sam Rayburn (D-TX), who served as Speaker of the House through much of the 1940s and 1950s. He is credited with declaring: "Any jackass can kick down a barn, but it takes a good carpenter to build one."[3] Throughout his term, Rayburn saw the need for more of the latter in Congress, and fewer of the former.[4] Such is no less true today.

The search for good carpenters – for "effective lawmakers," in our terms – is central to this book. Throughout, we aim to engage two broad questions in American politics. First, why are some members of Congress more effective than others at navigating the lawmaking process? And second, what does this variation across members imply for the organization of Congress and the creation of public policy in the contemporary American political system? In engaging the first question, we seek to uncover what personal characteristics, as well as institutional factors, contribute to (or detract from) a given legislator's effectiveness in Congress. Our investigation leads us to examine how factors such as gender, race, and previous experiences influence different legislators' careers and

---

[1] A *Real Clear Politics* analysis of public opinion polls that were conducted between January 5 and February 3, 2014, revealed that approximately 13 percent of Americans approved of the job Congress was doing, whereas more than 81 percent of Americans expressed disapproval. Retrieved from http://www.realclearpolitics.com/epolls/other/congressional_job_approval-903 .html, accessed on February 6, 2014.

[2] Related to this point, recent history is rife with examples of how other branches of government, and the president in particular (i.e., Howell 2003; Moe and Howell 1999; Oppenheimer 2013), may step in to fill the power vacuum when Congress is unable to formulate new policies, in spite of pressing national issues.

[3] For instance, see *Time Magazine*, "The Congress: The Prelude of the 83rd," January 12, 1953.

[4] Moreover, before becoming Speaker of the House, Rayburn served as a member, and then chair, of the Interstate and Foreign Commerce Committee, where he facilitated the creation and passage of numerous prominent pieces of legislation such as the Securities Act of 1933, the Securities Exchange Act of 1934 (which created the Securities and Exchange Commission), and the Public Utilities Act of 1935. As discussed in Caro (1982, chapter 18), Rayburn clearly demonstrated significant legislative skill in the years before he became Speaker.

their productivity in the U.S. House of Representatives, and how these features have varied in importance over time. In engaging the second question, we identify how the activities of effective legislators in different issue areas facilitate the creation of new public policies.

The concept that some members of Congress are more effective than others comports well with conventional wisdom and modern parlance. When Representative Dan Rostenkowski (D-IL) was forced to resign his chairmanship of the Ways and Means Committee in the wake of a scandal in 1994, commentators were quick to note that legislators

like Mr. Rostenkowski are needed who can close a deal, who can put together a majority behind a delicate piece of legislation, and few of them are left. His fall from power as chairman of the Ways and Means Committee changes the calculus of health insurance legislation this year and opens questions about how well the House of Representatives will be able to handle other difficult matters.[5]

Even those who traditionally criticized Rostenkowsi, such as *Chicago Tribune* columnist Mike Royko, readily conceded that he knew

how to cut through the bunk, make a deal, twist an arm, do a favor, call in a chit, and move point A to point Z without a lot of philosophical mumbo jumbo.... [These] are rare skills in Washington, where most congressional creatures – even their hired flunkies – are babbling exhibitionists.[6]

Finally, when Rostenkowski passed away in the summer of 2010, the obituaries and editorials upon his death were decidedly mixed in opinion as to whether his legacy would be that of a hero or a thief. Yet a common thread in nearly all of the memorials was that Rostenkowski was an incredibly effective legislator during his time in Congress.[7]

More recently (and not involving the specter of a scandal), in discussing the influence of Representative Henry Waxman (D-CA) in 2009, Speaker Nancy Pelosi (D-CA) argued that "almost every aspect of people's lives has been affected by

---

[5] Quote from Rosenbaum (1994). It is important to note that being an effective legislator should not necessarily be equated with being a policy wonk. Very few observers of congressional politics would argue that Rostenkowski was intimately familiar with the complicated details of many of the policies that he advanced through his committee; but, as Rosenbaum and others argue, Rostenkowski was quite adept at identifying what was politically feasible, and knowing who he could rely on (whether it be other Representatives or staff members) to cultivate the specific legislative details that would serve Representatives' varying needs, to engender their support.

[6] Quote from Royko (1994).

[7] A parsimonious sample of these sentiments can be found in Charles Madigan's April 13, 2010, editorial in the *Chicago Tribune*, entitled "Dealmaking and Downfall," in which he argues that "Rostenkowski delivered for Chicago in heroic proportions across the careers of five mayors, perhaps the only consistent and dependable piece of government from Daley to Daley. He made bold threats in exchange for dollars that saved theaters here or fixed messes there or helped rebuild neighborhoods. He sure loved his dealing.... He did business the way all smart businesspeople in Washington did business. He did it the way that worked."

Chairman Waxman – generic drug safety, clean air, so many things. ... [He] has really been an effective, effective legislator."[8] And these observations about Waxman's effectiveness were not reserved to his legislative allies. When Waxman assumed the chairmanship of the House Energy and Commerce Committee, Thomas Pyle, president of the Institute for Energy Research, noted that "Waxman is as liberal as it gets; and he's a very effective legislator." Thus, his rise to the chair position will provide "about as hostile a climate as there could possibly be" for energy providers.[9] Similarly, upon naming Representative Rahm Emanuel as White House Chief of Staff in November of 2008, president-elect Barack Obama commented, "No one I know is better at getting things done than Rahm Emanuel." And Republicans like Senator Lindsey Graham (R-SC) conceded, "Rahm knows Capitol Hill and has great political skills."[10]

These observations about varying degrees of legislative effectiveness are not confined to commentators and journalists. Political scientists have long believed that such classifications of "being effective" or "getting things done" are important to understanding legislative politics. In the 1950s, David Truman discussed how the effectiveness of skilled legislators influences the congressional agenda, in that "legislative skill, usually acquired only after considerable experience in the law-making body, creates its own following; less experienced or overly busy members will often be guided by the skilled veteran."[11] In the 1970s, Richard Fenno pointed to how legislative effectiveness is advertised by incumbents on the campaign trail, and how "to the extent possible – even if it requires a bit of imagination – members will picture themselves as effective users of inside power" when meeting with constituents.[12] Moreover, in the 1990s, David Mayhew eloquently noted that legislative effectiveness is ostensibly a necessary precondition for political career advancement: "Like power contenders in the Roman Republic who headed for Gaul or Spain to win battles, would-be presidents try to score points by showing they can actually do something – pass laws."[13] Hence, one would naturally suspect that a legislator's ability to move bills through the legislative process would have a direct bearing on the types of coalitions that she participated in, on her electoral security, and on the viability of her career progression onto higher office.[14]

More broadly speaking, it is fair to argue that individual and collective legislative effectiveness is a fundamental feature of practically every aspect of legislative policymaking, profoundly influencing American public policy. For example, scholarly research and conventional wisdom suggests that the majority party in Congress exerts substantial influence on policy outcomes, both through

---

[8] Quoted by O'Connor (2009).
[9] Quoted by Woellert (2008).
[10] Quotations taken from CNN.com, November 6, 2008.
[11] See Truman (1951, 344–345).
[12] See Fenno (1978, 137).
[13] See Mayhew (1991, 110).
[14] To avoid the awkward gender-neutral "he or she" and "his or her" language, we refer to generic members of Congress in feminine terms throughout the book.

its institutional advantages and in how it pressures its members. Yet little is known about how parties facilitate the strategic activities of their most effective members, who are crucial to advancing the parties' policy goals. With respect to representation, women and minorities serve a critical role within Congress. Yet does this role allow them to serve their constituencies as equally effective lawmakers? Additionally, the extent to which Congress as a collective body can develop meaningful policy solutions depends on the effectiveness of members and on how well such members are positioned within the organizational structure of Congress. The precise relationships between legislative effectiveness and these matters of partisan politics, representation, and policy advancement, however, have remained opaque. They are the focus of our inquiry.

Given the importance of these concepts, the legislative effectiveness of members of Congress is a surprisingly and sorely understudied topic in political science. While the above notable scholars recognize its importance in passing, and while an occasional article finds its way into scholarly journals, the questions of who can get things done in Congress, why, and with what effects have suffered from widespread neglect.[15] Far more often, members of Congress are characterized not in terms of their effectiveness, but instead solely by their party label or by their ideological stances, ranging from highly liberal to very conservative and everywhere in between.[16] Legislative scholars have spent enormous energy measuring the ideological *ideal points* of members of Congress, and rightly so. Based on *spatial models* of legislative politics, countless researchers have shed light on the role of political parties and party factions, on whether Representatives accurately represent their constituents, on the relationship between representation patterns (i.e., roll-call votes) and electoral success, on the match between descriptive representation by race and gender and substantive policy representation, and on the causes and effects of policy gridlock.

Yet we argue that all of these important topics (and many more) can instead be approached and examined through the lens of legislative effectiveness, and that such an approach will in many ways be more insightful. For instance, with a focus on members' effectiveness, we can study the importance of party status in advancing legislation through each stage of the lawmaking process, crucially uncovering where in the policy process majority-party members enjoy the greatest advantage. We can link the representation of women and minorities in Congress to their institutional strength, and thus better understand how the legislative strategies at their disposal influence the success or failure of their policy initiatives. And we can examine legislative stalemate across issue areas, yielding greater insight into how

---

[15] Throughout the book, we discuss earlier scholarly contributions relative to our own, with the greatest detail offered in Chapter 2.

[16] Fiorina (2011) and Mayhew (2011) both provide elegant recent reviews of prominent schools and thematic highlights in congressional scholarship over the past 40–100+ years. Clearly absent from either scholars' characterization of the literature is any body of work that speaks to some aspect of legislative effectiveness, as we have described it here.

political entrepreneurs and policy experts overcome policy gridlock. We take on all of these tasks here in an attempt to showcase the value of measuring legislative effectiveness and of using such measures to ask and answer questions, both new and old, about the workings of Congress.

More specifically, in Chapter 2 we develop a Legislative Effectiveness Score (LES) for each member of the House of Representatives in each Congress from the 93rd to the 110th (corresponding to the years 1973–2008). This chapter serves four broad purposes. First, it offers an example of applied measurement theory, illustrating how broad concepts in political science can be defined, how indicators of the concepts can be identified and then combined into a systematic measure, and finally how researchers can explore the measure's validity. Of course, the context for this exploration of measurement theory is the development of the LES. Here, as the second contribution for Chapter 2, we combine fifteen indicators of effectiveness, accounting for the number of bills introduced by each member of Congress and bill progression across five key lawmaking stages, for each of three levels of bill significance, all relative to the effectiveness of each other member of the House.

Third, we explore the robustness of the LES to alternative formulations, such as those that place different weightings on the various stages of legislative progression or those that take amendment activities more fully into consideration. And finally, we explore the characteristics of effective lawmakers, such as the importance of being a majority-party member, a committee leader, more senior, or from an electorally safe seat. In combination, in Chapter 2 we demonstrate how legislators with some degree of innate lawmaking abilities can cultivate a skill set and rely on their institutional positions to become highly effective in advancing their legislative agendas. We illustrate these findings by returning to the four lawmakers introduced at the start of this current chapter, offering an LES Scorecard for each and a discussion of why they became more or less effective in the 110th Congress.

In the subsequent chapters, we rely upon our measure of legislative effectiveness and expand it in a variety of directions to address some of the most important questions about the workings of Congress today. For example, in Chapter 3, we take an in-depth look at the initial finding that members in the majority party are more effective than members in the minority party. Although the vast majority of scholarly studies of party effects in Congress have focused on floor-voting patterns, there are good reasons to believe that the source of majority-party strength arises much earlier in the lawmaking process, specifically in the agenda-setting stage within congressional committees. Because the Legislative Effectiveness Scores are based on progressive stages across the lawmaking process, we can focus in on the relative importance of action in committees, the ability to overcome committee hurdles, and success on the floor of the House. In so doing, we isolate the relative importance of majority-party status for lawmaking success not only on the floor of the House, but also in committees and beyond the House chamber. Such an examination strongly establishes that majority-party effectiveness is found not based on voting behavior on the floor of the House. Rather, lawmakers within the majority party gain such a high degree of effectiveness based on the systematic exclusion of minority-party members' proposals from consideration in congressional committees.

In Chapter 4, we focus on other potential coalitions of members of the House, apart from their party affiliations. Because effective lawmaking requires the forging of significant coalitions, subsets of members who share common interests may band together and adopt coordinated strategies in order to achieve legislative success. In Chapter 4, we examine three such groups. First, scholars have long established that women bring different goals and ambitions to the legislatures in which they serve. Our initial analyses from Chapter 2 show that, all else equal, women are more effective than men. Here, we explore the legislative strategies adopted by female lawmakers to help advance their agenda items. We particularly note the tendency of women to try to achieve consensus, and how this perspective on lawmaking helps advance the interests of women, especially when they are in the minority party.

Second, we focus on the interests of African Americans in Congress. Like women, African Americans bring different legislative agenda items to Congress. However, unlike women, their proposals do not typically bridge partisan divides. Rather, African-American legislators, and their proposals, tend to reside on the liberal end of the Democratic Party. One possible strategy to achieve some degree of lawmaking success involves African-American lawmakers narrowing their policy portfolios to a small number of "black interest" bills, concentrating their efforts on such issues crucial to their constituencies. We establish that such a strategy, while possibly the best available, offers only a very limited payoff when Democrats are in the majority. When Republicans are in the majority, African Americans tend to limit their proposals still further, seeking often-symbolic policies that can pass through the Republican House. In contrast to their lack of success with Democrats, this part of their strategy works well.

Our final focus of Chapter 4 is on Southern Democrats. Given their moderate ideological position, Southern Democrats could (and did) sometimes bolt from the Democratic Party to join the Republicans in blocking Democratic initiatives or in advancing conservative causes. Because of their pivotal position, Southern Democrats may have been in a position to be even more effective than other majority-party Democrats throughout the 1970s and 1980s. On the other hand, by sometimes casting their lot with the Republicans, Southern Democrats may have been seen as unreliable, resulting in their proposals being dismissed along with those of minority-party Republicans. We test between these two alternatives, and find support for the latter. Specifically, when liberal members of the Democratic Party achieved a majority of House seats in the mid-1980s, they systematically excluded proposals of Southern Democrats from their governing coalitions, largely lumping them in with members of the minority party. Such a diminution of the effectiveness of Southern Democrats disappears when the Republicans assume majority-party status in the mid-1990s.

Crucial to these three examinations in Chapter 4 is the use of changing Legislative Effectiveness Scores over time. As the numbers of Southern Democrats declined and the ranks of African-American and female members of Congress increased, their strategies evolved and their successes and failures became more clear. By focusing on the LES measure across eras of Republican and Democratic control of Congress, we gain greater insight into how each of these minority groups fared both when in the majority party and within the minority party.

In contrast to the findings for individuals or groups of lawmakers in the earlier chapters, in Chapter 5 we turn our gaze to the institution of the House of Representatives as a whole. Specifically, we ask whether Congress can effectively overcome institutional hurdles to lawmaking and avoid being mired in policymaking gridlock. Here we move away from our overall Legislative Effectiveness Scores to generate a score for each member in each of nineteen issue areas that Congress commonly confronts. By focusing on each policy area separately, we establish that legislative gridlock is highly contextual. Some policy areas are many times more gridlocked than others. And the rates of policy gridlock vary within each issue area significantly from one Congress to the next.

Yet we argue that such patterns of gridlock across issue areas are far from random. Rather, congressional gridlock can be studied and understood based on a variety of characteristics of the policies themselves, and of the lawmakers who help to overcome legislative stalemate. In particular, in Chapter 5, we use issue-by-issue Legislative Effectiveness Scores to identify which issues are more partisan than others, which require greater expertise, and which feature a more prominent role for political entrepreneurs. These three factors vary across policies and over time. Together they go a long way toward explaining which issues are more gridlocked than others and how lawmakers may work together to overcome such gridlock.

Given the importance of political entrepreneurs in bringing about policy change, and given our interest in identifying highly effective lawmakers, in Chapter 6 we turn from our largely quantitative approach to a more qualitative assessment of the most effective legislators. Specifically, we identify the ten most-effective lawmakers across each of the nineteen issue areas explored in Chapter 5. We also find the ten most-effective members of each party in each Congress. In order to focus on the members themselves, rather than on the benefits of their institutional positions, we set aside party leaders and committee chairs. We then find that twenty rank-and-file members of Congress appear repeatedly (four or more times) on our top-ten lists, and we conduct a systematic qualitative assessment of the lawmaking habits common to these twenty highly effective members. Identifying five such habits, we note how new members of Congress can cultivate these habits in their own quests to become highly effective lawmakers.

Taken together, we believe that these chapters make a compelling case for studying the U.S. Congress through the lens of legislative effectiveness. Rather than viewing all members of Congress as merely Democrats or Republicans or solely in ideological terms, we argue that they should be seen as *lawmakers*, each with differing skills and abilities. Doing so can lead to countless new insights. But in order to attain such insights, scholars must embrace the formulation and analysis of systematic measures that capture how effective each lawmaker is. This is the endeavor that we begin with our measurement strategy as detailed in Chapter 2. There, we show how our measure is robust to alternative specifications and how it helps identify which lawmakers start down which lawmaking paths. For instance, those who fail in their lawmaking roles early in their careers tend to voluntarily retire from the House, while those who succeed tend to soon seek higher office.

Illustrations of the value of our measurement strategy then continue throughout the book. In Chapter 3, we establish how the measure's focus on different lawmaking stages can adjudicate debates about the locus of majority-party effectiveness in Congress. In Chapter 4, we illustrate how the measure's changing values over time allow scholars to study legislative strategies of coalition members within and apart from the majority party. In Chapter 5, we establish how legislative effectiveness varies in important ways across different policy areas. In Chapter 6, we show how the LES and its variants across issue areas can be used to identify the most highly effective lawmakers, and how these members can be studied to determine the habits that helped them attain legislative success.

Finally, in Chapter 7, we discuss the importance of legislative effectiveness for the overall well-being of the American democratic system. We offer examples of how scholars can take the focus on legislative effectiveness advanced here and use it to address numerous additional important research topics in political science. But we also note how a focus on legislative effectiveness may extend well beyond scholarly endeavors. Voters may be interested in whether their representatives are actually succeeding in carrying out the lawmaking tasks for which they have been elected. Interest groups may wish to target their efforts to the most effective lawmakers in order to best promote their specific policy goals. And lawmakers themselves may wish to become more effective, for themselves, their constituents, their parties, or the institution of Congress as a whole. Throughout this book, we offer an approach, framework, and set of measures that we hope will help in all of these endeavors.

However, in advancing our arguments, it is important to address two potential concerns that readers may have with our approach. First, we are quite sympathetic to the fact that some readers might have reservations about how we measure legislative effectiveness. As we allude to in this chapter and explore in greater depth in Chapter 2, there are many activities that might be indicative of a legislator's relative effectiveness in lawmaking that our measurement strategy does not (and, by design, cannot) capture. While we readily concede that many important aspects of lawmaking are here left unmeasured, we believe that the approach that we advocate has unambiguous value in understanding lawmaking processes. We are hopeful that the various analyses that we present in Chapter 2 will allay the concerns of even highly skeptical readers as to the relative virtues of our approach. Moreover, while we offer a new approach, we expect that ours will not be the final measure of effectiveness to be developed. Rather, we are hopeful that the measurement strategy that we propose and the analysis and findings that we present are sufficiently compelling to convince other scholars of the intellectual virtues of exploring legislative effectiveness further. To this end, we both welcome and encourage work by future scholars building directly on our measurement strategy and refining it further, perhaps to include various features of lawmaking that may be relatively underemphasized here.

A second potential concern that readers may have is that the topic of legislative effectiveness is of questionable relevance in understanding contemporary congressional politics. To many readers the only acceptable answer to the question, "Who are the most effective members of Congress?" at present may be, "None of them!" As alluded to above, current public evaluations of Congress are at an all-time low, likely due to prominent recent incidents of legislative dysfunction.[17] Even a casual observer of politics cannot escape the coverage of seemingly annual showdowns between Democrats and Republicans and between Congress and the White House over the budget and long-term fiscal commitments. The U.S. credit rating was downgraded. The federal government was shut down. Debts continued to mount. Meanwhile, Congress revealed itself as incapable of addressing policy problems ranging from gun control to environmental protection to immigration reform. Such concerns have contributed to the idea that we are living in a new era of contentious politics that transcends historical baselines for incivility and conflict. Whether due to the rise of the permanent campaign, the twenty-four-hour news cycle, increasingly ideologically polarized political parties, or other favorite explanations of scholars and pundits, Congress seems unable to govern. Unsurprisingly, there is a growing sentiment that those who serve in Congress simply cannot (and do not) engage in the practice of lawmaking.

In stark contrast to these claims, we argue that Congress continues to be best described as a lawmaking body. Thousands of new public policies are formulated in Congress each year, resulting in hundreds of new laws from one congressional election to the next. Moreover, these laws are not passed simply because they *have* to be passed.[18] Rather, what Congress does or does not do, what issues it confronts or neglects, what bills become law – all of these – depend largely on who the lawmakers in Congress are and how effective they are in their jobs. Some legislators hold particular institutional positions that enhance their abilities to address policy problems in politically attractive ways. Some legislators possess, either by natural endowments or cultivation over time (or both),

---

[17] Mann and Ornstein (2006, 2012) offer numerous examples of Congress as a "broken branch" of government.

[18] Some scholars suggest that must-pass legislation, such as through reauthorization bills, comprise the main focus of Congress today (e.g., Adler and Wilkerson 2013).

particular interpersonal skills that allow them to bring people together and convince them of the merits of their arguments.

Without a doubt, each legislator's party affiliation and ideological preferences interact with the internal organization and structure of the House of Representatives to advance or constrain her opportunities for influence in the lawmaking process. Yet these factors do not define the totality of her circumstances. Parties, preferences, and institutional rules do not dictate whether she will, or will not, emerge as more successful than others at moving her bills through the legislative process. Each member of Congress chooses how to use her abilities and the circumstances she confronts to represent her constituents and become an effective or ineffective lawmaker. The choices made by each lawmaker determine what the Congress can accomplish as a whole. At a time when cynicism about Congress (both within and outside of the institution) seems both insurmountable and well-founded, the search for effective lawmakers is perhaps as crucial as it has ever been. It is at times when institutions are failing that effective leaders are needed more than ever.

Is the Congress different today than it was thirty to forty years ago? In some ways, surely it is. But are the motives of those who hold office now so different from those who held office then? Here the answer is less clear, but we think probably not. Members of Congress continue to seek reelection, to be pulled in different directions by parties and constituents, and to attempt to improve public policies. The main tool they have at their disposal is that, in the U.S. Congress, the members themselves are tasked with making the laws. And throughout this book we document remarkable lawmaking successes, in Congress after Congress, across the past four decades. That is, we identify those members of the House who leveraged the benefits of their institutional positions (or transcended beyond them) to advance their causes and realize success, nearly always when the odds were against them. Such examples not only illustrate the theoretical scholarly claims we are advancing, but also lead us to believe that, despite contemporary challenges, effective lawmaking and legislative leadership are not lost to history. They may be more limited than observers might like, but they are undoubtedly present. And, if properly reinforced, they can achieve prominence once again.

2

Measuring Legislative Effectiveness

*Assessing the importance of floor decisionmaking is not easy. Ideally, the contri-
bution of each stage of the legislative process to the ultimate legislative product
could be determined, assigning weights to the various provisions of the legislation
according to some measure of their policy significance. Generalizing about all
legislation in a Congress by assigning weights to the individual measures according
to their significance would be the first step in assessing the relative importance of
the various stages of the process.*

– Steven S. Smith. *Call to Order: Floor Politics in the House and
Senate* (1989, p. 12)

*As the Congress came to a close, the lawmakers returned to their districts ready
to claim credit for their accomplishments and to advertise the positions they had
taken over the past two years. They would account for their actions and ask for
voters' support once again. Some would return home excited by the successes
they had achieved through their sponsored legislation. Others would draw
attention to broader issues and to their role in voting for or opposing the
proposals of their colleagues.*

*While each had carried their constituents' concerns to Capitol Hill a mere
twenty months prior, Representatives Pomeroy (D-ND), Oberstar (D-MN),
Kildee (D-MI), and McNulty (D-NY) returned from Congress in 2008 with
marked differences in their proven effectiveness as lawmakers. Pomeroy and
Oberstar had introduced the most legislation, with thirty-six and thirty-nine
bills, respectively. Yet their portfolios met vastly different fates. Oberstar saw ten
of his bills signed into law, while all but one of Pomeroy's bills died in committee
and none advanced to President Bush's desk for his signature. Kildee and
McNulty had more limited portfolios, introducing eleven and five bills, respectively; and they, too, had starkly different fortunes. By the end of the 110th
Congress, more than half of the bills that Kildee introduced had been signed into
law, whereas none of McNulty's five bills had made it to the White House.*

Looking simply at the input and output sides of this process, some preliminary statements can be made regarding each of these legislators' effectiveness at
advancing their agenda items through the legislative pipeline. For example, it
should be fairly uncontroversial to claim that Representatives Oberstar and
Kildee were more effective than Representatives Pomeroy and McNulty.
Beyond this straightforward claim, however, assessments become a bit murky.
On the one hand, for example, Oberstar might be viewed as arguably more
effective than Kildee, given that ten of his bills were signed into law, in comparison to Kildee's six. That said, in terms of the conversion rate from introductions
to law passage, more than half of Kildee's bills were signed into law, double
Oberstar's rate of conversion.

Putting aside raw numbers, there is also a matter of the content of the bills
that made their way to President Bush's desk. Of Oberstar's ten bills that were
signed into law, three could arguably be considered substantive and significant
measures, accomplishing such lofty purposes as supporting new water conservation measures and overhauling railway safety. In contrast, only one of Kildee's
bills achieved similar stature, revising and reauthorizing the Head Start program, while one of his other legislative successes was the naming of a post office
in Vassar, Michigan. Should these substantive differences be accounted for when
declaring one legislator more effective than another?

And what can be said about the relative effectiveness of McNulty and
Pomeroy? While neither lawmaker saw any of his bills passed into law, should
Pomeroy be viewed as potentially more effective than McNulty because he
introduced more bills, thereby advocating for more issues as part of Congress'
policy agenda? Should one also account for the fact that none of McNulty's bills
even passed out of the House, whereas one of Pomeroy's bills was voted out of
the House and was received in the Senate?

More fundamentally, what can explain why Oberstar and Kildee were so
much more effective than Pomeroy and McNulty? Upon returning to the House
in 2007, all four lawmakers looked so similar. Yet much changed with the
pounding of the opening gavel. Oberstar parlayed his seniority and his support
of key Democratic constituencies such as unions into chairmanship of the
Transportation and Infrastructure Committee. From there, he advanced the
interests of his district as well as the party's and country's goals toward maritime
pollution prevention, railway and airline safety, and infrastructure revitaliza-
tion. As chair, he helped ensure that twenty-five of his thirty-nine bills received
hearings or markups in committee, that twenty-seven reached the floor of the
House, and that twenty-two passed the House, even if he could not control their
fate in the Senate.

While not in line to be chair of the Education and Labor Committee,
Representative Kildee did gain an important position as chair of its
Subcommittee on Early Childhood, Elementary and Secondary Education. From
there, the lawmaker was well positioned to advance the part of his agenda focused
on children, such as with the Improving Head Start for School Readiness Act of

2007. Kildee's proposals outside of his privileged area achieved mixed success, however, as he was able to help the Saginaw Chippewa Tribe in its land interests but not the auto industry in its desired trade restrictions.

Representative McNulty also took on a subcommittee chair position on the Social Security Subcommittee of Ways and Means. This helped him move his sponsored bill on identity-theft protection out of committee, but did little to help with his district-favored proposals on textiles and hydroelectric projects. Finally, Representative Pomeroy did not rise to a chair position either of a committee or a subcommittee. The size of his legislative agenda may have matched the size of his home state of North Dakota, but without shared interests of other lawmakers and without a key institutional position, Pomeroy turned his attention away from his own sponsored legislation toward the communal tasks of the important Ways and Means Committee on which he sat.

These four stories make up but a small part of the hundreds of such narratives in each Congress that explain how and why ideas from back home become public policy for the nation. Much of the work of political scientists interested in legislative studies involves looking for systematic patterns across the hundreds of policymakers and thousands of sponsored bills in order to understand more broadly how legislatures produce public policy. In so doing, we must rely on simplifications. Rather than becoming bogged down in the details of each member's background and agenda, we seek ways to succinctly and accurately characterize lawmakers' activities. Summary measures are commonplace in studies of Congress, where party label, ideological ideal points, or vote share in the previous election quickly convey significant amounts of information about how we expect legislators to behave and what they are likely to accomplish.

For the purposes of this book, we need to develop a measure of each member's effectiveness at advancing her legislative agenda. Measurement is an important but difficult endeavor. It involves four main steps, each of which must be handled with care.[1] First, scholars must offer an explicit definition of the concept they seek to measure. Second, we must identify indicators of the defined concept. Third, we must combine the indicators into a set of scores that concisely capture the defined concept. Finally, such a score or measure should be assessed based on a variety of validation criteria.

The development of ideological ideal points for members of Congress provides a useful example of these four steps. First, scholars noted that they wished to assess members' positions on a commonly understood ideological

---

[1] These steps draw upon the tasks of measurement development and validation discussed by Adcock and Collier (2001).

scale ranging from liberal to conservative. Second, they determined that members' votes on key issues (or all issues) would provide the indicators of lawmakers' ideological positions. Third, scholars combined these vote patterns into scores, using more and more sophisticated econometric tools over time.[2] Finally, these scores were assessed in terms of how well they matched earlier versions of the scores, whether they aligned members similarly to measures of the ideologies of their districts, or whether they matched well-established patterns (such as Democrats voting in a liberal manner and Republicans voting conservatively). With these scores in hand, researchers found they could better address important issues in legislative politics than had previously been possible.[3]

Throughout this chapter, we follow the same four steps, here to construct and evaluate Legislative Effectiveness Scores (LESs). We begin by developing an explicit definition of the concept of legislative effectiveness that we intend to measure. We then discuss the indicators needed to adequately capture legislative effectiveness. We move next to the formal development of scores based upon these indicators. Finally, the bulk of the chapter assesses the validity of the Legislative Effectiveness Score measure based on a large number of criteria and analyses. Specifically, the legislative effectiveness of members is shown to be based on: (1) their innate abilities, (2) accumulated skill sets, (3) institutional positions, and (4) a broader set of considerations consistent with well-established expectations about the internal workings of the House of Representatives. The combination of these sections leads us to the conclusion that legislative effectiveness is an important concept that is well captured by the LES and that can be used to assess key issues in legislative politics like the role of political parties, the representation of minority groups, and the conditions for overcoming legislative gridlock.[4] Each of these later topics is then explored in subsequent chapters.

THE CONCEPT OF LEGISLATIVE EFFECTIVENESS

As we argued in Chapter 1, representation in U.S. legislative politics depends crucially on the ability of elected representatives to take the issues that are important to their constituents and translate them into public policy. Members

---

[2] Early attempts involved the simple averaging of how frequently members voted with a liberal group, such as the Americans for Democratic Action. Later methods involved patterns across all votes, examining the likelihoods of voting with particular coalitions under certain circumstances (Poole and Rosenthal 1997; Clinton, Jackman, and Rivers 2004).

[3] Yet even with such increasing sophistication, scholars still dispute the *meaning* of these scores, debating whether they capture individual policy preferences, district leanings, partisan pressure, or other considerations. These issues are engaged more explicitly in a recent review article by Clinton (2012).

[4] As part of a larger scholarly endeavor, we expect that the LES will likely be modified and improved upon by future researchers to be of even greater value.

of Congress vary substantially in their abilities to advance their legislative agendas, based both on their personal aptitude and on their institutional positions. Systematic differences across members in advancing agenda items can help us to understand the internal workings of Congress, the nature of representation in U.S. politics, and the ultimate fate of public policy proposals.

The key underlying concept is what we call *legislative effectiveness*. As concisely defined, legislative effectiveness is the proven ability to advance a member's agenda items through the legislative process and into law. This definition has four key components. First, we are discussing the "proven ability" of members. While many lawmakers may have great potential to bring about policy change, unless they use that potential to actually advance agenda items they are not considered effective by our definition. Second, we are interested in "advancing" legislation. This is a concept that is thus distinct from blocking the proposals of others. While we believe that placing obstacles in an opponent's path is also an important aspect of legislative policymaking, we are here focused on policy *change*, and specifically on who is able to bring about such change even in the face of such daunting obstacles.

Third, we are focused on the "member's agenda items," rather than the agenda items of the political party, the president, or even the member's constituents. While all of these other individuals and their preferences may shape the member's agenda items (likely in important ways), lawmakers have a great deal of choice and flexibility in deciding which issues to act upon and which to set aside. It is these choices that form the basis for evaluation of a member's effectiveness. Whether members are motivated by reelection-seeking or by such goals as attaining institutional power or formulating good public policy, passing legislation to please their constituents and to advance their policy agendas is an important component of being a member of Congress.[5] And it is on the grounds of such legislative advancements that we seek to evaluate each lawmaker's effectiveness.

Fourth and finally, we focus on movement "through the legislative process and into law." In so doing, we are arguing that effectiveness can be demonstrated at multiple stages of the lawmaking process, not simply in the passage of new laws. While such laws may be the ultimate goal, members may be effective at moving their proposed legislation through key committees and to the floor of the House. Yet even if they fail to gain passage of their bills on the floor, such members have demonstrated a level of effectiveness that will serve them well on other issues or in later Congresses.

---

[5] Mayhew (1974) establishes the benefit of building an understanding of Congress around the premise that members are single-minded seekers of reelection. Fenno (1978) elaborates on further goals of members, while noting that "members believe that their supporters want their representative to be influential in Congress, and that they take a certain pride in having an effective congressman – the more so when he is effective on their behalf" (139).

While including many aspects of the lawmaking process, by its nature this definition of legislative effectiveness also excludes various legislative activities and behaviors. The most successful members of Congress have skill sets that extend well beyond an ability to advance legislation. One could speak of their "fundraising effectiveness" with campaign contributors, their "electoral effectiveness" via constituent services, their "public relations effectiveness" in framing issues and position taking, or their "administrative effectiveness" in managing a large staff. Yet here we are interested in members of Congress as lawmakers, and thus are focused solely on their *legislative effectiveness*. While admittedly a limited part of the activities undertaken by representatives, in our view advancing legislation is so fundamental to a lawmaker's core purpose as to merit a central place in the study of legislative politics.

We are also excluding in our definition any exploration of whether the laws proposed by these members are *themselves* effective. Important work in the field of public policy analysis is done on a daily basis to assess the impact of policies. We are instead interested in where these policies come from. Without a doubt, many of the proposals advanced in Congress have negative impacts on certain segments of society and may be seen in very different lights by those with opposing ideological viewpoints. Indeed, the study of politics in Congress focuses on difficult choices, with winners and losers, where new policies are riddled with many of the same flaws as the status quo policies they are designed to replace. In studying legislative effectiveness, we are intending to assess not the effectiveness of the legislation itself, but the effectiveness of legislators in bringing about new public policies. While many of these new policies provide a brighter future for Americans, others do not have such fortuitous consequences.

INDICATORS OF LEGISLATIVE EFFECTIVENESS

With this definition in hand, the next step in developing and assessing a measure of legislative effectiveness is to identify a series of indicators that provide information about such effectiveness. We rely on fifteen such indicators, five for each major stage of the legislative process across each of three categories of legislation. Specifically, we consider: (1) how many bills each legislator introduces (BILL), and how many of those bills (2) receive action in committee (AIC), (3) pass out of committee and receive action on the floor of the House (ABC), (4) pass the House (PASS), and (5) ultimately become law (LAW). These five indicators are constructed separately for bills that are commemorative (C), bills that are substantive (S), and bills that are both substantive and significant (SS), as will be defined below. In combination, these fifteen indicators then form the basis for each member's Legislative Effectiveness Score.

In concrete terms, we first identify which legislator sponsored each bill in each Congress, and what happened to those bills at each stage in the legislative process. While undertaking such a task could be incredibly cumbersome, the availability of electronically accessible copies of the *Congressional Record* simplifies our task considerably. We rely on computer code written to collect all relevant information from the Library of Congress Web site, THOMAS, for every public house bill (H.R.) that was introduced into the 93rd–110th Congresses (1973–2008).[6] For every bill, we identify the sponsor and every step in the legislative process as identified in the "All Congressional Actions with Amendments" section of the bill's "summary and status" hyperlink. After collecting this information, we code the dates and incidence of each major stage of each bill's progression through the legislative life cycle. For example, we identify when the bill was introduced and referred to committee (and the identity of the committee or committees), as well as whether the committee held hearings, engaged in markup, sent the bill to subcommittee, reported the bill from committee, whether a rule was assigned to the bill on the floor, whether the bill was amended, whether it passed the House, whether it went to a conference committee, and so on.

Upon identifying the progress of every public House bill, we then identify how many bills each legislator sponsored as well as how many of those sponsored bills successfully completed subsequent steps in the legislative process in each Congress. Our specific indicators are thus: the number of bills that each member sponsored (BILL); and the number of those bills that received any action in committee (AIC), or action beyond committee (ABC) on the floor of the House. For those bills that received any action beyond committee, we also identify how many of those bills subsequently passed the House (PASS), and how many subsequently became law (LAW).

Drawing on these data, however, requires some sensitivity to variance in legislative content. More specifically, it could be argued (correctly in our view) that not all bills are of equal importance, and thus might not be equally indicative of a member's overall lawmaking effectiveness. Naming a post office can be achieved with considerably less legislative effort than reforming Social Security. To account for such variation, we categorize all bills as being either commemorative (C), substantive (S), or substantive and significant (SS). Our categorization is based on the following coding protocol. A bill is deemed substantive and significant if it had been the subject of an end-of-the-year write-up in the *Congressional Quarterly Almanac*.[7] A bill was deemed commemorative if it satisfied any one of several criteria, such as providing for a

---

[6] For the purposes of analysis, we confine our attention to House Bills, and discard all House Concurrent Resolutions, House Resolutions, and House Joint Resolutions. Our computer code utilizes the Ruby on Rails framework for the MySQL database system.

[7] This coding protocol is somewhat in line with the Anderson, Box-Steffensmeier, and Sinclair-Chapman (2003, 365) denotation of "hot" bills in the 103rd Congress – those that were the subject of a cover story in 1993–94 issues of *Congressional Quarterly Weekly Report*. It should be noted that *CQ Almanac* stories are not ex ante measures of bill significance, as bills that move further through the lawmaking process are much more likely to be mentioned.

renaming, commemoration, private relief of an individual, and the like.[8] Finally, all other bills, and any erstwhile commemorative bills that were also the subject of a *CQ Almanac* write-up were classified as substantive.[9] For each of these three categories of bills we relied on our five important stages of the legislative process to produce our final set of fifteen indicator variables.

As desired, these indicators match our definition of legislative effectiveness rather closely. As noted previously, we define legislative effectiveness as "the proven ability to advance a member's agenda items through the legislative process and into law." Thus, because they are based on actual bills and their fates, these indicators meet the "proven ability" concept. Moreover, different abilities may be revealed in advancing substantive and significant legislation than commemorative bills, so that categorization is also relevant. Because they focus on how far these bills move through the legislative process, the indicators match the "advancement" concept. Because we link each bill to its sponsor, the indicators capture each "member's agenda items." And the five stages capture "the legislative process and into law."

In relying upon these fifteen indicators, we are setting aside others that may at first glance be relevant to the defined concept of legislative effectiveness. For example, we are focused only on bill advancement instead of preserving the status quo through obstruction. While potentially important, indicators of which members are effective in obstructing legislation at which stages are unavailable.[10] We also only examine the sponsors of bills, rather than their cosponsors or others involved in bill advancement.[11] While cosponsors are helpful as indicators of who supports a piece of legislation, adding one's name

---

[8] Based on a complete reading of all bill titles, the following terms from titles are used to label them as commemorative: commemoration, commemorate, for the private relief of, for the relief of, medal, mint coins, posthumous, public holiday, to designate, to encourage, to express the sense of Congress, to provide for correction of, to name, to redesignate, to remove any doubt, to rename, and retention of the name. We then individually read each bill title containing these search terms, and removed it from the commemorative list if the bill also sought substantive policy changes.

[9] Hence, a small number of bills that had originally been designated as commemorative were upgraded to be classified as substantive bills. An example of such a bill is H.R. 9 in the 97th Congress ("A bill to designate components of the National Wilderness Preservation System in the State of Florida").

[10] One possible way to explore obstruction systematically may be to focus on what bills the chairs of committees and subcommittees allow to move forward. Some may only entertain legislation proposed by their own party's members. Others may narrow further based on ideology. Future work measuring such obstruction and linking it to legislative effectiveness as proposed here would be welcome.

[11] This method therefore does not account for legislators who do not sponsor many successful bills, but rather work behind the scenes to bring legislation to its fruition. While we believe that such legislators definitely exist and play an important role in lawmaking, they comprise a relatively small minority of all members of Congress and their actions are exceedingly difficult to assess in an objective manner. By focusing on the progression of the bills that members actually sponsor, we are capturing the most transparent and objective set of indicators of legislative effectiveness.

in support of a bill is a rather weak indicator of a lawmaker's ability to bring about policy change.[12]

Also excluded from our set of indicators are amendments to the bills studied here.[13] Many lawmakers may advance their agendas by embedding their legislative priorities in amendments offered in committee or on the House floor.[14] Moreover, our current set of indicators may give a sponsor too much credit for advancing her agenda, when the final law actually does not reflect her initial vision well at all due to significant amendments. This is a sufficiently serious concern to merit significant discussion and analysis. We carry out several such analyses in Appendix 2.1 at the end of this chapter. In so doing, we find that, whether we exclude all amended bills or whether we attribute effectiveness to successful amenders instead of to the bill's original sponsor, our ultimate measure of legislative effectiveness is impacted very little by such changes. Perhaps more importantly, using these alternative measures to study congressional institutions does not change the conclusions we reach upon setting amendments aside. Ultimately, we therefore rely on the simpler and more straightforward set of indicators that excludes bill amendment concerns.

Our study also excludes legislative institutions apart from the U.S. House of Representatives. We are not seeking to evaluate the effectiveness of legislators in other institutions, such as the Senate, state legislatures, or various legislative bodies around the world. Future works extending our approach to the U.S. Senate or to state legislatures would be most welcome, to the extent that measures of effectiveness could be used to shed light on important political processes within such

---

[12] While many scholars (e.g., Harbridge 2013) argue that cosponsorship reflects a legislator's earnest support for a measure, the potential reasons to engage in cosponsorship and the likely consequences of those decisions are varied, ranging from signaling the quality of the legislation (i.e., Kessler and Krehbiel 1996) to expressing a commitment to support the bill throughout the legislative process (i.e., Bernhard and Sulkin 2013). While recent scholarship has suggested that being at the center of a cosponsorship network is correlated with a sponsor's legislative success (e.g., Fowler 2006a, 2006b; Kirkland 2011; Cho and Fowler 2010), other studies show limited value from obtaining cosponsors (e.g., Wilson and Young 1997). These topics are clearly worthy of further study, but the uncertain value of cosponsorship coupled with endogeneity concerns lead us to set aside cosponsorship in our measure of legislative effectiveness.

[13] There are many ways in which the content of bills may be changed. Therefore, clarity in our assignment of credit is important. For instance, if several bills are considered by a committee and merged into a single bill, sponsors of those original bills receive credit for introduction and action in committee, while only the sponsor of the single combined bill receives credit for subsequent activities. In another example, some or all of the language of a bill may be replaced in committee, on the floor, or in the Senate, with the revised bill eventually becoming law. In our coding, the original sponsor receives credit for all stages, despite the change in content. Our assessment of amendments in Appendix 2.1 is therefore an important initial step in exploring these possibilities, as they impact measures of legislative effectiveness.

[14] For instance, a member who attaches a "rider" to an appropriations bill receives no added credit through our approach.

institutions. Of course, any such extensions must be sensitive to differences in lawmaking structures across institutions.[15]

Ours is also not the first study designed to measure and assess the effectiveness of lawmakers. Contrasting our indicators with those used in earlier studies is thus valuable. Previous research on legislative effectiveness has generally fallen into one of two categories. First, a body of scholarly research analyzes legislative effectiveness in U.S. state legislatures, often relying on elite surveys to generate reputational rankings of legislators. For instance, the most extensive set of surveys available is from the North Carolina state legislature, wherein a variety of political actors are asked to rate lawmakers on a series of criteria.[16] Such an approach is beneficial in being based on perceptions that extend beyond bill advancement, but also faces a series of perception biases and offers limited insights for those who do not regularly catch the eye of lobbyists or journalists.

Second, in contrast to these reputational-rankings approaches, scholars have also investigated the topic of legislative effectiveness at the national level by focusing on limited indicators of bill progression.[17] Most commonly, such work has relied on legislators' "hit rates" (also referred to as "success rates" or "conversion rates"), measuring the *percentage* of a legislator's sponsored bills that pass the chamber and/or become law, as a proxy for legislative effectiveness. Focusing on the percentage of bills passed, however, raises problems when comparing legislators who introduce significantly different amounts of legislation. As such, scholars have more recently turned to measuring legislative effectiveness primarily through the *number* of bills that a member sponsors that pass out of the House, and/or are enacted into law.[18]

For a variety of reasons, this second category of approaches is more desirable than reputational rankings for our purposes.[19] Because no systematic surveys of

---

[15] Exciting research on legislative effectiveness in Argentina and in Uganda is being conducted by Calvo and Sagarzazu (2011) and by Humphreys and Weinstein (2007), respectively.

[16] Meyer (1980, 564–565), for example studies legislative effectiveness in the North Carolina legislature by analyzing legislators' aggregate responses to the question, "Who are the five most influential members of the House?" Weissert (1991a, 1991b) and Padro i Miquel and Snyder (2006) also study the North Carolina legislature, but analyze a more substantial survey instrument that was administered to a collection of legislators, lobbyists, and journalists by the North Carolina Center for Public Policy Research.

[17] Such studies tend to build upon the early work of Matthews (1960), who focused on the U.S. Senate.

[18] This approach can be traced to Frantzich (1979). It was also employed by Moore and Thomas (1991) in their study of the U.S. Senate. More recently, Anderson et al. (2003), Cox and Terry (2008), and Hasecke and Mycoff (2007) have built on this approach to also analyze the number of sponsored bills that pass out of committee.

[19] This is not to say that the literature on state politics has embraced less objective measures of effectiveness than the congressional politics literature. Scholars such as Hamm, Harmel, and Thompson (1983), Saint-Germain (1989), Bratton and Haynie (1999), and Jeydel and Taylor (2003) have all analyzed the number (and rates) of bills that pass through different legislative hurdles as measures of effectiveness in state legislatures. Nor have all studies of Congress set aside survey-based measures of effectiveness (Hall 1992).

members of Congress have been conducted over time to evaluate one another's effectiveness, such indicators cannot be included in formulating our measure. Additionally, objective data about bill introductions and progression may be subject to fewer perception biases than such surveys, and these indicators allow straightforward over-time comparisons.

However, prior work relying solely on the number of bills that pass the House (or the analogous conversion rate) neglects certain aspects of the legislative process that are also related to our concept of legislative effectiveness.[20] While these later stages of the legislative process are crucial, and serve an important role among our indicators, we argue that earlier stages of the legislative process should not be neglected. Success at having one's bills receive attention in committee, a place on a legislative calendar, and the like is indicative of a lawmaker being able to move her agenda items forward.[21]

In Appendix 2.2, we assess the importance of including these earlier legislative stages among our set of indicators. We find that, even if one were only concerned with the extent to which a member's sponsored bills become law, crucial indicators of such success include: the number of that member's bills gaining action in committee, reaching the floor of the House, and passing the House, all in the previous Congress. This is true upon controlling for the number of bills the member introduced and the number of laws that member produced in the previous Congress. Put simply, accomplishments in early stages of the legislative process in one Congress are indicative of the ability to push those agenda items further through the process (and all the way into law) in later Congresses. For example, the attention generated through committee hearings may later translate into successful coalition building. Thus, including indicators of effectiveness at earlier stages of the process is an important step in the assessment of legislative effectiveness, as we have defined it.

THE LEGISLATIVE EFFECTIVENESS SCORE

Having defined the concept of legislative effectiveness and compiled fifteen indicators of effectiveness, we now combine these indicators into a single overall measure. From 1973 through 2008, across the 93rd through the 110th Congresses, 139,052 H.R. bills were introduced, 8,478 of which were commemorative, and 6,526 of which were substantive and significant. After classifying each bill into one of these three categories, we calculated an LES for each member i in each Congress t, as follows:

---

[20] Closely related to this notion of legislative effectiveness is the concept of legislative "entrepreneurship," which scholars such as Wawro (2001) and Schiller (1995) have measured by focusing on the number of bills that legislators sponsor and cosponsor in a given Congress. Effectiveness also captures the subsequent progress of members' efforts through later stages of the lawmaking process.

[21] Krutz (2005) engages these issues by analyzing which bills are most likely to be winnowed out as they proceed through the legislative process.

$$
LES_{it} = \left[
\begin{array}{c}
\left(\dfrac{\alpha BILL_{it}^C + \beta BILL_{it}^S + \gamma BILL_{it}^{SS}}{\alpha \sum\limits_{j=1}^{N} BILL_{jt}^C + \beta \sum\limits_{j=1}^{N} BILL_{jt}^S + \gamma \sum\limits_{j=1}^{N} BILL_{jt}^{SS}} \right) \\[4ex]
+ \left(\dfrac{\alpha AIC_{it}^C + \beta AIC_{it}^S + \gamma AIC_{it}^{SS}}{\alpha \sum\limits_{j=1}^{N} AIC_{jt}^C + \beta \sum\limits_{j=1}^{N} AIC_{jt}^S + \gamma \sum\limits_{j=1}^{N} AIC_{jt}^{SS}} \right) \\[4ex]
+ \left(\dfrac{\alpha ABC_{it}^C + \beta ABC_{it}^S + \gamma ABC_{it}^{SS}}{\alpha \sum\limits_{j=1}^{N} ABC_{jt}^C + \beta \sum\limits_{j=1}^{N} ABC_{jt}^S + \gamma \sum\limits_{j=1}^{N} ABC_{jt}^{SS}} \right) \\[4ex]
+ \left(\dfrac{\alpha PASS_{it}^C + \beta PASS_{it}^S + \gamma PASS_{it}^{SS}}{\alpha \sum\limits_{j=1}^{N} PASS_{jt}^C + \beta \sum\limits_{j=1}^{N} PASS_{jt}^S + \gamma \sum\limits_{j=1}^{N} PASS_{jt}^{SS}} \right) \\[4ex]
+ \left(\dfrac{\alpha LAW_{it}^C + \beta LAW_{it}^S + \gamma LAW_{it}^{SS}}{\alpha \sum\limits_{j=1}^{N} LAW_{jt}^C + \beta \sum\limits_{j=1}^{N} LAW_{jt}^S + \gamma \sum\limits_{j=1}^{N} LAW_{jt}^{SS}} \right)
\end{array}
\right] \left[\dfrac{N}{5} \right],
$$

where the five large terms represent the member's fraction of bills (1) introduced, (2) receiving action in committee, (3) receiving action beyond committee, (4) passing the House, and (5) becoming law, relative to all N legislators. Within each of these five terms, commemorative bills are weighted by α, substantive bills by β, and substantive and significant by γ. The overall weighting of $N/5$ normalizes the average LES to take a value of one in each Congress.[22]

Put simply, the LES captures the relative share of all legislative activities in any two-year Congress that can be attributed to each lawmaker. Several features of this construction are worth noting. First, because of the substantial differences in the number of bills that are introduced and the number of bills that advance to further stages (e.g., only 4.3 percent, or 5,960 bills, became law), our operationalization necessarily gives much greater weight to members who are more successful in later stages of the process (e.g., having a bill pass the House or become law) than earlier stages of the process (e.g., BILL or AIC). Thus, a member who introduces a large variety of bills mainly for symbolic purposes,

[22] Because our approach generates scores separately within each Congress, over-time comparisons must be made with caution, given different agenda sizes and productivity across Congresses.

but with little interest in moving them through the legislative process, will receive a quite low LES. The LES measure also captures intermediate stages, in addition to the introductory and concluding stages in the legislative process.

Second, throughout our analysis as reported here, we assign $\alpha = 1$, $\beta = 5$, and $\gamma = 10$, signifying that substantive and significant legislation exerts ten times the weight on the LES as commemorative legislation and twice as much as normal substantive legislation. These weights were chosen to reflect our view that advancing a substantive and significant bill is more difficult than moving general substantive legislation; and likewise, that advancing substantive legislation is a stronger indicator of legislative effectiveness than is moving commemorative legislation. In Appendix 2.3, we explore the effects of alternative weighting schemes. We find, first, that our results reported below for the institutional and personal predictors of legislative effectiveness are changed very little by alternative specifications, with $\alpha < \beta < \gamma$. Second, we find not only that the weighting scheme offered here has significant face validity, but also that it is among the best alternatives at constructing a measure of effectiveness that is highly correlated with the institutional and personal factors expected to be associated with effectiveness. Thus, this measure has a high degree of construct validity, as assessed more fully below.

Finally, the LES measure displays significant variation, ranging from the most effective legislator, Charles Rangel (D-NY), who had an LES of 18.69 in the 110th Congress (2007–08), to the 105 instances in our dataset where members of Congress have an LES equal to zero.[23] To give a sense of how Rangel attained such a high score, consider that the average member of the 110th House introduced fifteen substantive bills. Nearly one in three members introduced a bill deemed substantive and significant, and nearly one in two introduced a commemorative bill. Coming out of committee, the average member had only two substantive bills left in the legislative process; one in five members had a substantive and significant bill; and one in three had a commemorative bill still receiving consideration. While more than 75 percent of those remaining commemorative bills became law, less than half of the substantive and significant bills and less than one quarter of all substantive bills became law after passing out of committee. By comparison, Rangel introduced eight commemorative bills, six of which died in committee; but he also sponsored thirty-five substantive bills, eighteen of which found their way out of committee, fifteen of which passed the House, and seven of which became law. Moreover, for the far more selective substantive and significant category, Rangel sponsored eighteen bills, seventeen of which reached the floor, sixteen of which passed the House, and six of which became law. As a member of the majority Democratic Party and as chair of the Committee on Ways and Means, Rangel was well positioned to be effective. That he sponsored such measures as the Mortgage Forgiveness Debt

---

[23] The standard deviation of the LES across members is fairly steady at about 1.6 for each Congress in our dataset.

TABLE 2.1. *Average Impact of Various Activities on the Legislative Effectiveness Score*

	Commemorative (C)	Substantive (S)	Substantive and Significant (SS)
Introductions (BILL)	0.0023	0.0116	0.0231
Action In Committee (AIC)	0.0146	0.0732	0.1464
Action Beyond Committee (ABC)	0.0181	0.0904	0.1808
Passed House (PASS)	0.0223	0.1116	0.2232
Becomes Law (LAW)	0.0457	0.2285	0.4570

Note: The table shows the average impact on a member's Legislative Effectiveness Score caused by one bill of each type (commemorative, substantive, or substantive and significant) reaching a specific lawmaking stage (introduction, action in committee, action beyond committee, passing the House, and becoming law). For example, a substantive bill becoming law adds about 0.2285 to a lawmaker's LES above and beyond previous credit received for the bill having passed the House. These values are averages across the 93rd–110th Congresses (1973–2008).

Relief Act of 2007 (H.R. 3648), the Worker, Retiree and Employer Recovery Act of 2008 (H.R. 7327) and others that became law in the 110th Congress attests to his overall effectiveness.

To give a further sense of how the LES translates our fifteen indicator variables into a combined measure, consider the impact of each indicator on a member's LES. Table 2.1 illustrates the average effect of these indicators across the entire time period of our study. As can be seen, moving from top to bottom on the table, each legislative accomplishment at a later stage in the process has a greater impact on a member's LES. This is due to there being fewer such later activities than earlier activities. Indeed, the impact of one's sponsored bill becoming law is about twenty times as great as the mere introduction of that law, given that only about one in twenty bills becomes a law. Moving left to right on the table shows the weighting scheme we have assigned to different types of bills.

Bills passing through these stages also have a cumulative effect on the LES. For instance, if a member sponsors a substantive and significant bill that receives action in committee, reaches the floor, passes the House, and becomes law, that combined effort results in about a one-point increase in the member's LES.[24] A member who does nothing else but navigating such an important bill through to law thus receives about an average LES score. In contrast, a member who merely

---

[24] To an extent, one may argue that the final stage (between passing the House and becoming law) is beyond the lawmaker's control, depending instead on the Senate and the president. That said, the quality of the ideas in the bill and the nature of the supporting coalition remain important, and are certainly influenced by the lawmaker advocating the policy change.

introduces legislation and exerts no effort moving it forward would perform poorly on our score. Bill introductions themselves may be only a weak indicator of effectiveness, as members introduce legislation for reasons ranging from position taking to responsiveness to campaign contributions. Table 2.1 offers reassurance that the LES is not mainly a function of introductions that were not designed to move further in the lawmaking process. Indeed, a member focused only on introductions would have to sponsor more than 80 substantive bills (or more than 400 commemorative bills) to merely achieve the average score of other House members.

Turning back to our four members of interest, while Oberstar and Pomeroy introduced much more legislation than Kildee and McNulty, this increased introduction activity would not necessarily lead to significantly higher LESs. In the case of Oberstar, a sizable number of his bills were signed into law, yet all of Pomeroy's legislation died before reaching the president's desk. Hence, our measure would naturally rank Oberstar ahead of Pomeroy. Yet, even though Kildee introduced notably less than either of these Representatives, more than half of his bills (one of which was substantive and significant according to our coding protocol) were signed into law, which would likely cause him to score higher than either Pomeroy or McNulty (who, as noted, also did not see any of his legislation signed into law). In comparing Oberstar and Kildee, our methodology should likely rank Oberstar the higher of the two, given that he introduced more legislation, and had more bills (and more substantive and significant legislation) signed into law than Kildee. Indeed, a further consideration of these legislators' portfolios would reveal that Oberstar generally had greater success in advancing nearly all of his bills through the earlier stages of the legislative process than Kildee, which would be expected to contribute to a relatively high LES. Finally, our methodology would likely rank Pomeroy higher than McNulty given that he introduced more legislation, and had marginally more success advancing his agenda than McNulty.

In fact, the LESs that emerge from our estimation process reflect these expectations perfectly, with Oberstar scoring highest (12.97), followed by Kildee (4.488), then Pomeroy (0.631), and finally, McNulty (0.232). Figure 2.1 offers LES Scorecards for each of these four lawmakers, detailing their activities on each of our fifteen indicators, and then summarizing these activities through the single LES measure.

MEASUREMENT VALIDITY OF LEGISLATIVE EFFECTIVENESS SCORES

As noted at the outset of this chapter, measurement involves the four steps of: defining the key concept, compiling indicators, constructing a measure, and then assessing that measure's validity. Having accomplished the first three tasks, we dedicate the rest of this chapter to assessing the validity of the Legislative Effectiveness Scores. For our purposes, we engage in content validation and

The Lawmaker: **Earl Pomeroy** (D, ND) 110th Congress				The Lawmaker: **James Oberstar** (D, MN-8) 110th Congress		
LES: 0.631				**LES: 12.97**		
	c	s	ss		c	s	ss
BILL	0	36	0	BILL	1	32	6
AIC	0	0	0	AIC	1	18	6
ABC	0	1	0	ABC	1	20	6
PASS	0	1	0	PASS	1	15	6
LAW	0	0	0	LAW	0	7	3

The Lawmaker: **Dale Kildee** (D, MI-5) 110th Congress				The Lawmaker: **Michael McNulty** (D, NY-21) 110th Congress		
LES: 4.488				**LES: 0.232**		
	c	s	ss		c	s	ss
BILL	1	8	2	BILL	0	5	0
AIC	1	2	2	AIC	0	1	0
ABC	1	5	2	ABC	0	1	0
PASS	1	5	2	PASS	0	0	0
LAW	1	4	1	LAW	0	0	0

FIGURE 2.1. LES Scorecards for Four Lawmakers

Note: Scorecards show the number of commemorative (C), substantive (S), and substantive and significant (SS) bills (BILL) the lawmaker introduced, as well as how many received action in committee (AIC), action beyond committee (ABC), passed the House (PASS), and became law (LAW), resulting in the Legislative Effectiveness Score (LES), during the 110th Congress (2007–08).

construct validation.[25] Put simply, content validation seeks to assess whether there are key elements of the concept that are excluded and whether any inappropriate elements are included. Construct validity is judged by whether the measure matches well-established expectations about the concept being measured. Previously, we implicitly discussed content validity. For example, we excluded poor indicators of legislative effectiveness, such as cosponsorships or activities

[25] A third type of validation, "criterion validation," often compares a measure to known and true values of the underlying concept. Because there are no true values of legislative effectiveness, such validation is not relevant in our context.

apart from the legislative process itself. We also assigned greater weights to what seemed like better indicators of effectiveness, such as moving more important bills through Congress and of moving bills further through the legislative process.

Therefore, our remaining efforts focus on construct validation. That is, we seek to explore whether the Legislative Effectiveness Scores comport well with current understandings of the legislative workings of Congress, such as the important roles of political parties, committee leaders, representation, and race and gender effects.

To begin our assessment, we postulate that three key components are necessary to become a highly effective lawmaker: innate ability, the acquisition and cultivation of a critical skill set, and the sophisticated utilization of key legislative institutions. On its face, this argument is fairly consistent with commonplace discussions of effective members of Congress. In discussing the 2010 retirement of Representative David Obey (D-WI), for example, political commentator Norman Ornstein argued that his constituents were very lucky to have been represented by Obey for more than forty years, "one of the great legislators of our lifetime," a member of a class of "real" legislators "with a natural affinity for the legislative process, an ability to make laws, build coalitions and shape public policy."[26] This brief quote contains a number of elements central to our view about what makes an effective legislator – that effective members possess important skills, that they can cultivate these skills over time, and that these skills translate into a measure of effectiveness that captures the movement of legislation through Congress.

The innate abilities that produce effective legislators are not easily measured or quantified. Some lawmakers can simply engage in "the art of the possible" in ways that others cannot. They not only see policy solutions to pressing problems, but they also know the strategy of how to modify those theoretical solutions to make them politically viable. These are abilities that some members of Congress have at high levels and that others, even were they to dedicate all of their time and effort to cultivating, simply cannot achieve.[27]

And yet cultivating this critical skill set, rather than just relying on innate ability, is also part of becoming an effective legislator. Whether a member of Congress starts with high or low innate lawmaking ability, she can indeed improve over time. As members interact with their colleagues, they understand one another's passions and constituent needs. They come to know legislative rules and procedures, and they start to see broader coalitional possibilities than they had known before. This is an innocuous claim that likely resonates with observers of Congress and U.S. electoral politics. For example, political scientist

---

[26] Ornstein, Norman. 2010. "True Legislators Becoming Scarce in Congress." *Roll Call*. May 12.

[27] Mayhew (1991, 112–113) comments on these types of innate abilities in his discussion of presidential aspirants in Congress, noting that "[legislative skill] is a familiar checklist of talents including the abilities to set priorities, package proposals, time moves, court, persuade, and bargain."

Gary Jacobson (1999, 90) notes that "common to most incumbents' campaigns is an emphasis on the value of experience and seniority (for the capacity it gives members to serve the district more effectively)," presumably by advancing their legislative interests more easily than less experienced members.

Even the most skilled and studied lawmaker, however, is not able to accomplish anything by herself. Obtaining a committee chairmanship, having numerous like-minded colleagues, or being in the majority party all offer institutional possibilities not available to other members.[28] Without some ability to set the agenda, perhaps by holding various privileged institutional positions, even an otherwise skilled member's bills risk being lost among the thousands of other proposals entertained in any Congress.

These three simple factors – innate ability, cultivation of skills, and institutional positioning – help us understand which members get things done in Congress. And they serve as a first set of tests of the construct validity of Legislative Effectiveness Scores. Specifically, if this measure is truly a function of a legislator's innate abilities at bringing together legislative bargains, of cultivating those abilities across time, and of bolstering those abilities with privileged institutional positions, clear relationships should naturally emerge in the data in each of these three areas.

Innate Abilities

While innate ability is itself difficult to measure, such abilities likely manifest themselves in ways that are subject to systematic investigation. In particular, we hypothesize that innate abilities allow the same members to be effective in Congress after Congress, even in their earliest Congresses, and even as they move in and out of key institutional positions. To begin our assessment of this hypothesis, we simply correlate each member's LES in a given Congress with her LES in the previous Congress. It is important to note that there is nothing about the data-generating process that would lead us to expect a strong positive correlation over time absent tapping into common innate abilities of the same members over time. That is, at the start of every Congress, everyone's LES is identical. Only her actions of introducing bills and shepherding them through the lawmaking institutions within Congress elevates a member up from the score of zero that she would receive by doing nothing.

Supporting the concept of innate abilities yielding legislative effectiveness, there is strong initial evidence of similar scores persevering across a legislator's career from one Congress to the next. The coefficient of correlation between current LES_t and previous LES_{t-1} is 0.65. It is positive and significant, both statistically (p-value < 0.001) and in its substance, consistent with members

---

[28] For example, as Fenno (1973, 2–3) notes in his classic discussion of congressional committees, members of key committees "possess special capacities to affect the political fortunes of their House colleagues."

maintaining their effectiveness over time.[29] Simply put, members who are effective in the current Congress were likely effective in the previous Congress, and will continue to be effective in future Congresses.

Next, to the extent that we are truly capturing legislators' abilities to navigate the legislative process, these abilities should still exist even when they find themselves switching from being in the majority to being in the minority party (and vice versa). Given that our data include the regime change that occurred with the Republican takeover in the 104th Congress (1995–96), we can investigate this point by identifying the correlation between members' LESs in the 103rd and 104th Congresses, when their majority-minority statuses were reversed. For both majority- and minority-party members, we find that their LESs in the 103rd Congress are positively and significantly correlated with their 104th Congress LESs. That is, effective Democrats in the 103rd Congress were still relatively effective in the 104th Congress, even after they moved from being in the majority to being in the minority (and likewise for the Republicans). For Republicans, the correlation between their scores in the 103rd and 104th Congresses is 0.34, whereas the correlation across Congresses for Democrats is 0.24.[30]

Besides being apparent in the face of partisan regime changes, innate abilities should also help effective committee members become effective committee chairs. A simple way to assess this possibility is to identify the correlation between members' LESs in the Congress directly before they became committee chairs, and in the first Congress that they served as chair. Investigation reveals such a correlation to be positive (0.19) and statistically significant.[31]

Finally, innate ability in its rawest form can perhaps be best detected in a member's freshman LES. Just as we found that the average member maintains a similar LES from one Congress to the next, an ability-based effectiveness score should show a strong correlation between one's freshman effectiveness and one's sophomore effectiveness. One way to explore this possibility is to examine which members are above or below the median member of their freshman class, broken down by party (which is shown later to be a significant predictor of effectiveness). As we can see in a simple cross-tabulation in Table 2.2, there is a clear connection between members' freshman and sophomore term LESs. Members who were above the freshman median LES in their party in their

---

[29] The correlations discussed throughout this section are statistically significant at the level of $p < 0.001$, unless otherwise noted. That means that we have greater than 99.9 percent confidence that the relations uncovered here are not due to chance, but due to significant relationships across the variables of interest.

[30] Likewise, if we conduct a similar exercise and look at those members who were still in office when the next party regime switch occurred in the 110th Congress (2007–08), we obtain similar results. For Republicans, the correlation between their scores in the 109th and 110th Congress is positive and significant (correlation of 0.29), and the same holds true for the Democrats who moved into the majority in the 110th Congress (correlation of 0.20, p < 0.005).

[31] The p-value for this correlation is 0.02.

TABLE 2.2. *Effective Freshmen Become Effective Sophomores*

	Low Sophomore LES	High Sophomore LES	Total
Low Freshman LES	347	170	517
High Freshman LES	194	327	521
Total	541	497	1,038

Note: Illustrating the innate abilities of lawmakers, the table shows that, of the 1,038 House freshmen between 1973 and 2008 who became sophomores, there is consistency in the effectiveness of members across their first two terms in office. For example, 63 percent (327/521) of high-performing freshmen become high-performing sophomores, compared to just 33 percent (170/517) of low-performing freshmen. Members are determined to have "low" or "high" Legislative Effectiveness Scores based on whether they are below or above the median score of members of their party in their freshman and sophomore terms, respectively. The relevant test of statistical significance in the relationship between freshman and sophomore effectiveness in this table is: $\chi^2(1) = 97.90$ (p-value < 0.001).

first term were twice as likely to be above the sophomore median LES in their party in their second term as were below-average freshmen. Likewise, low-scoring freshmen were twice as likely to be low-scoring sophomores as were above-average freshmen.[32] These results suggest that, while there is certainly room for growth and improvement, legislators come to the chamber with a certain set of skills, and those that are successful early on continue to be successful, while those who are not effective tend to remain relatively ineffective in future terms.

Freshman Legislative Effectiveness Scores and Progressive Ambition

Could these innate abilities as detected, albeit imperfectly, by a member's freshman LES help predict that member's political future? Cursory analysis reveals some interesting findings. If we consider the most effective freshmen in the 98th Congress (1983–84), for example, we can identify several individuals who became prominent members of the House, or who advanced onto higher office. As shown in Appendix 2.4, those members who were in the top 10 percent of their freshman class included Rick Boucher (D-VA) and Alan Mollohan (D-WV), both of whom emerged as prominent members of the House of Representatives, as well as Bill Richardson (D-NM) and Barbara Boxer (D-CA), both of whom moved onto higher office. In contrast, none of the members in the top 10 percent of the 98th freshman class voluntarily retired from Congress. Most came to Congress with state legislative experience, perhaps accounting for part of their initial success. Consideration of other entering classes reveals other "rookie sensations" in the top 10 percent of their entering classes who became prominent in public life,

---

[32] The correlation between freshman LES and sophomore LES is 0.39 (p < 0.001).

TABLE 2.3. *Effective Freshmen Are More Likely to Soon Seek Higher Office*

	Does Not Seek Higher Office	Seeks Higher Office	Total
Low Freshman LES	592	68	660
High Freshman LES	531	98	629
Total	1,123	166	1,289

Note: The table shows that, of the 1,289 House freshmen between 1973 and 2008, those with initially high Legislative Effectiveness Scores were more likely to seek higher office within ten years. Specifically, 16 percent (98/629) of high-performing freshmen soon seek higher office, compared to just 10 percent (68/660) of low-performing freshmen. Members are determined to have "low" or "high" Legislative Effectiveness Scores based on whether they are below or above the median score of members of their party, respectively, in their freshman term. The relevant test of statistical significance in the relationship between freshman effectiveness and seeking higher office in this table is: $\chi^2(1) = 7.99$ (p-value = 0.005).

including Barney Frank (D-MA), who eventually chaired the Financial Services Committee, as well as the likes of Chuck Schumer (D-NY) in the 97th Congress (1981–82), David Price (D-NC) in the 100th Congress (1987–88), and Roy Blunt (R-MO) in the 105th Congress (1997–98).[33]

These examples are suggestive; yet, is there a more systematic relationship between the innate abilities revealed in freshman effectiveness and career prospects? Table 2.3 addresses this question head-on by identifying how many members who were above the median in their freshman cohorts (within their party) chose to seek higher office within their first ten years of being initially elected to Congress. For the purposes of analysis, we define "higher office" to be a Senate seat, a governorship, the presidency or vice presidency, or a mayor of a major city.[34] Our analysis demonstrates that those members who were in the upper half of their parties' freshman cohorts in terms of LES had 51 percent greater odds of seeking higher office during the first ten years of their congressional careers (98/629) than below average members (68/660).[35] Among the many prominent politicians who performed well as freshmen and soon sought higher office is Dan Quayle (R-IN), who was successful in his freshman term in

---

[33] For readers who might be relatively unfamiliar with these legislators, it is worth noting that Barney Frank ultimately served sixteen terms in the U.S. House, including as chair of the Financial Services Committee in the 110th and 111th Congresses, before retiring in 2012. Chuck Schumer is the senior senator from New York, having first been elected in 1998. David Price is a prominent Congress scholar, who has served in the House since 1997 (having previously served in the U.S. House from 1987–1995). Finally, Roy Blunt is currently the junior senator from Missouri, having been elected to the U.S. Senate in 2010; and he previously served as the minority whip in the House (and interim majority leader) during the 109th Congress.

[34] We thank Daniel Butler for generously providing us with these data.

[35] If we focus, instead, on whether legislators *ever* choose to run for higher office, we find that members who were in the upper half of their parties' freshman cohorts had 37 percent greater odds of seeking higher office at some point in their congressional careers.

TABLE 2.4. *Ineffective Freshmen Are More Likely to Retire Soon*

	Does Not Retire from Office	Retires from Office	Total
Low Freshman LES	574	86	660
High Freshman LES	573	56	629
Total	1,147	142	1,289

Note: The table shows that, of the 1,289 House freshmen between 1973 and 2008, those with initially low Legislative Effectiveness Scores were more likely to voluntarily retire from office within ten years. Specifically, 13 percent (86/660) of low-performing freshmen soon retired from office, compared to just 9 percent (56/629) of high-performing freshmen. Members are determined to have "low" or "high" Legislative Effectiveness Scores based on whether they are below or above the median score of members of their party, respectively, in their freshman term. The relevant test of statistical significance in the relationship between freshman effectiveness and voluntary retirement in this table is: $\chi^2(1) = 5.60$ (p-value = 0.018).

the 95th House (1977–78), moved over to the Senate in 1981, and ultimately became vice president under George H.W. Bush in 1989. John McCain (R-AZ) also falls into this category, standing above the median member's LES in his freshman cohort in the 98th Congress (1983–84) before moving over to the Senate in 1987, from where he launched two presidential bids (in 2000 and 2008). A more colorful representative of this class of high fliers is Rod Blagojevich (D-IL), who was elected to the House in the 105th Congress (1997–98), where he emerged as a leader in his freshman cohort. He ultimately ran (successfully) for Illinois governor in 2002, only to be impeached and removed from office in 2009 for attempting to sell the Senate seat vacated when Barack Obama became president.

An alternative way to engage this question is to ask whether members of Congress with less innate ability are more likely to retire voluntarily, perhaps because they do not find lawmaking to be the best use of their time in light of their poor performance. Table 2.4 presents similar analysis to Table 2.3 by identifying how many members who were above and below the median LES in their freshman classes (by party) chose voluntarily to retire during their first ten years in Congress.[36] As we can see, those members with a low freshman LES within their party have 46 percent greater odds of retiring voluntarily (86/660) than those members who were more effective during their freshman terms (56/629). Hence, not only does effectiveness seem a relevant consideration for career advancement, but early patterns of ineffectiveness are clearly related to members' choices to leave public life altogether. Among the many

[36] Although the temporal ordering of initial legislative effectiveness prior to retirement or to seeking higher office is suggestive, it is difficult to fully establish causation from these correlations. For instance, career goals and aspirations may drive both the effort to become effective and to seek higher office.

politicians in this category is J.C. Watts (R-OK), the former football star who was elected as a freshman to the 104th Congress (1995–96) and departed following the 107th Congress (2001–02) to become a lobbyist. The host of MSNBC's "Morning Joe," Joe Scarborough (R-FL), also falls into this category, as he was a relatively ineffective legislator compared to other members of his freshman cohort, and resigned within a few years, ostensibly to spend more time with his sons.[37] Whether these members leave because they are frustrated by their lack of effectiveness, or because they are offered fewer opportunities for career advancement than are other influential members in the chamber, is an open question and worthy of further study.[38] The fact that even the limited LES freshman snapshot helps to predict members' long-term career choices, however, provides further evidence that innate ability and initial effectiveness are crucial in understanding which members of Congress subsequently "get things done," as well as who moves up, and who moves on.

A Cultivated Skill Set

The above analyses lend some construct validity to the Legislative Effectiveness Scores, matching the expectation that legislative effectiveness is a product of innate abilities that carry forward from one term to the next and that shape the path of congressional careers. Yet there are many members in Table 2.2 who move up (or down) in relative effectiveness between their freshman and sophomore terms. And the correlations of members' scores over time may mask significant variation. Members can take significant steps to build up the skill set needed to be effective lawmakers. They can attempt various strategies and reinforce those that have the greatest success. They can learn from one another. They can build close working relationships with staffs and other members through connections from their home states, their parties, and the various caucuses to which they belong. One of the aggregate implications of these micro-level choices is that, over time, members should tend to become more effective.

Considering the effects of seniority on members' LESs is sufficient to demonstrate some degree of growth in the average member's skill over time. Recall that

---

[37] At the time of his resignation, Scarborough claimed that he had come to a "realization" that his sons were "at a critical stage of their lives and [he] would rather be judged at the end of his life as a father than as a congressman." ("Rep. Scarborough to Resign Seat," *USA Today*, May 29, 2001 retrieved from http://www.usatoday.com/news/washington/2001-05-25-scarborough.htm.)

[38] Interestingly, if we analyze whether a member *ever* chooses to retire voluntarily, we find that those members who were below the median freshman LES in their cohort within their party had only a 12 percent greater odds of retiring voluntarily across the course of their entire career in Congress, compared to those more effective freshman members. Hence, it is clear that some sort of self-selection is occurring during the first ten years of a member's career, which does not appear to be the case for those members who stay in Congress for longer periods of time, all of whom leave eventually one way or another.

the Legislative Effectiveness Scores are set to a mean of one. With that in mind, it is interesting to note that freshman members of Congress have an average LES of 0.365, while sophomores average 0.528. Members in their fifth term demonstrate an effectiveness level of 0.952, while those with ten or more terms of congressional service average 2.23.

This growth in effectiveness over time is indicative of members cultivating the crucial skill sets necessary to get things done in Congress. Moreover, this rise in LESs over time takes place also among members who are favorably endowed institutionally. Consider a member's first term as committee chair. There is much to be learned about being an effective chair. These new chairs' average LES is 4.19. After a few years of experience, however, the average chair is even more effective. For example, chairs in their third term of service and beyond average 5.37 for their LESs. Such growth in effectiveness may advocate against Republican-imposed term limits on chairs in recent Congresses. In short, whether serving as a rank-and-file member of Congress or as a committee chair, lawmakers have the ability to cultivate skills that result in greater legislative effectiveness, and they tend to take these opportunities to the tune of producing more legislation that finds its way further through the legislative process.

Institutional Positions

Many of the above facts and figures already support the idea that, beyond innate ability and the cultivation of critical skills over legislative careers, truly effective members of Congress achieve their legislative success by seeking and then utilizing key institutional positions. Moreover, some positions are more valuable than are others. Parties work hard to gain majority status and members covet committee chairmanships. One possible reason for such ambitions is that these institutional positions allow members to become much more effective lawmakers. Consistent with our expectations, the average LES of a committee chair is 4.78, while rank-and-file members average 0.800. This difference in means is highly significant, as is the difference in LES between the average majority-party member (LES of 1.45) and the average minority-party member (LES of 0.404).[39]

Figure 2.2 illustrates how seniority and institutional positions affect lawmakers' Legislative Effectiveness Scores. Committee chairs tend to be the most effective, followed by subcommittee chairs, followed by other majority-party members, and finally by members of the minority party. In each case, these scores tend to increase along with experience in the chamber, noted most significantly among those with committee and subcommittee chair positions. These findings should not be particularly surprising to students of Congress and

---

[39] These relationships are statistically significant with p < 0.001.

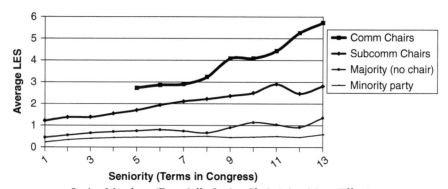

FIGURE 2.2. Senior Members (Especially Senior Chairs) Are More Effective

Note: The figure shows average Legislative Effectiveness Scores among House members from the 93rd–110th Congresses (1973–2008) between freshman term (Seniority = 1) and twenty-five years of service (Seniority = 13). Increased effectiveness with seniority is most evident for committee and subcommittee chairs, and for other members of the majority party.

its internal organization. Rather, these relationships provide further construct validity to the measurement of legislative effectiveness via the LES.

RELATION OF LEGISLATIVE EFFECTIVENESS SCORES TO EXISTING THEORIES OF CONGRESSIONAL POLITICS

We believe that legislative effectiveness provides a useful lens to understand the workings of Congress more generally. In the final methodological part of the chapter, therefore, we conduct analyses that serve two main purposes. First, to the extent that the variance in Legislative Effectiveness Scores is well explained by variables arising from existing theories of congressional politics, the construct validity of the LES is further established. Second, and simultaneously, to the extent that the LES is a valid measure of members' ability to advance their agenda items through the legislative process, these analyses set the stage for an assessment (and modification, as needed) of existing understandings of how congressional institutions and behaviors lead to policy outcomes.

Many theories of the legislative process have focused not on legislative effectiveness per se, but rather on the roles of such institutional and personal attributes as parties, the floor median, committees, race, gender, and ethnicity on the lawmaking process and on representation more generally. Although therefore not frequently articulated in terms of effectiveness, these theoretical contributions can be subjected to examination through the lens of legislative effectiveness, while at the same time helping us understand members' relative effectiveness. Based on previous scholarship, as well as on our preliminary analysis above, the following nine factors may well be related to a lawmaker's movement of bills through the legislative process.

Seniority Considerations

As noted above, we hypothesize that the cultivation of members' skills over time results in greater effectiveness. This claim is consistent with a longstanding body of research suggesting that, as legislators spend more time in Congress, they become better, and more effective, at lawmaking.[40] They have gained information and expertise regarding issues, other members' preferences, and the workings of the legislative process. As such, we would expect based on prior research, as well as on our preliminary analyses, that more senior legislators would have a heightened ability to navigate the nuances of legislative politics.

Previous Legislative Experience

Consistent with the argument about skill acquisition, one might expect that legislators who have previously served in their state legislatures would be more effective than legislators without similar experiences. To the extent that effectiveness is a talent that can be acquired and cultivated across time, state legislatures might serve as training grounds for members of Congress to develop skills that will help them in their future careers in the House. Such state-level political opportunities have long been considered a great benefit of U.S. federalism.[41] Because legislatures vary in their levels of professionalism, however, one might suspect that some legislatures serve as more rigorous proving grounds than others.[42] Hence, we might expect the influence of previous state legislative experience to vary depending on different levels of state legislative professionalism.

Party Influence

We have suggested that majority party control might provide the institutional advantage necessary for a substantial boost in legislative effectiveness for that party's members. A vibrant debate has developed over the past two decades regarding the extent to which political parties, and the majority party in particular, are influential in legislative politics.[43] Several theories posit different mechanisms of partisan influence, each with implications for the prospects of party

---

[40] Early work offering significant claims about seniority effects includes Fiorina (1977) and Mayhew (1974). In his studies of congressional careers, Hibbing (1991, 1993) argues that improved legislative "efficiency" (measured as a function of the percentage of sponsored bills that make it out of committee and pass the House) is likely to emerge across a legislator's career, and that it "may be due to the development of a better sense of what is and is not possible, or it may be due to better formal positions that usually come with increased tenure" (Hibbing 1991, 127).

[41] Paul Peterson (1995, 8) offers the example of early presidents and party loyalists establishing bases of support in their home states from which to gain national power and prominence.

[42] Squire (1992) offers a systematic measure and assessment of the relative professionalism of state legislatures.

[43] For early contributors to these debates, see Aldrich (1995), Cox and McCubbins (1993), Krehbiel (1993, 1999), and Rohde (1991).

members' legislative effectiveness. Broadly speaking, if the majority party is able to exercise influence over the legislative process at the expense of the minority party, then we would expect that members of the majority party would be more effective at moving bills through the House than would members of the minority party.

Legislative Leadership

A subset of strong-party theories has focused on the ways in which party leaders, in particular, are able to exert influence over the legislative process. Whether they engage in agenda setting, coercive arm-twisting to compel members to vote in accordance with their demands (as presumably occurred in the era of "Czar" Cannon), or whether their influence is less heavy-handed and is tantamount to legislative "vote-buying," one would expect that bills sponsored by majority-party leaders would be more likely to be considered in committee, receive attention outside the committee, and pass the House.[44] Alternatively, for bills sponsored by minority-party leaders, we might expect the opposite, with their efforts being suppressed by counteractive pressure on the part of majority-party leaders.

Committee Influence

Previously we tentatively found that institutional positions of committee leadership greatly influence members' possibilities for effective lawmaking. Such a finding is broadly consistent with the wide body of literature suggesting that committees facilitate political deal making.[45] Given this view of committee strength, some members of Congress may well benefit more than others. Chairs and members of the most powerful committees (Appropriations, Rules, and Ways and Means) should be disproportionately influential in comparison to the average member of the House. We would thus expect that bills sponsored by committee and subcommittee chairs (generally) and by members of the power committees would be more likely to be considered by their (and other) committees, more likely to reach the floor, and more likely to succeed in subsequent stages of the legislative process, which would result in greater effectiveness scores.[46]

---

[44] Jones (1968) offers a strong view of such arm-twisting, whereas Snyder and Groseclose (2000) and Herron and Wiseman (2008) explore the more subtle environment of coalition-building activities, and Cox and McCubbins (2005) highlight agenda setting. Recent work by Krehbiel, Meirowitz, and Wiseman (2013) explores the implications of having access to agenda control *and* the ability to buy votes for the legislative successes of party leaders.

[45] Key formative works on the nature and role of congressional committees in advancing policy agendas include Denzau and MacKay (1983), Shepsle and Weingast (1987), and Weingast and Marshall (1988).

[46] In addition to the analysis that follows, we also controlled for whether a legislator was a ranking minority member on a committee, and found that ranking minority member status is not correlated with a Representative's legislative effectiveness.

Ideological Considerations

In contrast to the proponents of strong-party theories and of deference to committees, an alternative perspective argues that legislative politics is majoritarian, and thus conducted in accordance with the policy preferences of a majority of members. Building on theories of a median voter deciding on outcomes along a single policy dimension, a number of scholars argue that policies reflecting the preferences of the median voter are most likely to pass the House.[47] Hence, if legislators propose policies close to their ideal preferences, we would expect that the fates of bills supported by those legislators who are closest to the median voter would be more favorable than those of more extreme liberals and conservatives. Therefore, more centrist legislators should be more effective.[48]

Race and Gender Considerations

Because they are drawn from demographic groups that are both currently and historically underrepresented in Congress (descriptively, speaking), female legislators and those from racial and ethnic minorities may be disproportionately active in advocating policies neglected by others.[49] While extensive scholarship has analyzed the experiences of female legislators and those from racial and ethnic minorities in state legislatures with varying results, much less work explores race and gender concerns in a broad, congressionally oriented framework.[50] Bringing issues onto the agenda that have been neglected previously, women and minorities may be particularly effective in seeing new solutions to important problems, or particularly ineffective in raising concerns that do not resonate with other lawmakers. Moreover, women and minorities might find natural coalitions of members in support of their legislation through such groups as the Congressional Black Caucus or the Congressional Caucus for Women's Issues.

Natural Coalition Partners

Coming from the same state might also present the possibility of a natural coalition, yielding greater legislative effectiveness. Because legislators from the same state

---

[47] Such median-voter models as those underpinning Krehbiel (1991) and Wiseman and Wright (2008) build upon the classic works of Duncan Black (1958) and Downs (1957).

[48] Alternatively, Woon (2008) suggests that, depending on their likely access to the agenda, certain legislators might moderate their bill proposals to enhance their chances of success, in contrast to others who will propose policies that are more consistent with their true policy preferences. Such strategic behavior would complicate the relationships between legislators' ideological positions and their relative effectiveness.

[49] See Gertzog (1984), Leader (1977), and Mezey (1978) for early work on the role of women in legislatures.

[50] Hamm, Harmel, and Thompson (1983) and Saint-Germain (1989) explore these issues at the state legislative level, with Anzia and Berry (2011) assessing the performance of men and women in Congress across a variety of measures.

might be relatively ideologically similar to each other, or face similar distributive pressures in trying to represent their constituents, a legislator might find coalition partners among the members of her delegation.[51] As such, one might suspect that legislators from states with larger congressional delegations would be relatively more effective than those from states with smaller delegations.

The Electoral Connection

Finally, legislators implicitly believe that their effectiveness in Congress is valued by their constituents.[52] Such a relationship could be based on the position taking involved in bill sponsorship, on credit claiming for advancing bills toward their fruition in law, or merely on the seniority that should translate into future effectiveness.[53] To the extent that voters value bill advancement on their behalf, one would expect a relationship between legislators' effectiveness and their electoral security.

Combined Together in Multivariate Analysis

While the above list of political concerns is not meant to be all-inclusive, these factors collectively represent a large set of considerations that we suspect would be related to a lawmaker's effectiveness. If these factors, on the whole, are unrelated to our measure of legislative effectiveness, such a finding would clearly call into question whether the LES is accurately capturing the key underlying concept relevant to so many areas of legislative studies. To identify whether (and how) systematic relationships might hold, we conducted ordinary least-squares regression analysis (with standard errors clustered by member to account for potential nonindependence of their scores over time), controlling for these different factors.[54] Data on members' party affiliation, gender, ethnicity, vote share in the previous elections, seniority, previous state legislative service, and party leadership positions were drawn from various volumes of the *Almanac of American Politics*.[55] Committee data were drawn from Charles Stewart's committee assignment website.[56] State legislative professionalism is operationalized as a weighted combination of the

---

[51] See Deckard (1972), Kessel (1964), and Truman (1956) for early explorations of the role of state delegations in Congress.

[52] Fenno (1978) offers examples of members of Congress making a case for reelection based on their self-proclaimed effectiveness.

[53] Mayhew (1974) discusses the position-taking and credit-claiming roles of members of Congress before the electorate.

[54] While we here explore the relationship between these key independent variables and members' LESs in a linear manner, it is worth noting that some of these relationships may be much more complex. For present purposes, our analyses show correlations between these many independent variables and the LES in order to demonstrate initial connections between important legislative phenomena and our new measure.

[55] Variable descriptions, summary statistics, and sources are given in Appendix 2.5.

[56] Data descriptions are offered in Nelson (1992) and Stewart and Woon (2005).

legislature's salary, staff, and time in session, relative to that of Congress.[57] Finally, legislators' left-right preferences are measured through the first-dimension DW-NOMINATE scores commonly used in the study of legislator ideologies.[58]

Our analysis from these regressions is presented in Table 2.5.[59] Model 2.1 simply shows the regression of the LES on the member's LES from the previous Congress, along with a constant. As discussed previously, and consistent with our innate abilities hypothesis, members show a strong positive correlation from Congress to Congress in their LESs. Model 2.2 includes variables capturing all nine factors from previous theories of legislative politics discussed above.[60]

Consistent with our initial explorations regarding members accumulating skills over time and relying on key institutional positions to aid in their effectiveness, the results in Model 2.2 reveal that a member's LES is clearly higher if she is more senior, if she is a member of the majority party, or if she is a committee or subcommittee chair.[61] Such findings comport well with existing research.[62] Given that scores have been normalized to be mean 1.0 within each Congress, the magnitudes of the coefficients imply that majority-party members and committee chairs are about two to five times more effective, respectively, than the average (nonmajority) member of Congress.[63]

---

[57] We use updated measures, based on the approach detailed in Squire (1992).

[58] These scores were developed by Poole and Rosenthal (1997).

[59] The results reported below are substantively identical to those that emerge if analysis is conducted on logged LES as a dependent variable. Results from a tobit analysis are also highly substantively similar.

[60] Model 2.2 excludes those legislators who do not have a lagged effectiveness score (so that the sample is identical to the one analyzed in Model 2.3).

[61] Many of the independent variables in the models presented here may be interrelated with the LES in complex ways. For example, endogeneity concerns exist regarding whether greater effectiveness may influence a member's vote share, committee assignment, or leadership position. Rather than attempting to establish causation in each case, our analysis features the exploration of associations. In our view, the possibility that effectiveness may *cause* changes in the independent variables, rather than being caused by them, only reinforces the importance of scholarship designed to study legislative effectiveness more fully.

[62] Drawing on various reputational rankings for the North Carolina legislature, for example, Meyer (1980, 564), Weissert (1991b), and Padro i Miquel and Snyder (2006) demonstrate that majority-party members and more senior legislators are perceived to be more effective lawmakers than junior and minority-party legislators. Frantzich (1979) demonstrates that majority-party, and more senior, House members have higher bill passage rates than minority-party or less senior members; his seniority finding is reinforced by Hamm et al.'s (1983) study of the Texas and South Carolina legislatures. More recently, Anderson et al. (2003) and Cox and Terry (2008) have also found that majority-party members, committee chairs, and senior members have relatively more bills advance out of committee and pass the House than their junior and minority-party counterparts.

[63] Consistent with the work of Adler and Wilkerson (2013), committee chairs' greater effectiveness is likely influenced by the fact that many high priority bills that go through committees (and are presumably guaranteed to pass, such as reauthorizations) are introduced on behalf of the committee by their chairs. Hence, consistent with our institutional positions hypothesis, holding such positions would clearly enhance these legislators' observed effectiveness at creating laws.

TABLE 2.5. *Determinants of Legislative Effectiveness*

	Model 2.1	Model 2.2	Model 2.3
Lagged Effectiveness Score	0.683***		0.474***
	(0.021)		(0.031)
Seniority		0.070***	0.010
		(0.010)	(0.007)
State Legislative Experience		−0.112	−0.092
		(0.096)	(0.058)
State Legislative Experience × Legislative Prof.		0.548*	0.401**
		(0.314)	(0.189)
Majority Party		0.547***	0.311***
		(0.067)	(0.045)
Majority-Party Leadership		0.299*	0.310**
		(0.174)	(0.139)
Minority-Party Leadership		−0.136**	−0.052
		(0.064)	(0.061)
Speaker		−0.464	−0.290
		(0.314)	(0.247)
Committee Chair		2.943***	2.099***
		(0.269)	(0.193)
Subcommittee Chair		0.765***	0.543***
		(0.095)	(0.064)
Power Committee		−0.259***	−0.119***
		(0.063)	(0.036)
Distance from Median		0.101	−0.104
		(0.143)	(0.089)
Female		0.121**	0.099***
		(0.060)	(0.038)
African American		−0.433***	−0.224***
		(0.103)	(0.082)
Latino		0.085	0.029
		(0.151)	(0.082)
Size of Congressional Delegation		−0.002	−0.001
		(0.003)	(0.002)
Vote Share		0.029**	0.031***
		(0.014)	(0.011)
Vote Share^2		−0.0002**	−0.0002***
		(0.0001)	(0.0001)
Constant	0.441***	−0.999**	−0.977**
	(0.019)	(0.512)	(0.394)
N	6297	6155	6155
Adjusted-R^2	0.42	0.42	0.56

Notes: Ordinary least squares estimation, robust standard errors in parentheses, observations clustered by member.
*p < 0.1 (two-tailed), **p < 0.05 (two-tailed), ***p < 0.01 (two-tailed).

However, the coefficient on Seniority suggests that the majority-party advantage is not completely overwhelming. More specifically, relatively senior minority-party members (those that have been in Congress for more than seven terms) may be as effective as the average majority-party member without such experience. The link between seniority and effectiveness offers one argument against instituting term limits for members of Congress.[64] The expertise developed on issues, as well as regarding which coalitions are feasible to bring about change, may be crucial to legislative effectiveness, and may be lost when a member leaves the House.

Our results reveal that the skill sets cultivated through state legislative experiences can translate into legislative effectiveness in Congress, but only under certain circumstances. Specifically, a mild degree of support for learning within the most professional state legislatures is found in the positive coefficient on the interaction between service in the state legislature and that legislature's level of professionalism. This suggests that House members who have served in more professionalized legislatures arrive in the U.S. Congress with less need for on-the-job training to become effective lawmakers. Alternatively, it might be the case that professionalized legislatures are a good screening mechanism for effective lawmakers, as only the most effective lawmakers in these legislatures seek higher office – namely, the U.S. Congress.

With respect to leadership positions, we find that majority-party leaders have slightly higher LESs. In contrast, minority-party leaders and the Speaker of the House have lower LESs, with the former of these differences being statistically significant.[65] While the negative coefficient on Speaker may be surprising at first glance, it is important to realize that our measure of effectiveness is based on how far legislators' bills advance in the legislative process. Because the Speaker of the House traditionally introduces few, if any, bills, and those bills that are offered are often controversial, it should not be surprising that the Speaker's bills might be less likely to advance than other bills. This is not to say that the Speaker is an ineffective lawmaker, but rather that the way we are conceptualizing effectiveness, as the ability of legislators to advance their bills through Congress, might not capture other notions of effectiveness, such as those exerted by the Speaker.

Model 2.2 also reveals that members of top committees (i.e., Appropriations, Rules, and Ways and Means) who are not chairs have lower LESs than rank-and-file members of the House.[66] This finding likely follows from the fact

---

[64] This argument is consistent with the position articulated by Hibbing (1993).

[65] These findings are *inconsistent* with the work of Frantzich (1979), Hamm et al. (1983), Padro i Miquel and Snyder (2006), and Weissert (1991b), who generally find that party and chamber leadership is positively related to various forms of perceived (or actual) legislative productivity and effectiveness.

[66] These findings are substantively identical if we define power committees to include the Budget Committee. Given that Appropriations, Ways and Means, and Rules have historically been

that much of the high-priority legislation that goes through these committees (e.g., Appropriations bills with a substantial likelihood of passage) is introduced by the committee chairs. Rank-and-file members of top committees tend to concentrate their efforts on the important areas governed by their committees, and therefore introduce less legislation than the average House member. Such tendencies naturally contribute to lower LESs for these members.

With respect to gender and race and ethnicity, women have higher LESs than men, while African-American legislators have lower LESs than whites, with no systematic differences between Latino members and the average member of Congress. These findings are consistent with some strands of the legislative politics literatures focused on race, gender, and ethnicity.[67] They are sufficiently intriguing that we dedicate much of Chapter 4 to discerning the conditions under which women and African Americans perform differently than their colleagues in Congress, based on the divergent strategic options for successful lawmaking available to them.

With respect to vote share, electorally safe members are at first more effective, but the relative impact of electoral safety on legislative effectiveness exhibits decreasing returns. This finding suggests that at-risk members might devote their efforts to activities other than legislative productivity (e.g., district casework, funneling federal funds to the district, and campaign fundraising), while somewhat safer members focus their attentions on becoming effective lawmakers. However, members from very safe electoral districts may feel less pressure to advance legislative agendas, and once again perform less well on our measure of effectiveness. In an alternative story about the relationship between legislative effectiveness and electoral success, if legislators are rewarded at the polls for their effectiveness, one would expect that the most electorally safe legislators would be those who are most successful getting legislation introduced and passed into law.

"exclusive" committees whereby Representatives could only hold seats on one of those three committees (and no other committees), these results likely reflect that fact that much of the legislation that moves through these three committees is sponsored by committee or subcommittee chairs; and perhaps members of these three committees devote most of their legislative energies to committee-centric matters, rather than other bills that would naturally advance through different authorizing committees.

[67] Saint-Germain (1989) and Bratton (2005), for example, find that female legislators experience higher rates of success than their male counterparts in several state legislatures; Bratton and Haynie (1999) find that African-American legislators are less successful in several state legislatures. In contrast, Hamm et al. (1983) find that ethnicity is not heavily correlated with number of bills (or rate of bills) that are sponsored and passed in the Texas and South Carolina House of Representatives; Thomas and Welch (1991) find that female state legislators are generally less successful than their male counterparts. In one of the few works that addresses these questions at the congressional level, Jeydel and Taylor (2003) find that legislative success is not clearly related to gender. Consistent with Anzia and Berry (2011), one possible explanation for our female legislator finding is that female candidates might be generically discriminated against in the electoral arena; hence, female candidates who are ultimately elected tend to have greater innate lawmaking ability than their average male counterparts.

These results, combined with existing studies that have yielded contradictory findings on this matter, suggest that the true relationship between electoral success and legislative effectiveness may require much additional work to disentangle.[68] Finally, we see that, controlling for other factors, a legislator's distance from the chamber median and the size of her state's congressional delegation are not generally statistically significant predictors of her LES.

Model 2.3 in Table 2.5 presents the results from a regression controlling for all of a legislator's personal and institutional attributes, as well as her lagged LES. As we can see from this model, a member's lagged LES continues to be positively related with her LES in the current Congress, even upon controlling for myriad personal and institutional attributes. This is consistent with our view that members have innate abilities that aid in their effectiveness over time.[69] The signs and significance of the coefficients on the different personal and institutional variables are generally substantively similar to those models without controlling for lagged LES. As before, key institutional positions of committee and subcommittee chairs and majority-party membership enhance members' effectiveness, as well, even controlling for their innate abilities.

Because the effects of state legislative experience and electoral margins are difficult to interpret due to their nonlinear interactive variables, Figure 2.3 illustrates these effect sizes. Holding all other variables at their average values, the figure shows three curves. The top curve represents the lawmakers who came to Congress with prior experience in the most professional state legislatures, such as California, New York, or Michigan. Rather than an average of 1.0, these lawmakers average around 1.3 on their Legislative Effectiveness Scores, indicating an ability to advance about 30 percent more legislation through Congress, all else equal. In contrast, the bottom curve shows a loss of about 10 percent in effectiveness for those members from less professional state legislatures, relative to members with no previous legislative experience (shown on the middle curve). Such a difference may just be a statistical artifact or may serve as tentative evidence that the lessons drawn from such state experience do not apply well to service in Congress.

The other noteworthy characteristic of Figure 2.3 is the curved nature of the effects, moving left to right on the figure.[70] As was mentioned previously, these nonlinear effects seem to indicate that the most effective lawmakers are those from somewhat, but not completely, safe districts. This finding is consistent

---

[68] Studies of success in the electoral realm relative to the legislative realm (e.g., Frantzich 1979; Padro i Miquel and Snyder 2006; Weissert 1991b) are preliminary and conflicting, suggesting that much more work is needed in this area.

[69] There may also be other factors, beyond innate abilities, that help account for consistent patterns over time.

[70] This figure originally appears in: Volden, Craig, and Alan E. Wiseman. 2012. "Legislative Effectiveness and Representation," in Lawrence C. Dodd and Bruce I. Oppenehimer (eds.). *Congress Reconsidered*, 10th Edition. Washington, DC: CQ Press (pp. 237–264).

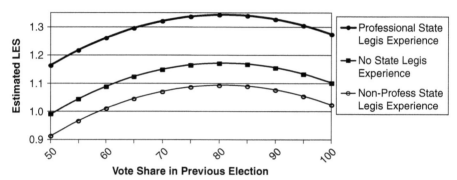

FIGURE 2.3. Moderately Safe Members and Those with Experience in Professional State Legislatures Are More Effective

Note: The figure shows estimated Legislative Effectiveness Scores among House members from the 93rd–110th Congresses (1973–2008) based on Model 2.3 from Table 2.5, holding other variables at their means (modes for binary variables). Lawmakers from moderately safe seats are more effective than those holding at-risk or uncontested seats. State legislative experience is only positively related to legislative effectiveness in the House if that experience was in a highly professional state legislature. Otherwise, such experience is actually negatively related to legislative effectiveness.

with those in closely contested seats dedicating their resources to electoral and constituency activities, those from very safe seats feeling less compelled to build up their lawmaking portfolios, and those in between being both most motivated and best able to advance a significant legislative agenda.[71]

One final point of interest from Table 2.5 is the adjusted-R^2 statistic of Model 2.3. The value of 0.56 suggests that about 56 percent of the variance in a member's LES can be explained by her lagged LES score (i.e., how effective the member was in the previous Congress), and the personal and institutional circumstances that she faces in the current Congress.[72] Hence, although each member engages in numerous activities resulting in her LES in any given Congress, the underlying factors of innate ability, acquired skills, and institutional position, coupled with considerations from earlier theories of legislative politics, go a long way toward explaining who "gets things

---

[71] One interesting exception to the pattern in Figure 2.3 is that, within the majority party, electorally vulnerable (below 60 percent vote share) freshmen (LES average of 0.53) outperform their safer colleagues (LES average of 0.38) at a statistically significant rate (p = 0.002). Consistent with anecdotal evidence, for this small grouping of lawmakers, party leaders may attempt to aid their junior colleagues' electoral fortunes by promoting their sponsored bills (and, in some cases, by making them the sponsors of likely-to-pass party-favored legislation).

[72] The remaining variance means that some members outperform or underperform relative to the average expectations given their personal characteristics and institutional positions. High-performing lawmakers (such as those with very positive "residuals") are explored in much more detail in Chapter 6.

done" in Congress.[73] In sum, the construct validity of the LES is strongly supported by the variation in this measure matching well-established expectations about lawmaking in Congress and about the types of members who are best able to advance their agendas.[74]

SUMMARY AND NEXT STEPS

Why are some members of Congress more effective than others at moving their legislative agenda items forward? What does such effectiveness tell us about the inner workings of Congress and its role in shaping public policy for the United States? To answer these questions in a systematic and quantitative fashion, we engaged in a measurement activity yielding what we refer to as Legislative Effectiveness Scores. The LES is developed upon combining fifteen key indicators of each member's legislative advancements in each Congress into a single measure that captures the essence of legislative effectiveness. The content of this measure matches key stages of the legislative process as well as the importance of the bills being analyzed. In its construction, this measure matches expectations about legislative effectiveness arising from theoretical understandings of the institution of Congress.

Specifically, consistent with members having innate lawmaking abilities, we find significant correlations from one Congress to the next in each member's LES, including in the move from freshman term to sophomore term, from majority party to minority party, and from committee member to committee chair. These innate abilities, as judged by a lawmaker's freshman LES, also tell us something about lawmakers' own perceptions of their legislative effectiveness. Less effective members choose to leave the institution and enter private life; more effective members seek to take their talents to higher offices. Consistent with the importance of institutional positioning and the accumulation of lawmaking skills over time, we find that members of the majority party, and especially subcommittee and committee chairs, enjoy enhanced effectiveness, and that the LES for these groups increases with their experience in Congress. We also find that members' scores are well explained by such

---

[73] Moreover, these findings are not driven merely by the difference between members who exert a high level of effort and those who are disengaged from the legislative process. For example, an analysis along the lines of that reported in Table 2.5 solely on the subset of engaged legislators (those introducing ten or more pieces of legislation) yields substantively similar results.

[74] The totality of this work argues *against* the view of Adler and Wilkerson (2013, esp. chap. 7) that the "must-pass" status of bills (and *not* the sponsors themselves) is mainly what drives lawmaking in Congress. An alternative way of understanding that work is that characteristics of lawmakers are important in explaining the fate of certain types of bills relative to others (and that researchers must be careful in how to classify different types of bills). Such a finding is consistent with our approach of subsetting bills into the three categories of commemorative, substantive, and substantive and significant. Looking at subsets of bills by issue area also yields important findings for bill success and policy gridlock, as illustrated in our Chapter 5.

additional theoretically derived factors as electoral success, leadership positions, race, gender, and personal characteristics.

In combination, the analyses reported here lead us to believe that we have generated an important measure of a concept – legislative effectiveness – that can now be used to better understand congressional politics. We began this chapter with a discussion of the body of legislation that was introduced by four members of the 110th House of Representatives, and a consideration of the fates of their various bills. While these members' goals and achievements are important when studied individually, we believe that studying them collectively and finding patterns across such members can be even more powerful. Legislative Effectiveness Scores allow us to cardinally rank Representatives Pomeroy, Oberstar, Kildee, and McNulty, as well as other members of Congress in sensible ways, setting the stage for further investigations throughout this book and beyond.

For example, we found members of the majority party to be generally more effective than their minority-party counterparts. While this finding comports well with some significant strands of legislative scholarship, a natural question remains regarding the source of this majority-party advantage. For example, is the majority-party leadership able to compel members of its caucus to vote in favor of its agenda, ensuring at the final passage stage that its members are more effective than are members of the minority? Alternatively, is the majority party able to bottle up legislation that is unfavorable to its interests in the committee system, so that only majority-party-favored legislation advances to the floor (and ultimately to the president's desk)? These types of questions about where and how party influence is exerted are central to the debate on the role of parties in Congress, and they are precisely the types of inquiries that we engage in Chapter 3.

Turning to other findings, it is intriguing that female lawmakers appear to be systematically more effective than their male counterparts, particularly given previous research suggesting that female members of Congress are institutionally disadvantaged when compared to men. While our large-sample analysis suggests the robustness of women's enhanced effectiveness, it begs the question: how do women achieve greater effectiveness than men in Congress? At the same time, it is intriguing, and perhaps deeply troubling, that African-American lawmakers appear to be systematically *less* effective than their white counterparts. Such a finding raises broad questions regarding the efficacy of minority representation in the U.S. Congress. Do African-American legislators appear to be less effective because of specific strategies that they choose to employ in the chamber, or are they subjected to some form of institutional disadvantage or racism given their policy stances or agendas? Evidence of the latter possibility would be particularly troubling in light of the measures that the federal government has undertaken since the 1960s to enhance the number of minority representatives in Congress (such as the development of majority-minority congressional districts). What is the benefit of expanding descriptive representation of minorities in Congress if they arrive to a chamber that systematically undermines their agendas? In Chapter 4, we explore in greater detail the activities of three "minority" groups in Congress – women, African Americans, and Southern Democrats – to establish and explain their effectiveness in and out of the majority party and across key stages of the lawmaking process.

Finally, does our metric help explain the aggregate production of new policies in the U.S. Congress? Is it true that policy entrepreneurs are generally necessary to bring about policy change? If so, do these policy entrepreneurs appear to be effective legislators in the ways that we are defining effectiveness? And can the most influential policies coming out of Congress be attributed to the members we find to be most effective? At a time when the United States is facing unprecedented challenges in the realms of health policy, financial services regulation, environmental matters, and other policy areas, it is important to engage such questions of where leaders come from, how they can facilitate policy change, and which changes they will help bring about. The latter chapters of the book are dedicated to these questions of how Congress overcomes legislative gridlock and what strategies propel its most effective members to lawmaking success.

APPENDICES TO CHAPTER 2: MEASURING LEGISLATIVE EFFECTIVENESS

Appendix 2.1: The Effect of Amendments on the LES

As constructed in Chapter 2, each member's LES is based on her sponsored bills, their progress through five stages of the legislative process, and the nature of the bills in terms of their substantive significance. What is set aside in such measurement construction is the extent to which sponsored bills are subsequently amended. Such an omission may be inconsequential for bills that are only modified slightly or for those that are not amended at all. However, occasionally the full text of bills is eliminated with entirely other language inserted, or other major modifications are made. While the policy extent of such modifications cannot be judged without a line-by-line assessment of the bill wording, some assessment of the impact of amendments on the LES measure is desirable. In this appendix, we report the results of analyses designed to explore how the inclusion or exclusion of information about amendments affects the LES and its usefulness as a measure of legislative effectiveness.

To do so, we track the successful amendments offered to each bill on the floor of the House of Representatives.[75] Such data are available for the 97th Congress

---

[75] This analysis neglects the extent to which bills are modified in committee (data on which are unavailable), amendments in the Senate, changes in conference committees, and the degree to which these amendments modify the original language or intent of the bill. Therefore, we offer here only a partial analysis of the role of amendments in modifying the Legislative Effectiveness Scores. That said, the additional impact of committee and Senate amendments would need to be much more substantial than that of House floor amendments in order to significantly diminish the credibility and usefulness of the LES measure, based on the analysis offered here.

(1981–82) and beyond, thus limiting our dataset somewhat. Although less than two percent of all bills introduced in the House are subsequently amended on the floor, these tend to be substantive and significant pieces of legislation and those that pass the furthest through the legislative process; they must therefore be considered carefully. Hence, we construct two alternative legislative effectiveness scores. In the first, we restrict our analysis solely to the subset of bills on which there were no successful floor amendments. We again construct scores based on the equation given in Chapter 2, but now alter the scaling based on this reduced number of bills. The resultant scores are once again normalized to mean of 1.0 for each Congress.

In a second revised measure, for each amended bill, we assign half of the credit for the bill's movement through the legislative process to the sponsor and the other half to the lawmakers who offered successful amendments to the bill, divided equally among the successful amenders.[76] With such credit now assigned not only based on sponsorship but also on amendment activities, we once again utilize the main equation from Chapter 2 to generate new legislative effectiveness scores, again weighted to a mean of 1.0 per Congress.

With these two new measures in hand, we conduct the regression analysis from Model 2.3 of Table 2.5 not only on the original Legislative Effectiveness Scores (now restricted to the Congresses for which we have amendment data) but also on these revised measures. The results are reported in Table 2A.1.

The results show remarkable consistency across these three alternative measures. Nearly all variables' coefficients take similar values in terms of their substantive and statistical significance. Yet two minor differences appear that may be indicative of what is lost by omitting amendment data in the construction of the LES. First, the coefficient on Majority Party is smaller in Model 2A.3 than in the earlier models, indicating that one tactic used by the minority party with some effect is the offering of successful amendments on the floor. Second, Seniority, Speaker, Committee Chair, and Subcommittee Chair all have smaller positive (or more negative) values in Models 2A.2 and 2A.3 than in Model 2A.1. This suggests that the bills sponsored by these individuals are more prone to be amended, perhaps due to their substantive and significant nature. While suggestive, these differences are not statistically significant.

Therefore, setting these two points aside, the remarkable similarities across these three models indicates that the interpretations put forward throughout this book based on the LES measure as constructed without including amendments are very likely to hold true upon a more systematic inclusion of such amendments. The inclusion here of amendments is costly in terms of lost data for the 93rd through 96th Congresses, and this analysis indicates that such costs are not

---

[76] Other weights on the amount of credit given to amenders yield largely similar results.

TABLE 2A.1. *Effect of Floor Amendments on Legislative Effectiveness Scores*

	Model 2A.1 LES	Model 2A.2 Unamended Subset LES	Model 2A.3 Amended LES Attributing Half of Score to Amenders
Lagged Score	0.416***	0.442***	0.453***
	(0.037)	(0.034)	(0.035)
Seniority	0.022***	0.014*	0.014*
	(0.008)	(0.009)	(0.008)
State Legislative Experience	−0.065	−0.065	−0.074
	(0.065)	(0.071)	(0.062)
State Legislative Experience × Legislative Prof.	0.338*	0.348*	0.305*
	(0.196)	(0.206)	(0.180)
Majority Party	0.417***	0.416***	0.368***
	(0.056)	(0.059)	(0.057)
Majority-Party Leadership	0.361**	0.393**	0.345**
	(0.171)	(0.194)	(0.155)
Minority-Party Leadership	−0.076	−0.060	−0.070
	(0.073)	(0.088)	(0.075)
Speaker	−0.434	−0.814***	−0.604***
	(0.289)	(0.226)	(0.223)
Committee Chair	2.364***	2.119***	2.123***
	(0.238)	(0.254)	(0.223)
Subcommittee Chair	0.486***	0.360***	0.390***
	(0.082)	(0.081)	(0.072)
Power Committee	−0.167***	−0.291***	−0.221***
	(0.045)	(0.049)	(0.040)
Distance from Median	−0.198*	−0.162	−0.177
	(0.116)	(0.126)	(0.122)
Female	0.130***	0.135***	0.121***
	(0.045)	(0.046)	(0.041)
African American	−0.141*	−0.102	−0.121
	(0.082)	(0.101)	(0.083)
Latino	0.032	0.025	0.017
	(0.086)	(0.097)	(0.082)
Size of Congressional Delegation	−0.002	−0.002	−0.002
	(0.002)	(0.002)	(0.002)
Vote Share	0.037***	0.042***	0.040***
	(0.013)	(0.015)	(0.013)
Vote Share^2	−0.0002**	−0.0003***	−0.0002***
	(0.0001)	(0.0001)	(0.0001)
Constant	−1.217**	−1.317**	−1.246***
	(0.487)	(0.530)	(0.468)
N	4008	4008	4008
Adjusted-R^2	0.54	0.48	0.54

Notes: All analyses in the table include only the subset of data for which amendment information is available for the current and previous Congress. Ordinary least squares regressions are used, with robust standard errors shown in parentheses, and observations clustered by member.
*p < 0.1 (two-tailed), **p < 0.05 (two-tailed), ***p < 0.01 (two-tailed).

outweighed by the benefits of modifying the measure to exclude amended bills or to boost the scores of successful amenders.

Appendix 2.2: The Role of Earlier Stages in the Production of Laws

We argue throughout Chapter 2 that legislative effectiveness is best captured by Legislative Effectiveness Scores that combine members' activities across five important stages of the lawmaking process. An alternative view of legislative effectiveness is that earlier stages of the lawmaking process are not important, as the attainment of success in these stages alone does not ultimately change public policy the way that enactment of a law does.

Our view is that legislative effectiveness can be better measured by also including earlier stages, because they establish the proven ability to move legislation forward, even if they do not bring about new laws in each instance. If we are correct, then effectiveness at earlier stages in the legislative process should predict success at later stages. Moreover, based on our argument that legislative effectiveness is partly based on the innate abilities of lawmakers, this effect should persevere from one Congress to the next.

To explore these conjectures, in this Appendix we rely on the dependent variable of the number of laws enacted in each given Congress that were sponsored by each lawmaker. We seek to explain this number of successful enactments with actions at each legislative stage in the previous Congress.

Table 2A.2 presents the results of a series of ordinary least squares (OLS) regressions.[77] Each of these regressions controls for all of the independent variables used in Model 2.3 of Table 2.5, with the exception of the Lagged LES. The first five models also include variables capturing the number of sponsored bills in the previous Congress that reach each of the five stages used to construct the LES.[78] Each of these models shows significant evidence that accomplishments in the previous Congress, even at earlier stages of the legislative process, positively impact the number of laws produced by a lawmaker in the current Congress. For example, each additional bill receiving action in committee in one Congress is associated with 0.128 more laws arising in the next Congress from the sponsored bills of this member. Interestingly, the best fitting estimate of current law production arises for Model 2A.7, which accounts for the number of bills in the previous Congress passing the House. Such bills, if they do not become law in that Congress, are perhaps among the most likely proposals to become law in the subsequent Congress.

To explore the possibility that such findings are merely the result of controlling for members of Congress who are particularly active in sponsoring bills both in the previous and current Congress, in Models 2A.9 through 2A.13 we also

---

[77] The alternative of negative binomial regressions, given the count data for the dependent variable, yields substantively similar results to those reported here.

[78] Due to collinearity concerns, each stage is entered separately here.

TABLE 2A.2. *Explaining Laws with Activities in Previous Congress*

	Model 2A.4	Model 2A.5	Model 2A.6	Model 2A.7	Model 2A.8	Model 2A.9	Model 2A.10	Model 2A.11	Model 2A.12	Model 2A.13	Model 2A.14	Model 2A.15	Model 2A.16	Model 2A.17
Lagged Introductions ($BILL_{t-1}$)	0.011*** (0.002)					-0.001 (0.003)					-0.008*** (0.003)			
Lagged Action In Committee (AIC_{t-1})		0.128*** (0.013)					0.115*** (0.013)					0.048*** (0.010)		
Lagged Action Beyond Committee (ABC_{t-1})			0.191*** (0.017)					0.176*** (0.017)					0.105*** (0.018)	
Lagged Passed House ($PASS_{t-1}$)				0.238*** (0.019)					0.219*** (0.019)					0.152*** (0.024)
Lagged Becomes Law (LAW_{t-1})					0.364*** (0.034)					0.337*** (0.034)				0.131** (0.052)
Current Introductions ($BILL_t$)						0.018*** (0.003)	0.014*** (0.002)	0.012*** (0.002)	0.012*** (0.002)	0.013*** (0.002)	0.020*** (0.003)	0.013*** (0.002)	0.012*** (0.002)	0.012*** (0.002)
Adjusted-R^2	0.30	0.35	0.38	0.39	0.38	0.32	0.37	0.40	0.41	0.40	0.40	0.41	0.41	0.41

Notes: $N = 6154$ in all models.

Results are from ordinary least squares regressions.

All control variables (other than lagged LES) used in Model 2-3 in Table 2.5 are included in these models, also.

Robust standard errors are shown in parentheses, with observations clustered by member.

*p < 0.1, **p < 0.05, ***p < 0.01 (two-tailed).

control for the number of bills sponsored by the lawmaker in the current Congress. These models reaffirm that legislative activities at all stages beyond sponsorship in the previous Congress are associated with enhanced production of laws in the current Congress.

To further explore whether there is merely a correlation of the same members producing more laws in each Congress, in Models 2A.14 through 2A.17, we also control for the number of laws produced in the previous Congress, which is positive and statistically significant in each of these models. Although now the number of bills sponsored in the previous Congress is negatively related with current law production, all later stages are significant positive indicators of subsequent production of laws.

Taken together, these results present the following picture. Members of Congress vary in their legislative effectiveness. Early stages of the legislative process, from receiving action in committee, to shepherding their bills to the floor of the House, through passing the House, all show which members are particularly effective. Effectiveness at such stages is indicative that these members will be able to produce more laws in both the current and subsequent Congresses. Therefore, a measure such as the LES that accounts for such earlier stages better captures the underlying concept of legislative effectiveness than does a measure relying merely upon the number of laws that a legislator produces.

Appendix 2.3: Alternate Weights on Types of Legislation

To generate the Legislative Effectiveness Scores used throughout this book, we rely on the main equation in Chapter 2 and assign relative weights to commemorative, substantive, and substantive and significant bills of one, five, and ten, respectively. Although these weights can be justified in terms of their content validity, and although the measure as a whole is assessed throughout the chapter in terms of its construct validity, this Appendix explores these particular weightings in more detail.

Specifically, we construct alternative legislative effectiveness scores holding the weight of substantive and significant bills at 10 and allowing the weights on the other types of bills to take any integer value between 1 and 10.[79] We then treat these new scores as the dependent variable in regressions that match Model 2.3 of Table 2.5, which is our full model designed to explain the institutional and personal factors that result in higher or lower degrees of legislative effectiveness.[80]

---

[79] We therefore set aside weighting schemes that assign a zero value to any of these categories or weighting schemes that assign greater weight to other categories than to substantive and significant bills.

[80] The lagged dependent variable used in each model matches the weighting schemes used for the dependent variable.

Two main findings emerge from this series of analyses. First, for all such regressions for which the weights are assigned with commemoratives lowest and substantive and significant laws the greatest, the main findings offered in Table 2.5 and discussed in the text continue to hold true. Although coefficients naturally change, the substantive interpretations of the relations among the key variables are robust to a wide array of alternative weights. Such is not the case when commemorative bills are weighed at a significantly higher level than substantive bills, indicating that such an alternative approach to generating legislative effectiveness scores would tap into some other underlying concept, one which does not meet our definition of legislative effectiveness very well.

Second, one aspect of the construct validity analysis for the LES as conducted in Chapter 2 was an assessment of the degree to which the variance in the LES is well explained by the key variables arising from earlier theoretical and empirical works on congressional politics. Put simply, Model 2.3 in Table 2.5 had an adjusted-R^2 value of 0.56. In Table 2A.3, we report the adjusted-R^2 values for each of the 100 regression analyses carried out with the various weighting schemes discussed previously.

Across all of these models, the weighting scheme of 1-5-10 that we use has the second highest adjusted-R^2 value, slightly behind only the 1-6-10 weighting scheme. Models assigning greater or lower weights to substantive bills perform less well, as do those assigning greater values to commemorative bills. Although

TABLE 2A.3. *Moderate Weights for Substantive Bills and Low Weights for Commemoratives Yield the Most Predictive Model*

Adj. R^2 Values	Substantive Weight:									
Commemorative Weight	1	2	3	4	5	6	7	8	9	10
1	0.51	0.54	0.55	0.56	*0.56*	<u>0.56</u>	0.56	0.56	0.56	0.55
2	0.51	0.53	0.55	0.56	0.56	0.56	0.56	0.56	0.56	0.55
3	0.51	0.53	0.55	0.55	0.56	0.56	0.56	0.56	0.56	0.55
4	0.50	0.53	0.54	0.55	0.55	0.56	0.56	0.56	0.55	0.55
5	0.50	0.52	0.54	0.55	0.55	0.55	0.55	0.55	0.55	0.55
6	0.49	0.52	0.53	0.54	0.55	0.55	0.55	0.55	0.55	0.55
7	0.48	0.51	0.52	0.53	0.54	0.54	0.55	0.55	0.55	0.54
8	0.47	0.50	0.52	0.53	0.53	0.54	0.54	0.54	0.54	0.54
9	0.47	0.49	0.51	0.52	0.53	0.53	0.54	0.54	0.54	0.54
10	0.46	0.48	0.50	0.51	0.52	0.53	0.53	0.53	0.53	0.53

Note: The table shows the adjusted-R^2 calculations for the equivalent of Model 2.3 from Table 2.5 run on 100 alternative Legislative Effectiveness Scores created using bill weights ranging from 1 to 10 for both commemorative and substantive bills, while leaving the weights on substantive and significant bills at 10. The greatest adjusted-R^2 occurs with weights of 1 and 6 (shown <u>underlined</u>), while that used throughout the book is very similar, with weights of 1 and 5 on commemoratives and substantive bills, respectively (shown in ***bold and italics***).

our goal in developing a weighting scheme was not to maximize the adjusted-R^2 of Model 2.3, the fact that this model is easily one of the best performers on this criterion lends additional construct validity to the measure. Moreover, nothing about this set of robustness analyses points to the need to modify our weighting scheme away from the weights used to construct the LES used throughout this chapter and the book as a whole.

Appendix 2.4: Examples of Effective Freshmen

The following table lists the top freshmen in the 98th Congress (1983–84), as referenced in the text of Chapter 2, to examine the background and fate of these highly effective members of Congress.

TABLE 2A.4. *Freshmen in Top 10 Percent of Their Cohort in LES in 98th Congress*

Name	LES	State Legislature?	Subsequent Political Position
Rich Boucher (VA)	2.501	Yes	In House until 2011 (112th Congress)
Katie Hall (IN)	2.143	Yes	Lost reelection bid (99th Congress)
Bill Richardson (NM)	1.991	No	Secretary of Energy, governor of New Mexico until 2011
Barbara Kennelly (CT)	1.346	No	Lost bid for governor (1998)
Barbara Boxer (CA)	1.326	No	Currently in U.S. Senate
James McNulty (AZ)	1.199	Yes	Lost reelection bid (99th Congress)
John Bryant (TX)	1.080	Yes	Lost bid for Senate (1996)
James Clarke (NC)	0.940	Yes	Lost reelection bid (99th Congress)
Alan Mollohan (WV)	0.895	No	In House until 2011 (112th Congress)

Appendix 2.5: Descriptive Statistics

TABLE 2A.5. *Descriptive Statistics of Independent Variables for Table 2.5*

Independent Variables	Description	Mean	Std. Dev.
Seniority[a]	Number of terms served by member in Congress	5.205	3.964
State Legislative Experience[a]	Equals "1" if member served in state legislature	0.487	0.500
State Legislative Professionalism[b]	Squire's index of state professionalism relative to Congress	0.290	0.150
Majority Party[a]	Equals "1" if member is in majority party	0.569	0.495
Majority-Party Leadership[a]	Equals "1" if member is in majority-party leadership	0.016	0.125
Minority-Party Leadership[a]	Equals "1" if member is in minority-party leadership	0.017	0.131
Speaker[a]	Equals "1" if member is Speaker of the House	0.002	0.042
Committee Chair[c]	Equals "1" if member is a committee chair	0.050	0.218
Subcommittee Chair[a]	Equals "1" if member is a subcommittee chair	0.249	0.432
Power Committee[c]	Equals "1" if member serves on Rules, Appropriations, or Ways and Means	0.251	0.434
Distance from Median[d]	|Member *i*'s DW-NOMINATE score – Median member's DW-NOMINATE score|	0.353	0.223
Female[a]	Equals "1" if member is female	0.088	0.283
African American[a]	Equals "1" if member is African American	0.065	0.246
Latino[a]	Equals "1" if member is Latino/Latina	0.035	0.185
Size of Congressional Delegation[e]	Number of districts in state congressional delegation	18.350	13.990
Vote Share[a]	Percentage of vote received in previous election	68.530	13.890

Data sources:
[a] Constructed by authors based on *Almanac of American Politics*, various years.
[b] Constructed by authors based on updates to Squire (1992).
[c] Constructed by authors based on Nelson (1992) and Stewart and Woon (2005).
[d] Constructed by authors from DW-NOMINATE scores provided by Keith Poole.
[e] Constructed by authors.

3

The Keys to Majority-Party Effectiveness in Congress

> *The fact is that no theoretical treatment of the United States Congress that posits parties as analytic units will go very far.*
>
> – David Mayhew, *Congress: The Electoral Connection* (1974, 27)

> *First, let me admit that if I were writing* The Electoral Connection *today I would back off from claiming that "no theoretical treatment of the United States Congress that posits parties as analytic units will go very far." Still, I have not seen any evidence that today's congressional party leaders "whip" or "pressure" their members more frequently or effectively than did their predecessors thirty years ago.*
>
> – David Mayhew, *Congress: The Electoral Connection* (2nd Edition, 2004, xvii)

The victors were celebrating across Michigan that night. In the Upper Peninsula, Bart Stupak was celebrating his reelection to an eighth term in Congress. On November 7, 2006, the Roman Catholic, pro-life, former police officer once again handily defeated the same Republican he had overcome in 2002 and 2004, each time more than doubling his opponent's vote share.

Far to the southeastern part of the state, Joe Knollenberg was celebrating a much tighter race. Also a white, male, Roman Catholic, seven-term member of Congress, the incumbent was feeling the changing nature of his district – still able to rely on the Republican-leaning city of Troy and the conservative suburbs of Oakland County, but noticing the rising tide of Democratic support near Detroit, and a Democratic surge in the 2006 election year more generally. The previously safe Republican had to spend nearly $3 million to defeat his Democratic opponent by six points. Yet, despite a more uncertain race, and thus a more satisfying victory, Knollenberg's celebration was perhaps a bit less enthusiastic than that of the Stupak camp.

Although their demographic characteristics, congressional seniority, and electoral outcomes matched each other closely, the lawmaking fates of these two Michiganders were about to reverse entirely. Elsewhere in the country, beyond the control of either member, Democrats were replacing Republicans in key congressional seats, moving their party from about a dozen seats shy of a majority to about a dozen seats above a majority. Such a switch would elevate Stupak into the majority party, where he had not been since his first term, prior to the 1994 elections. In a reversal of fortunes, Knollenberg would return to the minority status he had only experienced briefly in his first term.

What would such changes mean for these two now fairly senior lawmakers? Would they continue to promote the causes that had won them electoral success and recognition back home? Would their proposals receive the same degree of consideration in committees and subcommittees, where much of congressional lawmaking takes place? Would those that reach the floor of the House face party-line votes, meaning certain defeat for Knollenberg and success for Stupak? How would the tightly divided Senate and end-of-term President Bush respond to these lawmakers' initiatives?

In Chapter 2 we developed Legislative Effectiveness Scores to compare the lawmaking skills and successes of members such as Knollenberg and Stupak. We demonstrated how those scores could be used as a lens through which to view the inner workings of Congress, capturing the personal and institutional factors that undergird major theories of legislative politics. Among the note-worthy findings, we uncovered a majority-party effect, wherein members of the majority party outscored minority-party members. Consistent with that finding, it is perhaps unsurprising that Stupak's LES rose from 0.631 in the 109th Congress (2005–06) to 3.144 in the 110th (2007–08). In comparison, Knollenberg's 3.539 LES plummeted to 0.138 as he entered the minority party.

What we had not been able to capture in such an overview, however, was exactly *why* party status mattered so much. At which stage in the legislative process does control of the majority party dictate the fate of a member's law-making activities? Are the levers of partisan policymaking pulled in committees or on the floor? Can a minority-party member with a good idea still work her way through the lawmaking process, or is Congress too partisan of an institution today to allow for policy outcomes to be driven by proposal strength? And has the nature of party politics in Congress changed dramatically over the past four decades, as the increasingly polarized rhetoric in the media and in Washington might suggest? In this chapter we confront these questions, both in general and in determining the congressional fates of the two members from Michigan – Knollenberg, who would be defeated in 2008, and Stupak, who would retire two years later.

WHERE'S THE PARTY IN THE U.S. HOUSE OF REPRESENTATIVES?

To many casual observers of Congress, policymaking is a partisan activity. Parties advance platforms. They have agendas. Republican initiatives are pitted against Democratic proposals. And being in the majority party helps – a lot.

To legislative scholars, the process is much more complex. As the quotes by David Mayhew at the start of this chapter suggest, considering parties as monoliths with all members voting with the party is not the best approach to understanding policymaking in Congress. Especially in the 1970s, when Mayhew initially advanced his argument, party labels were far from sufficient to explain voting patterns. Many Southern Democrats were conservative enough to prefer to vote more often with Republicans than with Northern Democrats on the floor of the House. Academics and journalists found modifiers, such as "liberal," "moderate," and "conservative," useful in describing members and grouping them together.

Scholars, in particular, used spatial models to illustrate the alignment of members of Congress from liberal on the left to conservative on the right.[1] And, during the 1970s and 1980s, conservative Democrats overlapped considerably with liberal Republicans, forming a moderate center, which has since diminished greatly.[2] Because parties are only as strong and cohesive as their members want them to be, such distributions of preferences played a major role in how scholars theorized about parties in Congress.[3]

In one prominent advance, David Rohde and John Aldrich put forth a theory of *conditional party government*.[4] They argue that when majority-party members are tightly aligned in their ideological preferences and when their preferred policy positions differ significantly from those of the minority party, then these members endow their leaders with the ability to advance a tight partisan agenda. No such strong party will arise if its members are ideologically diverse or if the majority and minority parties prefer policies that are quite similar. As these scholars claim, parties will act in a unified manner, but only under the right conditions.

Of course, in the extreme case in which all members want the exact same policies as their copartisans, such a spatial model would collapse to simple bloc voting, with all majority-party members voting in favor of their party's proposal and all minority-party members voting against it. Indeed, Keith Krehbiel argues that, under the conditions of conditional party government, party leadership is irrelevant, as the party's members want to vote together, even without any pressure from the party.[5] In his *parties-as-preferences* view, political parties appear to be strong not because of coordination or because of leaders' influence,

---

[1] Krehbiel (1988) offers a helpful review of the spatial model of legislative politics and its usage in political science up through the 1980s.

[2] Numerous scholars (Bartels 2008; Fiorina, Adams, and Pope 2006; Hetherington 2009; and McCarty, Poole, and Rosenthal 2006) discuss polarization in contemporary legislative politics in the United States.

[3] Recent explorations of the endogenous nature of party strength include Volden and Bergman (2006), Patty (2008), and Diermeier and Vlaicu (2011).

[4] Most prominently, these arguments emerge from Rohde (1991), Aldrich (1995), and Aldrich and Rohde (2000a, 2001).

[5] This is part of an extensive line of argumentation about political parties in Congress found in Krehbiel (1993, 2003, 2007).

but merely because of shared preferences, with liberals embracing the Democratic label and conservatives affiliating themselves with the Republicans.[6]

As a majority-based institution, the most crucial member of the House of Representatives in such a preference-based spatial theory is the centrally located *median*, long understood in the Median Voter Theorem.[7] The appearance of partisan agendas and majority-party strength may therefore arise merely because of a close alignment between the preferences of the overall floor median and the median within the majority party, rather than through leaders forcing their members to toe the party line.[8]

Neither the extreme view of unified partisan voting blocs nor that of parties as mere correlations of ideological preferences resonated strongly with legislative scholars. For example, Gary Cox and Mathew McCubbins argue that majority-party members could do better than to individually vote in line with their ideological preferences.[9] Because there are many benefits of governance that could be directed to majority-party members and their districts, and because these members share similar outlooks on governance, they benefit from becoming more cohesive than their mere preferences alone would suggest. In essence, majority-party members form a "legislative cartel," giving their leaders the carrots and sticks necessary to enforce agreements that collectively serve the party members' interests.

In a refined version of this theory, Cox and McCubbins specify the mechanism of majority-party influence in greater detail.[10] They advance a theory of *negative agenda setting*, in which the key role of the majority party arises from keeping items off of the agenda that would not benefit a majority of members in the majority party.[11] Proposals that move current status quo policies away from the majority party, such as liberal proposals when the Republican Party holds a majority, do not see the light of day. Majority-party members hold a majority of seats on each policy committee and subcommittee, and act on behalf of the party to kill proposals not in the party's interest, including most bills sponsored by minority-party members.

Although there are many other important theories of parties in Congress, these views are leading contenders in explaining the role of parties in

---

[6] Minozzi and Volden (2013) present a theory and evidence of parties playing a coordinating role on floor votes, issuing a call to join with copartisans that extremists are more likely than moderates to heed.

[7] The idea that candidates in elections converge to the median position of voters, and that policy in legislatures similarly converges to the median, builds upon the formative work of Black (1948) and Downs (1957).

[8] Wiseman and Wright (2008) track the alignment between the floor median and the majority-party median across numerous Congresses over time.

[9] Their defining work on this subject is Cox and McCubbins (1993).

[10] These arguments are best advanced in Cox and McCubbins (2002, 2005).

[11] Analytically, the majority-party median assumes a role that is analogous to the committee median in Denzau and Mackay's (1983) seminal model of committee gatekeeping.

policymaking.[12] They lead to the following three hypotheses that we explore in an attempt to identify the keys to majority-party effectiveness in Congress.

Partisan Preferences Hypothesis: Members near the majority-party median will be more effective in advancing their proposals than members further away from the majority-party median.

Consistent with the conditional party government theory, as well as with the view that apparent party strength arises due to preference alignment, the Partisan Preferences Hypothesis suggests that members near the heart of the majority party should outperform those further away.[13] If majority-party status involves little more than preference alignment, or if it is highly dependent on the conditions of close alignment within the majority party set against a distant minority party, then properly controlling for spatial preferences should erase any evidence that majority-party status by itself results in greater legislative effectiveness.

Party Leaders Hypothesis: Majority-party members will endow their leaders with powers to enforce party discipline, making the leaders particularly effective.

Although leadership could take a variety of forms, the most blatant would be a hierarchical assignment of complete control to the party leaders. Were this the case, leaders would take up the party's agenda, introduce proposals on their members' behalf, and insist on party-line voting. Although we believe this to be an overly simplistic characterization, and although party leaders could use the mechanisms of party control to advance *any* party member's proposed bill, such direct leadership effects are worthy of examination.

Parties in Committees Hypothesis: Majority-party members' proposals will be privileged in committees. Committee and subcommittee chairs will be particularly effective.

This third hypothesis reflects negative agenda setting, wherein minority-party members should see less success in committees than do majority-party members. How exactly that committee effect works remains an open question. It could be that committee and subcommittee chairs will be particularly effective members, as we already began to uncover in Chapter 2. Alternatively, all majority-party

---

[12] Smith (2007) offers a helpful overview and assessment of this voluminous literature. Recent contributions to this literature have wrestled with questions of how exactly parties influence the legislative process and policy outcomes (e.g., Anzia and Jackman 2013; Carson, Monroe, and Robinson 2011; Jackman 2014; Jenkins, Crespin, and Carson 2005; Jenkins and Monroe 2012; Krehbiel, Meirowitz, and Wiseman 2013; Minozzi and Volden 2013).

[13] Spatial theories often feature similar proposals arising from members located across broad segments of the political spectrum, as they understand the strategic nature of which bills will pass. In contrast, where members can incorporate a costly quality (or valence) to their bills, the ideological locations of their proposals correlate instead more closely with their true preferences (e.g., Hirsch and Shotts 2012; Hitt, Volden, and Wiseman 2011). It is in this light that preferences may matter both for lawmakers' proposals and for their ultimate legislative effectiveness.

members may receive some enhanced recognition in committees relative to minority-party members.

EMPIRICAL EXAMINATIONS OF PARTIES IN CONGRESS

Scholars of parties in Congress have extensively examined all of the theories discussed previously. The typical approach has been to focus on roll-call votes on the floor of the House (or the Senate). As the argument goes, if parties are important analytical units, we should see extensive numbers of partisan votes, wherein most Democrats vote against most Republicans.[14] If partisanship extends beyond ideological preference alignments, such party voting should be evident above and beyond the liberal or conservative preferences of members.[15] If the conditions must be just right for the party to band together for a collective purpose, coordinated party voting should be enhanced when those conditions are met.[16] And, if proposals against the majority party's wishes are left off the agenda, a majority of the majority party should rarely find themselves on the losing end of votes.[17]

Yet we argue that this focus on floor votes is far too narrow to understand the role of parties in Congress.[18] As we discussed in Chapter 2, lawmaking involves much more than voting on already well-formed proposals. To be effective, lawmakers must formulate solutions to public policy problems. They must promote those solutions to a group of like-minded legislators. They must craft those solutions into bills, survive a rigorous review in committees and subcommittees, and navigate the legislative calendar just to get to the floor-voting stage.

---

[14] A wide body of literature has investigated the presence (or absence) of party strength by analyzing various roll-call based measures of party voting cohesion. Prominent examples of such work include Collie (1989), Collie and Brady (1985), and Sinclair (1978). Lebo, McGlynn, and Koger (2007) develop a novel theory of "strategic party government" and test the implications of their theory by relying on various cohesion indices. Krehbiel (2000) provides a review and critique of such approaches for assessing the potential impacts of parties in legislatures.

[15] Several scholars have attempted to isolate the impact of partisan pressure of roll-call decisions, holding the influence of policy preferences constant. Important contributions to this debate include Snyder and Groseclose (2000, 2001), Krehbiel (2003), and McCarty, Poole, and Rosenthal (2001).

[16] Aldrich and Rohde (2000a), for example, explore the empirical implications of the conditional party government theory in the context of legislative organization. Roberts (2005) and Roberts and Smith (2003) explore several of the theory's other implications.

[17] Cox and McCubbins (2002, 2005) have denoted situations in which a majority of the majority party finds itself on the losing end of a roll call as a "party roll." They have investigated the relationships between majority-party roll rates and the preferences of pivotal actors in the majority party to establish evidence in support of their party cartel theory. Several scholars including Carson, Monroe, and Robinson (2011), Clinton (2007, 2012), Hirsch (2011), Krehbiel (2007), Schickler and Pearson (2009), Stiglitz and Weingast (2010), and Wiseman and Wright (2008) have investigated the implications and limitations of roll rate analyses.

[18] Carrubba, Gabel, and Murah (2006) and Clinton (2007) note the problems inherent in analyses of roll-call votes, which are themselves endogenous outcomes of earlier strategic decisions, and thus biased in a variety of ways.

To explore these hypotheses, then, we engage all of the major stages of the lawmaking process, both before and after floor votes. We do this through a four-step process. First, we assess the overall Legislative Effectiveness Scores of members of the majority and minority parties, to understand why majority-party members outperform minority-party members on the whole. Second, we break these scores down by the multiple stages of the lawmaking process, to assess whether majority-party strength arises from differences in proposals advanced, in committee activities, in floor voting, or in action beyond the House. Third, we conduct a series of regressions to discern which factors – whether preferences, leadership, or committee roles – account for the bulk of the enhanced legislative effectiveness of majority-party members. Finally, we examine how these factors have changed over time, from the early 1970s through today. The totality of our approach suggests that party effects are not mainly based on floor-voting patterns, and therefore that legislative scholars focused on floor voting have largely been looking in the wrong place to understand parties in Congress.[19]

LEGISLATIVE EFFECTIVENESS ACROSS PARTIES

While legislative scholars tend to think about members of Congress in terms of their party *status* – majority or minority – members of the voting public tend to focus on party *affiliations* – Democrat or Republican. Our Legislative Effectiveness Scores characterize the degree to which lawmakers advance their legislative proposals through the House of Representatives and into law. To the extent that Republicans generally advocate for more limited government than do Democrats, one may wonder whether the LES measure is biased in such a way that Democrats score higher because of their more activist agendas. Before turning to an assessment of majority-party status, we therefore highlight differences between Republicans and Democrats.

Figure 3.1 presents LES Scorecards averaging the values across the 99th–110th Congresses (1985–2008), first for all Democrats and then for all Republicans. Over this time period, each party held majority control for twelve years, making them comparable on party-status grounds. The first noteworthy characteristic of the scorecards is the average LES, which is just under the

---

[19] This is not to say that scholars have altogether ignored the role of parties and leaders in committees in Congress (see, for example, Dion and Huber 1996, 1997; Evans 1991, 2011; Krehbiel 1991; Schiller 1995; Smith and Deering 1997). Rather, as committees diminished in power following the reforms of the 1970s and as parties became more polarized in recent decades, the amount of scholarship on committees in Congress has fallen and that on parties has increased. We argue that parties and committees need not be treated as substitutes; rather, a focus on how committee structures aid partisan goals remains crucial. As such, based on our findings, we advocate more work on parties in committees, both theoretically and empirically. Moreover, empirical work based on data at the committee stage may be even more enlightening than the current trend of looking for party effects on floor votes.

The Lawmaker: **Average Democrat** 99th–110th Congresses		
LES: 0.957		
	c	s	ss

	c	s	ss
BILL	0.65	11.66	0.82
AIC	0.18	1.48	0.68
ABC	0.23	0.80	0.66
PASS	0.22	0.60	0.54
LAW	0.14	0.27	0.25

The Lawmaker: **Average Republican** 99th–110th Congresses		
LES: 1.045		

	c	s	ss
BILL	0.51	11.38	0.61
AIC	0.14	1.44	0.46
ABC	0.19	1.06	0.49
PASS	0.18	0.82	0.40
LAW	0.13	0.37	0.17

FIGURE 3.1. LES Scorecards Show Little Difference in Legislative Effectiveness Between Democrats and Republicans

Note: LES Scorecards reveal no substantial difference in average Legislative Effectiveness Scores (LES) between Democrats and Republicans. They show the number of commemorative (C), substantive (S), and substantive and significant (SS) bills (BILL) the average lawmaker in each party introduced, as well as how many received action in committee (AIC), action beyond committee (ABC), passed the House (PASS), and became law (LAW). These Scorecards capture all Democrats and all Republicans in the 99th–110th House of Representatives (1985–2008), a period when Democrats and Republicans each held the majority for a comparable number of years.

normalized 1.0 for Democrats and just above that average for Republicans, indicating no pro-legislation bias making Democrats' scores higher than Republicans. Focusing on the first column, there is very little difference between Democrats and Republicans in their use of commemorative (C) legislation. As always, the Scorecard from top to bottom shows the progression of bills from their introduction (BILL) to action in committee (AIC), action beyond committee (ABC), passing the House (PASS), and finally becoming law (LAW). Although Democrats introduce commemorative bills at a somewhat higher rate, the average number of commemorative laws looks very similar across parties.

As shown in the middle column, both Democrats and Republicans on average introduce between eleven and twelve substantive (S) bills per lawmaker per Congress. The fates of these bills differ somewhat, however, with 3.3 percent of Republicans' substantive bills becoming law compared to just 2.3 percent for bills introduced by Democrats.[20] This enhanced effectiveness of Republicans on substantive legislation is offset by Democrats' greater success in substantive and

---

[20] The average Republican sees 0.37 of the substantive bills that she introduces become law; hence 0.37/11.38 = 0.0325 (approximately 3.3 percent). A similar calculation, drawing on the numbers in Figure 3.1, yields the analogous percentage of Democratic-sponsored substantive bills that become law.

The Lawmaker: **In Majority Party** 93rd–110th Congresses		
LES: 1.452		
	C	S	SS
BILL	1.13	16.73	1.30
AIC	0.21	1.88	1.07
ABC	0.26	1.21	1.10
PASS	0.24	0.93	0.91
LAW	0.17	0.45	0.43

The Lawmaker: **In Minority Party** 93rd–110th Congresses		
LES: 0.404		
	C	S	SS
BILL	0.97	13.82	0.17
AIC	0.18	0.77	0.09
ABC	0.23	0.38	0.07
PASS	0.22	0.30	0.06
LAW	0.15	0.15	0.03

FIGURE 3.2. LES Scorecards Show Substantially Greater Legislative Effectiveness Among Majority-Party Members

Note: LES Scorecards reveal substantial differences in average Legislative Effectiveness Scores (LES) between majority- and minority-party members. They show the number of commemorative (C), substantive (S), and substantive and significant (SS) bills (BILL) the average lawmaker in each party introduced, as well as how many received action in committee (AIC), action beyond committee (ABC), passed the House (PASS), and became law (LAW), during the 93rd–110th Congresses (1973–2008).

significant (SS) areas, as detailed in the rightmost column. Here, on average, four bills are introduced across every five Democrats, compared to three bills introduced for every five Republicans. For this set of bills, which, as detailed in Chapter 2 receive mention in the *Congressional Quarterly Almanac*, the success rate of moving from bill to law is about 30 percent for both parties' lawmakers. Thus, over this time period, Democrats are responsible for more of the laws that are deemed substantive and significant according to our measure, whereas Republicans produce more substantive legislation that does not receive as much widespread attention. The combination of these factors accounts for the nearly indistinguishable overall scores between Democrats and Republicans.

In comparison to these small differences across party affiliations, Figure 3.2 shows the scorecards that reveal massive differences based on party status. Now exploring all Congresses in our dataset (1973–2008), the average LES of majority-party members is 1.452, more than *triple* that of minority-party members' 0.404 score.[21] These scorecards reveal a small difference in the overall rate of bill introduction, with the average majority-party member introducing about nineteen bills, to about fifteen bills for minority-party members. The largest difference here is in substantive and significant bills, where majority-party

[21] One might imagine that majority-party status would be even more valuable under unified government, with the president and Senate sharing the partisan leanings of the House. This does not appear to be the case empirically, however, with just more than a 1.0-point LES difference between majority- and minority-party averages under both unified and divided government.

members introduce far more than do minority-party members. Rather than minority-party members being devoid of big ideas, however, we believe this difference arises mainly from those members' big ideas not moving far through the legislative process and thus not meriting the same amount of attention in the *Congressional Quarterly Almanac*.

Indeed, the most noteworthy aspect of the party-status scorecards arises in the transition from the bill introduction stage (BILL) to the committee stages, whether bills receive action in committee (AIC) through hearings, markups, and votes in committees or subcommittees, and whether bills receive action beyond committee (ABC) and placement on the legislative calendars as movement toward a floor vote. Specifically for the center column of substantive bills, the power of the majority party comes into full light. Whereas 5.5 percent of minority-party members' bills receive committee attention, that rate is doubled to 11.2 percent for bills of majority-party members. Even more dramatically, 7.3 percent of majority-party members' substantive bills reach the floor of the House, three times the rate for minority-party members. This is even setting aside the substantive and significant legislation, where more than 95 percent of the bills receiving action beyond committee have been introduced by majority-party members.

Based on these Scorecards alone, we find immense support for the Parties in Committee Hypothesis. By the time bills reach the floor of the House, where the vast majority of legislative politics scholarship has focused in attempts to discern the effect of political parties, the battle is already over. Majority-party members have won, and minority-party members have lost. And, indeed, upon reaching the floor of the House, little further partisan differences are noticeable. The rates of conversion into law for bills reaching the floor of the House differ little for majority- and minority-party members. Those proposals by minority-party members that survive the winnowing process of committees perhaps have sufficiently high value or broad enough support so as to be no more threatened on the floor or beyond the chamber than are proposals by majority-party members.[22] Overall, 50 percent of bills by minority-party members that reach the floor of the House actually become law, compared to 41 percent for majority-party members.[23]

We illustrate these differences across stages of the legislative process in Figure 3.3, which combines all types of bills, without regard to their commemorative or substantive natures. As shown in the figure, majority-party members introduce about 25 percent more bills overall than do minority-party members. The strongest partisan activities then emerge in committee, where majority-party members receive a boost. In terms of action in committee (AIC), majority-party members enjoy a 200 percent increase over the typical minority-party member,

---

[22] Krutz (2005) offers a systematic examination of the winnowing process in Congress.
[23] A significant part of this difference is clearly due to a different mix of commemorative, substantive, and substantive and significant bills at this stage across parties.

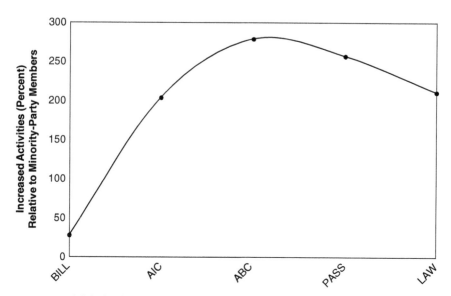

FIGURE 3.3. Majority-Party Activities Outpace Those of the Minority Party, Especially in Committee

Note: The figure shows the percentage by which majority-party activities surpassed minority-party activities for the average member of the House across the five stages of lawmaking. For instance, while the average majority-party member introduces about 25 percent more bills (BILL), this advantage climbs to 200 percent more bills receiving action in committee (AIC), and nearly 300 percent more receiving action beyond committee (ABC). Because minority-party members' bills outperform those of majority-party members in floor voting and beyond the House, however, such advantages diminish in the House passage stage (PASS) and in bills becoming law (LAW).

thus tripling the amount of active legislation at that stage. For action beyond committee (ABC), this majority-party advantage reaches nearly 300 percent, indicating that about four out of every five bills reaching the floor of the House has been sponsored by a member of the majority party. Consistent with the previous discussion, upon reaching the floor, this majority-party advantage diminishes somewhat, with minority-party members' bills achieving greater success in floor votes and beyond the House, on average, than those of majority-party members.[24]

In sum, if the relevant question is, "Where is the party in the House of Representatives?" the key answer emerging is "In committees!" From the point of view of majority-party leaders and their members, such an approach to bottling opponents' proposals up in committee is quite attractive for a variety

---

[24] In Appendix 3.1, we revisit these overall stage-by-stage trends while controlling for all of the other factors raised in Chapter 2, in order to illustrate that these broader patterns are robust to the full set of controls.

of reasons. For instance, floor votes on some such proposals might divide or embarrass the majority party, and some may even end up passing the House if given a vote on the floor.

The above aggregate statistics arise from the immense efforts of individual members of Congress and their staffs. For example, when in the majority party in the 109th Congress (2005–06), Joe Knollenberg developed a tightly focused agenda. Representing a manufacturing district in Michigan, he sponsored the American Manufacturing Competitiveness Act and the Stop Counterfeiting in Manufactured Goods Act. The latter proposal resonated with his colleagues, and soon became law, as did the appropriations bill he sponsored. Of the nine bills he introduced, three became law, one that we deem substantive, and two substantive and significant. In the next Congress, Knollenberg reintroduced the American Manufacturing Competitiveness Act, as well as other items left unfinished in his previous busy term. He expanded his agenda a bit further, to perhaps resonate with ideas also held by Democrats, toward high-tech research in one bill and fuel efficiency in another, sponsoring eleven bills in total. Unlike his previous success, not one of these proposals received action in committee – no hearings, no markups, no votes, nothing.

Knollenberg's newfound fate was one to which Bart Stupak had grown familiar. None of his thirty-seven sponsored bills in the 108th Congress (2003–04) had received any action in committee. His thirty sponsored bills in the 109th (2005–06) met with a similar fate. Members of Stupak's party went so far as to seek a discharge petition to bring to the floor one of his bills that was bottled up in committee, but secured only 135 of the 218 signatures needed. Upon gaining majority-party status, Stupak grew even more ambitious, sponsoring fifty bills in the 110th Congress (2007–08), and found more success than in all twelve of his years in the minority party combined. Seven of his substantive bills moved beyond committee, along with one commemorative and one substantive and significant bill. Of those nine, six passed the House and three became law, including the Online Pharmacy Consumer Protection Act of 2008. This was his most prominent lawmaking success since he was last in the majority party. In his freshman term, Stupak, the former police officer, drew attention to a new drug epidemic in northern Michigan, crafted legislation targeting the availability of ephedrine (used in the production of methamphetamine or "meth"), and saw his Domestic Chemical Diversion Control Act of 1993 signed into law by President Clinton. Representative Stupak's proposals did not shift significantly between these two successes, but the institution had shifted around him.

PARTISAN ADVANTAGE IN ITS COMPONENT PARTS

While the previous analyses and narratives are revealing, they are also each limited in a variety of ways. For example, the summaries across stages in Figure 3.3 treat all bills alike; and absent from the above accounts are other factors such as seniority or institutional positioning that we now know influence the effectiveness of majority-party members. Therefore, many questions remain. For instance, is the overall elevated LES merely due to a spatial ideological alignment of majority-party members? Are majority-party members more senior on average than minority-party members and thus better able to leverage their experience into lawmaking success? What is the role of party leaders and committee leaders?

To address these questions systematically, we return to an analysis of the overall LES for each member. The benefit of this overall measure is that it captures all of the major stages of the lawmaking process and it assigns weights to each piece of legislation based on its substantive significance. Thus, it provides an overall view of who is accomplishing what in Congress. As shown in the scorecards of Figure 3.2, at an aggregate level, majority-party members score a full point higher on our metric than do minority-party members, a tripling of their average LESs.

In this section, we assess the degree to which that total partisan effect can be explained by various component pieces. Specifically, in line with the three hypotheses derived from the previous literature, we explore whether the total direct party effect is reduced substantially upon controlling for the indirect effects of ideological distribution, party leadership, and committee control. To do so, we return to a series of regressions, similar to those conducted at the end of Chapter 2, in order to isolate the main partisan effects and break them into their component parts.

Model 3.1 in Table 3.1 includes a single explanatory variable to account for variance in the LES dependent variable across members. Consistent with the scorecards from Figure 3.2, we find that Majority Party takes a coefficient of 1.073, indicating that majority-party members score about 1.4, relative to the approximate 0.4 LES for minority-party members.

To explore the Partisan Preferences Hypothesis, we include an additional variable in Model 3.2. Distance from Majority-Party Median uses the DW-NOMINATE scores discussed in Chapter 2, giving lower values to members who are closely aligned with the middle of the majority party and greater values to those further away.[25] If the party effect uncovered in the first model arises due mainly to these spatial preferences, with those further away from the heart of the majority party dismissed for making unwelcome proposals, the coefficient on this new independent variable should be negative and significant. As shown, it is negative, although it fails to achieve a high level of statistical significance in the specification of Model 3.2. Moreover, the coefficient on Majority Party remains close to 1.0, indicating that the overall partisan effect is little diminished upon accounting for parties in terms of preference alignment in this way.

---

[25] In contrast, in Chapter 2 we included an independent variable capturing the distance between the member's ideal point and the floor median. Such a variable was not statistically significant in Model 2.3 of Table 2.5.

TABLE 3.1. *Partisan Determinants of Legislative Effectiveness*

	Model 3.1	Model 3.2	Model 3.3	Model 3.4	Model 3.5
Majority Party	1.073***	0.951***	0.945***	0.157**	0.164***
	(0.055)	(0.090)	(0.090)	(0.064)	(0.055)
Distance from Majority-Party		−0.209	−0.205	−0.196**	−0.300***
Median		(0.127)	(0.127)	(0.096)	(0.075)
Majority-Party Leadership			0.306	0.549***	0.289**
			(0.235)	(0.197)	(0.138)
Minority-Party Leadership			−0.024	−0.015	−0.043
			(0.042)	(0.042)	(0.061)
Speaker			−0.604*	−0.043	−0.314
			(0.358)	(0.359)	(0.247)
Committee Chair				3.616***	2.082***
				(0.295)	(0.193)
Subcommittee Chair				1.111***	0.541***
				(0.082)	(0.064)
Constant	0.386***	0.537***	0.535***	0.519***	−0.818**
	(0.012)	(0.094)	(0.094)	(0.072)	(0.392)
Chapter 2 Controls?	No	No	No	No	Yes
N	7884	7884	7884	7884	6155
Adjusted-R^2	0.11	0.11	0.11	0.42	0.56

Notes: Ordinary least squares estimation of member Legislative Effectiveness Scores, with robust standard errors in parentheses, and observations clustered by member.
*$p < 0.1$ (two-tailed), **$p < 0.05$ (two-tailed), ***$p < 0.01$ (two-tailed).

Model 3.3 allows for an assessment of the Party Leaders Hypothesis, by now adding indicator variables for whether the given member is in the Majority-Party Leadership, Minority-Party Leadership, or Speaker. As we had found previously, leaders in the majority party gain a small advantage, leaders in the minority party face difficulty, and the Speaker introduces very few bills herself. As before, these additional controls do not make the direct partisan effect go away, nor do they diminish that effect much from its previous size.

In Model 3.4, however, we turn to the Parties in Committees Hypothesis, which already received substantial support previously. Here we explore whether the majority-party advantage in committees results largely from committee leaders, by including indicator variables for whether the member under investigation is a Committee Chair or Subcommittee Chair. Coefficients on both of these variables are positive and highly significant in statistical terms. Therefore, once again, this analysis leads to the conclusion that party influence takes place in committees. These committee-based majority-party actors account for nearly all of the direct partisan effect uncovered previously. Now the total party effect of 1.073 for Majority Party in Model 3.1 has diminished to 0.157 in Model 3.4.

Model 3.5 adds all of the control variables introduced in the analysis of Legislative Effectiveness Scores in Chapter 2.[26] Collectively, these leave the direct effect of Majority Party at about the same magnitude as was uncovered in Model 3.4. These final two models are much more fully specified than the earlier models in the table. Upon such controls, the effects of preferences and of party leaders come into sharper view. Consistent with the Partisan Preferences Hypothesis, the coefficient on Distance from Majority-Party Median is negative and statistically significant. The average member of the minority party is 0.73 units away from the majority-party median according to this ideological preference measure. Such a distance accounts for between a 0.1 and 0.2-point drop in the LES for minority-party members based on spatial considerations alone. Some support also emerges in these latter models for the Party Leaders Hypothesis, with majority-party leaders outperforming other majority-party members. Yet this effect is small and does little to explain the overall majority-party effect.

The nature of the Ordinary Least Squares regressions run in Table 3.1 allows us to characterize the relative weights of the component parts resulting in the total majority-party effect found in Model 3.1. Specifically, that total effect is comprised of a *direct effect* – the amount still evident in the Majority-Party coefficient of Model 3.4 – and *indirect effects* for each of the preference, leadership, and committee variables that resulted in the reduction of the direct effect. Figure 3.4

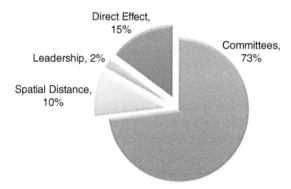

FIGURE 3.4. Committees Account for Nearly Three-Fourths of Enhanced Majority-Party Effectiveness

Note: The figure shows the component parts that make up the total boost in effectiveness for majority-party members over minority-party members. About 73 percent of the difference can be attributed to committee and subcommittee chairs, whereas much smaller portions are directly attributable to member preferences in their ideological spatial distances from the party median or to party leaders. About 15 percent of the total effect remains as a direct party effect through the analyses of Table 3.1, upon which this figure is based.

----

[26] Specifically, we include all but one of the variables found in Model 2.3 of Table 2.5. Distance from Median is excluded due to its correlation with the variable Distance from Majority-Party Median included here.

illustrates how that total effect is divided up into its component parts, based on the results of Model 3.4.[27]

As shown in the figure, spatial distance, via the Distance from Majority-Party Median measure, does account for about 10 percent of the total majority-party LES effect. The indirect effects of the three leadership variables account for merely 2 percent of that total effect.[28] In contrast, Committee Chair and Subcommittee Chair combine to account for nearly three-fourths of the total enhanced effect of majority party on LES. This is once again strong support for the Parties in Committees Hypothesis. The remaining direct effect of majority party (15 percent in the figure) is left unexplained, and could be due to such factors as majority-party members other than committee and subcommittee chairs still outperforming minority-party members within legislative committees.

PARTIES IN COMMITTEES OVER TIME

In two separate ways, we have found support for a committee-centered explanation of the increased effectiveness of majority-party members. Specifically, majority-party members are much more likely to gain attention and success in committees for their legislative proposals. And most of the enhanced LES for majority-party members arises through the effectiveness of committee and subcommittee chairs. Such effects are averages, however, of all of the Congresses from 1973 through 2008. These average effects may mask changes over time. Congress today is described as a more partisan and polarized institution than it has been in the recent past. We know that congressional reforms of the 1970s diminished the power of committees.[29] Moreover, when the Republicans took control of the House following the 1994 elections, they sought to further reduce the power of committee chairs by establishing term limits for chair positions.[30] Did either of these reforms decrease the indirect committee effect shown in Figure 3.4? And has the total effect of party increased over time along with greater polarization?

To answer these over-time questions, we reran Models 3.1 and 3.4 from Table 3.1 on a Congress-by-Congress basis. We then plotted the total effect, the indirect effect of parties in committees, and the remaining unexplained direct

[27] The relative size of an indirect effect, for, say, preferences is $b_2 b_{X_2 X_1}$, where b_2 is the coefficient on Distance from Majority-Party Median in Model 3.4 and $b_{X_2 X_1}$ is the coefficient on Majority Party from a simple regression of Distance from Majority-Party Median on Majority Party. The sum of all indirect effects and the remaining direct effect equals the total effect uncovered in Model 3.1.

[28] This set of variables may well paint too limited a picture of party leaders, who may also play roles such as demanding or enabling opponents' legislation to be killed in committee.

[29] For the role of parties and leaders following such reforms, see Rohde (1991).

[30] Evans and Oleszek (1997) and Aldrich and Rohde (1997–98) provide parsimonious overviews of the institutional reforms that were implemented in the House following the Republicans' rise to the majority in the 104th Congress.

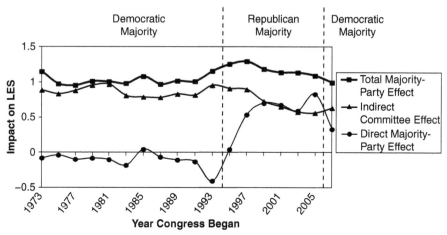

FIGURE 3.5. Committees Account for Nearly All of the Enhanced Majority-Party Effectiveness Until Republicans Control the House

Note: The figure shows a steady boost in effectiveness of about one point in Legislative Effectiveness Scores (LES) between majority-party members and minority-party members. Through 1994, this gap is almost entirely explained by enhanced effectiveness of committee and subcommittee chairs, leaving no difference between other majority-party members and minority-party members (direct effect of nearly zero). Upon Republicans assuming the majority in 1995, however, committee effects explain less of the total partisan boost, with rank-and-file members of the majority party outperforming their minority-party counterparts.

effect over time in Figure 3.5. The bold line on the top of the figure shows the total direct effect of party. Consistent with earlier analyses, it averages just above 1.0. This effect is fairly steady throughout the 1970s and 1980s, and then rises as the Republicans assume majority-party control in the 104th Congress (1995–96). The peak during the early years of the Republican majority then gives way to a diminished party effect over the next decade, back to traditional levels.

What is more remarkable is the extent to which that overall enhanced majority-party LES is explained away by the role of committee and subcommittee chairs. Throughout the period of Democratic control ending in 1994, the indirect committee effect accounts for nearly all of the total effect of parties. Committee and subcommittee chairs significantly outperformed minority-party members and members of their own party. Indeed, the remaining direct effect of Majority Party was essentially zero throughout this time frame, meaning that rank-and-file members of the majority party who did not hold chair positions performed no better than minority-party members on their LES measures.

The story changes substantially under the Republican majority. Consistent with the idea of diminishing the clout of chairs and spreading around the majority party's power, a wide gap opens up on the right part of Figure 3.5

between the total party effect and the indirect committee effect. Relatedly, the direct effect of being in the majority party rises significantly over this period. Put succinctly, under the Republicans, both committee and subcommittee chairs as well as rank-and-file majority-party members outperformed those in the minority party. While in the majority from 1973–94, rank-and-file Democrats' average LES was a mere 0.49. In contrast, following the Republican Revolution, majority-party non-chairs averaged 0.78. While the ideas of minority-party members were still dismissed, proposals of all Republicans became advantaged, not just the initiatives of those in top committee and subcommittee roles.[31] Although there is limited data to draw a full picture, Democrats in the 110th Congress (2007–08) seemed to be moving back away from the Republican model, with a decrease in the direct effect of party and a slight increase in the committee-based indirect effect.

One wonders, therefore, whether Representative Stupak would have been as effective a majority-party member in the 110th Congress if he had not assumed a subcommittee chair in Energy and Commerce within the new majority party. Representative Knollenberg's LES rose from 0.378 to 1.966 when he became a subcommittee chair in 2001. However, consistent with the broader pattern of effectiveness across majority-party members, Knollenberg's LES remained high as he moved across institutional positions in the majority party, diminishing only following the Republicans' defeat in 2006.

The democratization of effective lawmaking across members of the Republican Party need not indicate that the effect of parties has moved out of committees and onto the floor of the House. Rather, it could merely be the case that a broader array of majority-party members' bills is given greater attention in committee than ever before, while minority-party members' bills are still largely set aside. Returning to the aggregate numbers from the previous sections bears this claim out. From 1973–94, majority-party Democrats introduced 24 percent more legislation than minority-party members, but had 282 percent more bills find their way through committee. Following the 104th Congress, from 1994–2006, those rates are *identical* for majority-party Republicans, with 24 percent more introductions and 282 percent more bills reaching the floor. The

---

[31] One factor that may play something of a role here is the support in lawmaking and credit claiming that Republican leaders offered to electorally vulnerable junior Republicans. Yet such a strategy appears in our data even prior to Republicans attaining majority-party status in 1995. Also perhaps relevant to these findings, in the 104th Congress the Republican leadership advanced high profile legislation through the Appropriations Committee, rather than various authorizing committees, as had been common practice previously (Aldrich and Rohde 2000b; Maraniss and Weisskopf 1996). Hence, chairs of authorizing committees likely had relatively fewer prominent bills move through their committees' jurisdictions. The fact that such a pattern holds beyond the 104th Congress is intriguing, however, given that, after receiving significant political pushback, Speaker Newt Gingrich and others in the Republican leadership decided to revert back to the conventional practice of advancing authorizing legislation through authorizing committees (Aldrich and Rohde 2000b, 29).

relative introduction rates of the majority-party members to minority-party members have remained constant over time, and parties are acting in committees as they have in the past.

The difference that has emerged, then, is that following the Republican rise in 1994, the proposals of a much broader group of majority-party members than merely the committee and subcommittee chairs were advancing further in the legislative process than had been the norm in previous Congresses. This may have been a natural response to the very large influx of new Republican law-makers in the 1994 elections and in surrounding years. New members tend to resist seniority norms whereby policymaking influence is consolidated among committee and subcommittee chairs.[32]

One further difference over time is in the *size* of agendas that majority-party members have been trying to move through Congress and in the *capacity* of the institution to handle their proposals. Prior to the 104th Congress (1995–96), majority-party members averaged twenty-two bills introduced. That number tightened to fourteen introductions after the 104th Congress. Yet, whereas 2.0 bills per majority-party member passed the House in an average Congress in the earlier era, that capacity rose by ten percent to 2.2 bills per majority-party member per Congress in the more recent era. Recent increased productivity may be offset by bicameral difficulties and broader institutional gridlock, however, with the average majority-party member producing 1.0 law per Congress recently, compared to 1.1 prior to the 104th Congress. We raise concerns about legislative gridlock once again in Chapter 5 with a focus on many different specific areas of public policy.

For now, our research illustrates the usefulness of Legislative Effectiveness Scores in adjudicating among the sides in the debates over major issues in legislative politics. Consistent with the conditional party government theory of Aldrich and Rohde, we find that preferences of members relative to one another do indeed help explain the overall effectiveness of the majority party. However, such a preference-based approach is limited, leaving behind a large unexplained portion of the enhanced effectiveness of being a majority-party member. Moreover, the increased effectiveness of majority-party members has not varied significantly between 1973 and the present, despite significant changes in the conditions that Aldrich and Rohde highlight.

Instead, our findings are even more consistent with the negative agenda setting theory of Cox and McCubbins. The enhanced effectiveness of majority-party members arises because the bills of minority-party members are largely ignored and killed in committees. Moreover, upon accounting for the role of committee and subcommittee chairs, little is left to explain regarding the enhanced effectiveness of majority-party members. That said, the story that emerges here is not quite as clean as the negative agenda setting view might

---

[32] Similar patterns of resistance and reform occur at various points in congressional history (e.g., Rohde 1991, Schickler 2001).

suggest, with at least two puzzles remaining. First, the proposals of minority-party members perform equally well as those of majority-party members, if not better, on the floor of the House. Why might this be? Second, the relative effectiveness of committee and subcommittee chairs changed significantly in Republican-controlled Congresses. How does this seeming democratization of ideas across majority-party members fit into scholarship that focuses mainly on the ideological location of proposals rather than on the lawmakers who propose them? Work on parties in Congress remains unfinished, and our study suggests a fruitful approach of looking at lawmakers in their roles before and beyond floor voting for additional evidence.[33]

CONCLUSION

We began this chapter with the stories of two members of Congress from Michigan, whose lawmaking fates changed dramatically on a single election night in 2006. Despite his reelection, Joe Knollenberg's party lost majority status and his proposals never again saw the light of day. That election flipped the switch on his political power. The *Detroit News* had previously declared him to be "arguably the state's most powerful Republican." Now, seeing his slim electoral margin, the Democratic Congressional Campaign Committee targeted Knollenberg for defeat in the next electoral cycle. No longer able to make the case that he was a powerful subcommittee chair and an influential member of the majority party, Representative Knollenberg went down to defeat in 2008. Although his career lasted two years longer than many of his colleagues who were defeated in 2006, his fate was essentially sealed the same night. His legislative proposals were dead on arrival and the surge of Democratic support in Michigan for Barack Obama was more than he could overcome.

In contrast, Bart Stupak had been dealt a very favorable hand in the 2006 elections. Having survived a dozen years in the minority party, he was ready to use his institutional power to advance his legislative goals and the interests of his constituents. Stupak's ultimate legislative fate came not from a lack of power, but perhaps from overplaying the cards he held. In late 2009 and early 2010, the pro-life representative led a small group of Democrats who claimed they would not vote for President Obama's health care reforms without an amendment restricting coverage for abortions. Finally realizing the bill would be defeated without his support, Stupak withdrew his opposition upon receiving a pledge from the president of an executive order barring federal funding of abortions

---

[33] The approach we use here may also be valuable in exploring the relative power of majority parties in other institutions such as the U.S. state legislatures. There, scholars have thus far found substantial variance in partisan policymaking advantages (e.g., Anzia and Jackman 2013), and have been building tools to measure such concepts as partisan ideological differences (e.g., Shor and McCarty 2011).

through the new law.[34] His changing positions made Stupak a top enemy of both pro-choice and pro-life groups, and in the end made him a target of Tea Party activists, opposed to such a large government intrusion into health care. A few short weeks after the president signed the Patient Protection and Affordable Care Act, Representative Stupak announced that he would retire from Congress. Had he remained in the minority party, his good electoral fortunes would likely have continued for some time. He would have averted his health care fiasco, but would have remained frustrated and ineffective as a lawmaker.

Both Knollenberg and Stupak flourished as lawmakers when in the majority and wilted in the minority. Matching conventional wisdom and the aggregate findings from Chapter 2, majority-party status is immensely valuable. However, in recent decades, political scientists have debated just how the majority party attains its success. Does that success arise from merely a close ideological alignment of members? From a strong hierarchical leadership and influence over floor voting? From institutional prerogatives, such as the agenda-setting powers of committees?

In this chapter, we used the lens of legislative effectiveness to reach three main conclusions. First, most of the power of the majority party resides in committees, where the proposals of majority-party members are far more likely to receive hearings, markups, and votes. Their bills are nearly four times more likely to reach the floor, and even more so for substantive and significant legislative proposals. This committee-based decision making accounts for about three-fourths of the enhanced lawmaking success of members of the majority party.

Second, upon reaching the floor, minority-party members are no longer disadvantaged relative to majority-party members. On the whole, minority-party members have greater success once their bills find their way out of committee. While much of that success arises from a larger portion of commemorative bills in their mix of floor votes, minority-sponsored substantive legislation that reaches the floor is no less likely to pass the House or to become law than are bills sponsored by majority-party members. Perhaps the proposals of minority-party members that run the gauntlet of the majority-party-biased committee system are stronger and qualitatively better in some way, thus overcoming any residual bias against them on floor votes. In terms of political science scholarship, these two findings indicate that much of the work on parties designed to detect party influence based on floor voting patterns alone is misdirected. Studies focused on legislative activities beyond floor voting, such as our focus on legislative effectiveness, may well be better suited to uncovering the true nature of political parties in Congress.

Finally, we find that not all party members are equal. Through the period of Democratic control, committee and subcommittee chairs were highly effective

---

[34] Ultimately, for political reasons that we discuss in Chapter 5, the House needed to pass the exact same version of the legislation that had previously passed the Senate, making amendments impossible. Nonetheless, the discussions that Stupak led factored significantly into subsequent policy debates.

by our measures, while rank-and-file Democrats were no more effective than Republicans. When the Republicans took control of Congress, however, they sought to reduce the control of committee and subcommittee chairs, and in so doing spread the enhanced effectiveness from being in the majority party to a broader array of Republicans.

In Chapter 4, we advance this last theme further, exploring inequalities across members of the same party. We seek to explain why women tend to be more effective than men, all else equal. We assess why African Americans receive lower Legislative Effectiveness Scores. And we examine whether Southern Democrats used their pivotal positions as moderates in the 1970s and 1980s to enhance their legislative effectiveness, or whether Northern Democrats dismissed their ideas as they did those of Republicans.

APPENDIX 3.1: THE DETERMINANTS OF BILL PROGRESSION IN CONGRESS

In Chapter 3, we note an increasing share of bills by the majority party remaining in the legislative process throughout the committee stages and a declining share through subsequent stages. In particular, the illustration in Figure 3.3 makes this relationship quite apparent. However, that figure was based on raw numbers, without any analysis of the other considerations beyond majority-party status that may have resulted in increased or decreased lawmaking success through various stages of the legislative process. In this appendix, we report the results of a series of OLS regressions that control for all of the independent variables raised in Chapter 2 in assessing the partisan nature of the number of bills introduced and their progression through Congress and into law.[35]

The results are shown in Table 3A.1, which includes the same specification of independent variables across five different dependent variables. Here, we concentrate our discussion merely on one key independent variable – the indicator of whether a member is in the Majority Party, shown in the top row of the table. The dependent variable in Model 3A.1 is the total number of bills introduced by each member. As the analysis reveals, all else equal, members of the majority party introduce approximately the same number of bills as minority-party members. Any differences detected in the body of the chapter are explained away by the greater number of introductions by committee and subcommittee chairs, among other variables.

Models 3A.2 and 3A.3 show the influence of congressional committees. The coefficients on Majority Party indicate approximately a five-point increase for majority-party members in the percent of their bills receiving action in committee and the percent moving beyond committees, respectively. The means for these two dependent variables are 15.4 and 11.9, meaning that the

---

[35] The lag of each member's LES is now excluded, as the LES is no longer the dependent variable.

TABLE 3A.1. *The Determinants of Bill Progression in Congress*

Dependent Variable	Model 3A.1 — Total Bills Introduced	Model 3A.2 — Percent of Member's Bills Receiving Action in Committee	Model 3A.3 — Percent of Member's Bills Receiving Action Beyond Committee	Model 3A.4 — Percent of Bills Receiving Action Beyond Committee That Pass the House	Model 3A.5 — Percent of Bills Passing House That Become Law
Majority Party	0.233 (1.097)	5.020*** (0.669)	5.263*** (0.574)	-5.260*** (1.584)	-9.080*** (2.217)
Seniority	0.369*** (0.110)	0.363*** (0.094)	0.376*** (0.090)	-0.205 (0.144)	0.080 (0.198)
State Legislative Experience	-3.003** (1.328)	0.769 (1.210)	1.953* (1.142)	5.074*** (1.737)	-0.473 (2.550)
State Legislative Experience x Legislative Prof.	3.358 (3.792)	-0.895 (3.341)	-4.037 (3.176)	-11.484** (5.118)	-1.789 (7.165)
Majority-Party Leadership	-3.055* (1.749)	5.007*** (1.924)	5.440*** (1.948)	3.616 (2.526)	-0.937 (3.951)
Minority-Party Leadership	-2.123 (2.164)	-1.036 (1.476)	-0.364 (1.582)	3.925 (3.743)	3.404 (5.786)
Speaker	-12.363*** (1.933)	-1.776 (7.199)	15.213 (10.109)	17.180*** (2.865)	27.677*** (8.377)
Committee Chair	7.271*** (1.973)	12.885*** (1.672)	16.801*** (1.647)	-1.045 (1.719)	1.004 (2.211)
Subcommittee Chair	5.284*** (0.940)	8.006*** (0.846)	6.365*** (0.769)	-0.838 (1.174)	-2.559 (1.601)
Power Committee	-1.042 (1.012)	-2.111*** (0.728)	-0.873 (0.700)	3.878*** (1.149)	8.398*** (1.728)
	-3.024	-2.929**	-0.218	-4.214	-7.879*

Distance from Median					
	(2.443)	(1.430)	(1.296)	(3.362)	(4.400)
Female	1.888*	-2.498***	-0.776	-4.060**	-3.163
	(1.145)	(0.735)	(0.735)	(2.017)	(2.714)
African American	-5.852***	-0.289	0.714	3.338	-1.248
	(1.421)	(1.078)	(1.308)	(2.355)	(2.775)
Latino	-6.130***	3.017*	4.065***	1.133	-2.228
	(1.792)	(1.757)	(1.565)	(2.757)	(3.746)
Size of Congressional Delegation	0.044	-0.023	-0.003	0.032	-0.014
	(0.035)	(0.024)	(0.022)	(0.038)	(0.053)
Vote Share	0.602***	0.177	0.128	-0.328	0.619
	(0.203)	(0.159)	(0.144)	(0.315)	(0.451)
Vote Share^2	-0.004***	-0.001	-0.001	0.002	-0.003
	(0.001)	(0.001)	(0.001)	(0.002)	(0.003)
Constant	-7.823	3.256	-0.116	99.916***	36.410**
	(7.283)	(5.680)	(5.150)	(11.560)	(16.488)
N	7641	7572	7572	4465	4144
Adjusted-R^2	0.07	0.17	0.20	0.01	0.02

Notes: Ordinary least squares estimation, with robust standard errors in parentheses, and observations clustered by member.
* p < 0.1 (two-tailed), ** p < 0.05 (two-tailed), *** p < 0.01 (two-tailed).

majority-party effect is relatively large. These findings are consistent with the illustration in Figure 3.3. In addition to this overall effect for members of the majority party, committee and subcommittee chairs and majority-party leaders all substantially outperform other majority-party members in receiving attention for (and the success of) their bills in committees.

Models 3A.4 and 3A.5 show that the enhanced majority-party effectiveness ends once bills pass out of committee. No longer are chairs and leaders substantially advantaged in passage through the House or in navigating through the Senate and president into law. While, on average, 83 percent of bills reaching the floor actually pass the House, this percentage is about five points lower for the bills of majority-party members. Likewise, the average of 54 percent of House-passed bills becoming law is comprised of about a 9 percent higher rate for minority-party members than for majority-party members. These findings are consistent with decreased effectiveness for majority-party members at stages beyond committees. On the whole, these more detailed analyses reinforce support found throughout this chapter for the Parties in Committee Hypothesis.

4

A Tale of Three Minorities

We were too limited to be all things to all black people in America.[1]

– Louis Stokes (D-OH), 2007

When Marjorie Holt entered Congress in 1973, she joined what seemed to be a permanent minority. The previous period of Republican control lasted only two years, and ended with the 1954 elections. Holt's party would not return to the majority until 1995, long after she would leave the House. But, unlike many of her colleagues, she did not come to Congress to pad her resume and simply vote no against the Democratic agenda. Entering Congress at age fifty-two, she was interested in advancing policies and making a difference. Doing so would be a challenge.

Holt came from Maryland's heavily Democratic 4th district, which included Annapolis and parts of Anne Arundel County. Yet, rather than taking stands that were immediately popular with majorities back home, Holt staked out the conservative positions that she felt were right for the country and then tried to win over her constituents and congressional colleagues.[2] *She supported prayer in schools, opposed school busing for desegregation purposes, and advocated for constrained budget growth. In a strongly Democratic Congress, she described her first term as "swimming through the sharks."*[3] *But she supported Democratic initiatives when she could, partly in the hopes of building bipartisan support for her own proposals, proclaiming, "As they say in my state's lottery, 'You've got to play to win.'"*[4] *Continuing her attempts to "win," Holt stuck with her proposals, even upon initial failures.*

[1] Quoted as part of the "Louis Stokes Oral History Interview," retrieved from www.c-spanvideo.org/program/Stoke, accessed December 6, 2012.

[2] For details of Holt's policy positions and campaigning, see Baker (1978).

[3] Interview with Frank Gregorsky, retrieved from www.exactingeditor.com/MarjorieHolt.html, accessed on December 7, 2012.

[4] As reported by Rowe (1977), Holt's articulation of this sentiment was greeted by applause from Democratic members of the House. Moreover, even earlier in her career, Holt had cultivated such a

In Congress after Congress, she advocated the same issues, in the traditional "women's issues" areas of education and gender discrimination, as well as in other areas such as budgetary policy. She introduced and then reintroduced bills to prohibit federally ordered racial desegregation in schools, provide relief for sex discrimination claims against insurance companies, and repeal the Davis Bacon Act, which mandates that federal contractors pay workers no less than prevailing local wages. Perhaps most notable were her many attempts to limit the growth of federal expenditures. She described coalition-building efforts on her substitute amendment to the Democratic budget in 1978 as exhilarating: "As I offered my arguments, it was really exciting to see one Democrat after another decide that it was a good idea. It passed by one or two votes and Speaker Tip O'Neill became very excited and came down to the floor, where he and Jim Wright twisted enough arms to defeat the amendment."[5]

While she could not defeat the majority leadership on that issue, Marjorie Holt's perseverance paid off on other areas, such as with her successful proposal to improve medical facilities for veterans, an issue important in her district.[6] She sponsored an average of thirty-three bills per Congress across her seven terms, compared to just twenty-one bills for the typical minority-party member over this time period. Her persistence and efforts to build coalitions across partisan divides paid off, with at least one of her bills reaching the floor in six of her seven Congresses, and with an average Legislative Effectiveness Score of 1.06 across her final four Congresses, more than double that of the typical Republican.

As a Democrat, Louis Stokes experienced a different Congress than did Marjorie Holt. Yet, as an African American in the 1960s and 1970s, his challenges were no less daunting. In his initial terms in Congress, among less than a dozen African-American lawmakers, Stokes felt a responsibility not only to represent his district back home in Cleveland, but also to represent blacks across the country.[7] He sponsored an average of twenty bills in each of the 93rd through 96th Congresses (1973–1980) on such wide-ranging public policy topics as home foreclosures, armed forces discharges, low-income energy subsidies, and youth job creation. Yet none of them became law, nor did they reach the floor, nor did they even receive hearings or markups in committee. His fellow

---

strong following among Democrats that Democratic members of the Maryland legislature would often invite her to their fundraisers, as well as attend her political events.

[5] Interview with Frank Gregorsky, retrieved from www.exactingeditor.com/MarjorieHolt.html, accessed on December 7, 2012.

[6] H.R. 3278, "A bill to amend title 10, United States Code, to provide additional standards for determining the amount of space to be programmed for military retirees and their dependents in medical facilities of the uniformed services, and for other purposes," became Public Law 97–337 when signed by President Reagan on October 15, 1982.

[7] Fenno (2003, 31) describes Stokes's policy preferences as highly congruent with "the policy needs of the black community in Cleveland."

Democrats were not attracted to his proposals, and his legislative strategies were not working.

Many of his black colleagues found their proposals meeting similar fates, and felt individually and collectively limited in their numbers, their resources, and their influence. Embracing a different strategy, Stokes helped found the Congressional Black Caucus (CBC) in the early 1970s. Recognizing their limited power, but understanding the structure of the House, the CBC set about to gain representation on the three most powerful committees, eventually landing Shirley Chisholm (D-NY) onto the Rules Committee, Charles Rangel (D-NY) onto the Ways and Means Committee, and Stokes himself onto the Appropriations Committee.[8]

Beyond Appropriations, Stokes served as Chair of the Select Committee on Assassinations during the 95th Congress (1977–78) and Chair of the Ethics Committee (formerly known as the Committee on Standards of Official Conduct) in the early 1980s. These various roles allowed him to undertake significant procedural and institutional reforms as well as investigations, all while directing appropriations funds back to his district.

Although he could have attempted to leverage his positions of influence to introduce and pass substantive legislation further addressing concerns of his constituents, Stokes instead largely abandoned such lawmaking activities. Rather, he tightened his legislative agenda, introducing an average of only five bills per Congress from the 97th through 105th Congresses (1981–1998). Despite some notable successes in the Intelligence Authorization Acts of 1988 and 1989 and the Veterans Affairs and Housing and Urban Development Appropriations Acts of 1994 and 1995, for the eleven terms in the majority party from the 93rd–103rd Congresses, Stokes's record featured nine with a Legislative Effectiveness Score even below the minority party average. When Democrats became minority-party members, Stokes found some common ground on which to work with Republicans, on raising awareness of the Underground Railroad, and on the plight of sports fans. Yet his minority party position, coupled with the death of his politician brother (Carl Stokes, in 1996) made continued service as a congressman sufficiently unattractive that Stokes retired in 1998.

As neither a woman nor an African American, W.C. "Dan" Daniel did not feel the pressure experienced by Marjorie Holt or Louis Stokes to serve as a surrogate representative of all American women or all blacks in the United States. Rather, he could focus his lawmaking attentions on his constituents, such as in addressing the farming concerns and other parochial considerations

---

[8] Details of Louis Stokes's congressional career and the founding of the CBC are offered in the Louis Stokes Oral History Interview, retrieved from www.c-spanvideo.org/program/Stoke, accessed December 6, 2012. Swain (1995, 36–44) and Tate (2003, 104–110) discuss the development of the CBC and its efficacy in legislative policymaking.

of his "Southside" Virginia district, extending from Richmond to the southern border of Virginia, from the tidewater region west to the Blue Ridge Mountains. Indeed, the largest portion of his legislative portfolio dealt with agricultural issues and other matters that were directly relevant to the day-to-day lives of rural Virginians.

Given the substantial number of rural districts nationwide during Daniel's early years in Congress (he was first elected in 1968), he had a natural coalition for some of his proposals. As a Democrat, he could perhaps also count on his majority-party status. As an incredibly electorally secure member, having run unopposed in nearly every election, Daniel had the freedom to devote his energies to lawmaking activities instead of to electioneering. And, as a conservative Southern Democrat, he was part of a potentially pivotal group. Indeed, throughout the Civil Rights Era and extending into Daniel's early congressional career, Southern Democrats played an important role. Tending to be more conservative than other Democrats, they would occasionally break ranks and vote with Republicans in a "conservative coalition." Daniel stood as a textbook representative of this group, having been elected with the support of the "Byrd Organization," a party machine that dominated Virginia politics in the middle of the twentieth century.[9] Such a pivotal and possibly powerful position might well lead to deference and preferential treatment from Northern Democrats.

While these potential advantages would be expected to provide boosts to Daniel's lawmaking career, his proposals were marginalized and he was among the most ineffective Democratic lawmakers in the House. His Legislative Effectiveness Score never exceeded 1.0, and instead averaged 0.23, less than the average of members in the minority party. Moreover, from 1973 until 1988, only four of Daniel's sponsored bills ever made it out of committee and onto the floor of the House, and only one bill was ever signed into law.[10]

In Chapter 3 we explored the substantially enhanced legislative effectiveness of members of the majority party and demonstrated the central role of the committee system. The previous three examples, however, illustrate that majority-party status alone is insufficient to explain individual lawmaking patterns. Marjorie Holt was more than twice as effective as other members of the minority party, whereas Louis Stokes and W.C. Daniel were less effective than minority-party members during the bulk of their terms in the majority party. Are these three lawmakers merely outliers, not representative of the larger workings of

---

[9] Daniel represented one of the two Virginia districts that George Wallace carried when he ran for President in 1968, in an area where some of the political bosses preferred to shut down the public schools than desegregate in compliance with *Brown v. Board of Education.* Barone, Ujifusa, and Matthews (1979, 899–900) and Barone and Ujifusa (1987, 1231–1232) provide parsimonious summaries of the political considerations of Daniel's district over the course of his career.

[10] H.R. 5580, the "North Atlantic Treaty Organization Mutual Support Act of 1979" became Public Law 96–323 when signed by President Jimmy Carter on August 4, 1980. Representative Daniel passed away in January 1988, which likely influenced his LES in his final Congress.

Congress? Or are their stories indicative of further overarching tendencies that must considered in order to understand the effectiveness of lawmakers in Congress?

In this chapter we argue that individual members vary considerably in how they navigate the party system in Congress to advance their legislative agendas. Put bluntly, no member of Congress is endowed with the constitutional or procedural authority to be an effective lawmaker all by herself. Her proposed bills may end up in committees or subcommittees of which she is not a member. On the floor of the House, her vote is but one of hundreds. And beyond the House, she is not even a formal actor. Rather, each bill sponsor must rely on informal powers. She must convince others that the problem she is focusing on demands attention, that her proposal helps fix that problem, that others will join in to make their combined efforts worthwhile, and that moving forward is politically viable and electorally responsible.

Often this long journey begins with a coalition-building effort among like-minded individuals who share common interests and face common problems. We focus here on three such minority groups, each of which is individually too limited to unilaterally bring about policy change. Women, African Americans, and Southern Democrats have some commonalities that may position them well (or poorly) to navigate the partisan institutions in Congress and to become highly effective lawmakers. Substantial literatures exist on the legislative behaviors of women and African Americans and on the coalitional considerations of Southern Democrats. We argue that such behavioral tendencies of members of each legislative minority group interact with the partisan institutions in Congress to impact the successes of lawmakers within each group, both within and outside of the majority party.

Most succinctly, the consensus-building activities of women in Congress pay particular dividends when they are in the minority party, during which time the fate of their legislative proposals in committee and on the floor rests crucially on gaining support from those across the aisle. For African Americans, possible biases against their agenda items coupled with how thinly they are spread across institutional positions limit their legislative effectiveness. However, such difficulties are more pronounced when African Americans are in the majority party, a time during which their effectiveness should be enhanced, but is not. Finally, for Southern Democrats, their role in the conservative coalition made them unreliable and unattractive partners to Northern Democrats. As the ranks of the Northern Democrats and more-liberal Southern Democrats swelled and Congress started to become more polarized, the conservative Southern Democrats were pushed aside, leaving them much less effective than their more liberal counterparts in the majority party. Moreover, during the period that we analyze, when in the minority party, Southern Democrats were also superfluous to Republican efforts to advance a conservative agenda; their legislative agendas were as quickly discarded as those of their Northern Democratic colleagues.

Throughout the rest of the chapter, we advance these narratives one by one, and evaluate them in terms of the relative effectiveness of each group both within the majority and the minority parties. We demonstrate variations in their patterns of effectiveness across four decades of congressional history, and we link those differences in legislative effectiveness to the five stages of lawmaking that we have analyzed in earlier chapters: from bill introductions through the committee process and floor voting and into law. Before beginning, however, it is important to clarify our definition of *Southern Democrat*. Rather than classifying all Democrats who were elected from Southern states as Southern Democrats, we restrict our definition to include only non-African-American Southern Democrats. African-American Democrats elected in the South have certainly not shared the conservative leanings and policy preferences traditionally held by Southern Democrats, thus lumping them together would be a mistake. Likewise, to enhance comparability, when comparing Southern (non-African American) Democrats to "Other Democrats" (commonly called "Northern Democrats"), we exclude African Americans from the subsample of consideration.[11]

THE LEGISLATIVE EFFECTIVENESS OF WOMEN IN CONGRESS

Scholarship on the role of women in legislatures has made significant contributions in uncovering when and why women run for political office, how voters respond to male and female candidates, and how men and women differ in their proposals and legislative styles upon entering the legislature.[12] Much less is known, however, about how the differences between the legislative behaviors of men and women influence their lawmaking effectiveness, or ultimately what public policies they help to bring about. Because our interest is in legislative effectiveness, we first review what is known about the differences in behavioral tendencies between men and women in Congress and U.S. state legislatures. We then explain and examine how these behavioral tendencies interact with party status in order to enhance the lawmaking effectiveness of women in Congress, particularly for women in the minority party.

Many scholars have identified gender as an important variable for explaining political behavior in legislative institutions. For example, numerous studies have demonstrated that female legislators are more likely than their male counterparts

---

[11] Given the relatively small number of Southern African Americans in Congress across our time period, this restriction has little effect on the support for the hypotheses raised and tested. But it does help solidify the view that we are considering a mostly conservative-leaning faction of the Democratic Party.

[12] This section draws heavily on the work of Volden, Wiseman, and Wittmer (2013a). More specifically, slightly altered versions of Figures 4.1 and 4.2, as well as the motivation and explication of the analysis presented in these figures, appeared earlier in: Volden, Craig, Alan E. Wiseman, and Dana E. Wittmer. 2013a. "When Are Women More Effective Lawmakers than Men?" *American Journal of Political Science* 57(2): 326–341.

to sponsor legislation that focuses on "women's issues," such as education, child care, and family health.[13] Additional gender differences have also been found in such areas as leadership styles, constituency service, and communication patterns in hearings.[14] Taken together, this literature collectively points to substantial differences between the behaviors of male and female members of Congress and state legislatures, such as in women's desires to build consensus across party lines.

Having identified these differences, a natural question is, "How, if at all, do these differences translate into members' legislative effectiveness?" On this point, an interesting puzzle has arisen. On the one hand, scholars have uncovered numerous potential institutional limitations that women face in their day-to-day lawmaking, especially as minority participants in a classically "old boys club."[15] Yet, in many cases, female legislators have *not* been found to be systematically less effective than men in their lawmaking roles.[16] Indeed, our aggregate findings in Chapter 2 suggest that, controlling for all else, women are *more effective* lawmakers than men.

If it is true that female legislators face challenges in gaining acceptance and in turning the legislative agenda toward topics typically neglected by the average male legislator, what lawmaking strategies do they use to nevertheless become equally or more effective than their male counterparts? Among the many possible explanations, two emerge most cleanly from the scholarly literature. First, there is a great deal of emphasis on how women in legislatures feel they must work harder than men to achieve similar lawmaking success.[17] This concept was colorfully described by Texas politician Ann Richards: "After all, Ginger Rogers did everything that Fred Astaire did. She just did it backwards and in high heels." A nationwide survey conducted by the Center for American Women and Politics (CAWP) shows this pattern most starkly, with 74 percent of female state legislators reporting working harder than their male colleagues.[18] Part of the high

---

[13] See, for example, Barnello and Bratton (2007), Boles (2001), Bratton and Haynie (1999), Burrell (1994), Carroll (2001), Poggione (2004), Reingold (1992), Saint-Germain (1989), Sanbonmatsu (2003), Swers (2002), and Thomas and Welch (1991, 2001).

[14] Jewell and Whicker (1994) and Rosenthal (1998) compare the leadership styles of men and women in legislatures. Richardson and Freeman (1995) and Thomas (1992) explore gender differences in how lawmakers interact with their constituents. Kathlene (1994) explores how male and female legislators experience different patterns of deference in committee hearings.

[15] For instance, Thomas (2005, 252) demonstrates that approximately one-quarter of all female state legislators expressed concerns about discrimination, citing issues such as "getting people to respect me as a woman," "being a woman in an old boys club," "isolation of women members," and "having my male counterparts deal with me on their level."

[16] Given variance across legislatures, across the circumstances in which female legislators find themselves, and across methods of analysis, it is not surprising that the evidence has been somewhat mixed in this regard (e.g., Anzia and Berry 2011; Bratton and Haynie 1999; Jeydel and Taylor 2003; Lazarus and Steigerwalt 2011; Saint-Germain 1989).

[17] Reingold (1996) finds support for this claim among state legislators.

[18] For details, see CAWP (2001). Lawless and Fox (2005) provide further examples of this phenomenon.

level of effort exerted may arise from pressure on female legislators to serve as "surrogate representatives," serving all women, even those beyond their legislative districts.[19]

Second, the propensity of women to engage in consensus-building activities may bolster their legislative effectiveness. Previous research has argued that there are significant differences between the political approaches employed by male and female lawmakers, with women being more collaborative and consensual, and men being more individualistic and competitive.[20] For example, surveys characterize women in state legislatures as "more committed team players than men" and find that "gender differences are more pronounced with respect to activities that involve communication and compromise."[21] Whether such differences are rooted in the particular challenges that women face as lawmakers or in broader underlying male-female differences is difficult to judge.[22] For our purposes, we merely note that previously established gender differences in legislative behavior may well impact the relative effectiveness of men and women in Congress.

Moreover, we argue that these behavioral tendencies interact in important ways with the political party effects found to be so significant in Chapter 3. Although these feminized strategies of cooperation, conciliation, and consensus building may be undervalued and therefore hinder female legislators in some settings, such leadership approaches may be quite valuable under certain political circumstances.[23] Specifically, cooperation and consensus building may help female legislators effectively work with members in the majority party, even when they themselves are members of the minority party.[24] Members of the

---

[19] Carroll (2002) and Mansbridge (2003) explore the nature of surrogate representation.

[20] See, for example, Jeydel and Taylor (2003), Rinehart (1991), Rosenthal (1998), and Thomas (1994). Duerst-Lahti (2002a, 23) outlines a comprehensive overview of proto-attributed gender differences. Masculine traits are individuation, instrumental, rule-focused, dominate, power over, competition, hierarchy, speak out, public sphere, and breadwinning; in contrast, feminine traits are connection, contextual, relationship focused, collaborate, power to, cooperation, web-center, listen well, home sphere, and caregiving.

[21] Carey, Niemi, and Powell (1998, 101) describe their survey and its results in great detail.

[22] Although situational effects undoubtedly matter, numerous laboratory experiments (e.g., Kennedy 2003) find female subjects to prefer cooperation and universalistic solutions much more than the competitive processes and outcomes that men prefer. In addition, Sanbonmatsu, Carroll, and Walsh (2009, 20–21) note that female candidates for state legislative offices are more likely than men to say that they are motivated to serve for specific public policy considerations, which points to another behavioral tendency that might influence bargaining and negotiation styles of men and women.

[23] Scholars have argued that Congress has been, and continues to be, a masculinized institution. Hence, traits that are typically ascribed to women are thought to be undervalued, or even detrimental. And although increased "feminization" in leadership styles has occurred at the state level (Jewell and Whicker 1994), it appears as if legislative professionalism and feminization are negatively related (Duerst-Lahti 2002b).

[24] Consistent with this argument, Senator Barbara Mikulski has claimed that female legislators "check our party at the door and work really on civility" (Alvarez 2000).

minority party could easily step into an obstructionist role. But those who care deeply about bringing about policy change, and those who have the skills to build consensus across party lines, may continue to work hard and serve as effective lawmakers. Cultivation of coalition partners in the majority party is crucial to success in the committee and floor voting stages of the lawmaking process. As stated in the following hypothesis, we believe that the behavioral tendencies of female legislators interact with the institutional considerations women face when in the minority party to make them more effective lawmakers than their male counterparts.[25] Absent such institutional constraints, consensus building across parties is not nearly as valuable, as the majority party is typically well-situated in the House of Representatives to proceed without minority party support.

Women's Effectiveness Hypothesis: *In the minority party, women are more effective than men. In the majority party, women and men are likely to be equally effective.*

Below, we explore how the positions that African Americans and Southern Democrats find themselves in, when part of the minority or majority party, likewise influence their effectiveness. That said, in order to keep our theoretical expectations and empirical findings most closely linked, we turn now to the evidence regarding the effectiveness of women in and out of the majority party.

Despite the extensive scholarly work on the behavioral differences between men and women in legislatures and the significant scholarship on the role of the majority party, very little research has attempted to identify: (a) whether legislators' behaviors change depending on their party status, and (b) how these behavioral changes correspond to legislative outputs. Given the data that we have collected to create our initial Legislative Effectiveness Scores, we are in a unique position to engage precisely these questions. As discussed in detail in Chapter 2, a member's LES is based on the number of bills that she introduces, and the fates that each of those bills experience as they move forward in the lawmaking process, from potentially being the focus of committee debate, to floor debate, to passing the House, and ultimately being signed into law, all weighted by each bill's significance. Hence, not only can we identify whether a member's legislative effectiveness is higher or lower than the average member of the House (perhaps depending on party status), but we can also begin to identify the stages in which these differences in effectiveness arise. Doing so allows us to test our hypothesis above and to explore its underlying causes.

---

[25] Volden, Wiseman, and Wittmer (2013b) investigate whether women might also be more effective lawmakers than men because they engage in a degree of issue specialization, which induces deference on the part of other lawmakers. While their analysis demonstrates that women generally focus their efforts on particular substantive areas, they find little evidence of deference within the chamber, as women are not more successful in advancing legislation in these specialty areas in comparison to other issue areas.

In Table 2.5 of Chapter 2, we sought to explain the variance in the LES with a variety of personal and institutional variables. Controlling for such considerations as majority-party status, seniority, committee and subcommittee chairs, and many others, we found an effect of 0.10 for women. Given the average LES value of 1.0, this finding implies that women are about 10 percent more effective as lawmakers than are men by our measure, all else equal. However, if we explore this effect for women in the majority party and women in the minority party separately, by adding such conditional variables to our fully specified model from Chapter 2, further insights arise.

Specifically, in such a model, the coefficient on an indicator variable for women in the minority party takes a value of 0.11, which is clearly positive and statistically significant.[26] Substantively, this value is especially sizable in comparison to men in the minority party, whose average LES is 0.39. Controlling for differences across genders in such other considerations as seniority, leadership positions, and so on, minority-party women are thus approximately 28 percent more effective than are minority-party men.

A somewhat different story emerges for women in the majority party. Once again, an indicator variable for such women takes a positive coefficient, now one of 0.08. However, statistically, this effect is no different from zero (p = 0.22), partly due to a great deal of variance in the relative effectiveness of majority-party women from one another and over time. In substantive terms, the typical male lawmaker in the majority party scores an LES of 1.49. Therefore, controlling for all else, women in the majority party are only about 5 percent more effective than majority-party men, perhaps explaining why such an effect is not detected as being statistically significant.

Such findings offer initial support for the Women's Effectiveness Hypothesis. Yet we take two further steps that help explain when and why the above results come about. We look first at patterns over the decades of our study and then explore differences between men and women at each of the lawmaking stages that make up the Legislative Effectiveness Score.

Whereas the results described previously arise from regressions that combine all Congresses together, we can conduct the same analysis for each Congress separately.[27] Doing so shows the extent to which the effectiveness of women in the majority and minority parties varies over time. Figure 4.1 illustrates the coefficient values for minority-party women and majority-party women in each Congress from 1973 through 2008. The circles, connected by

---

[26] Further details of these models and specifications are offered in Table 4.1, described in the final section of this chapter. Statistical significance on this variable gives us more than 99.9% confidence in the enhanced effectiveness of minority-party women being systematic, rather than arising due to randomness (p < 0.001).

[27] For such OLS regressions, and similar regressions in the other sections of this chapter, we include all of the same control variables as in the full Model 2.3 of Table 2.5, with the exception of the lagged LES variable, which is here excluded due to the cross-sectional nature of each regression.

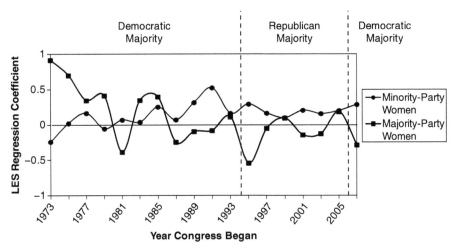

FIGURE 4.1. When Are Women More Effective Than Men? Steadily So in the Minority Party, Decreasingly So in the Majority Party

Note: The figure shows the relative effectiveness of women compared to men, controlling for all other factors discussed in Chapter 2, from seniority to committee leadership. The circles along the thin line show the boost in Legislative Effectiveness Scores (LES) for women in the minority party, relative to men in the minority party, indicating greater effectiveness in each Congress since 1980. The squares along the thick line show the relative LES boost for women in the majority party, relative to men in the majority party. The enhanced effectiveness of majority-party women prior to the mid-1980s has given way to women having similar or lower effectiveness compared to men in the more recent, polarized Congresses.

the thin line show the coefficients on an indicator variable for women in the minority party. As can be seen, this variable took positive values in all but two of the Congresses (93rd and 96th, both in the 1970s). In every Congress since 1980, women in the minority party have outperformed men in the minority party, regardless of whether that minority party is made up of Democrats or Republicans. Such consistency helps explain the statistical and substantive significance across all Congresses combined, as described previously.[28]

In contrast, there is much more variance for the coefficient on women in the majority party, shown in Figure 4.1 by the squares connected by the thick line. Here, perhaps a distinction can be drawn between the years 1973–1985 (corresponding to the 93rd–99th Congresses) and 1987–2007 (corresponding to the

---

[28] The inconsistency in findings across the earlier Congresses is likely influenced by the relatively lower numbers of women in the minority caucus during these years, in comparison to more recent Congresses.

100th–110th Congresses). Six of those seven earlier Congresses featured majority-party women being more effective than majority-party men.[29] Yet eight of the latter eleven Congresses featured majority-party women as less effective than their male counterparts. It is possible that the consensus-building activities of women were more valuable among majority-party women during the less-polarized early Congresses of the 1970s and 1980s than the more-polarized Congresses of recent years. It is also possible that Democratic women were better able to bridge the gaps between Northern and Southern Democrats that were more prominent in the earlier era.[30] Yet, regardless of the reasons behind the changing effectiveness evident in the figure, the totality of the evidence provides further support for the Women's Effectiveness Hypothesis, with consistently enhanced effectiveness for women in the minority party that is not equally reflected among majority-party women.

Finally, we look not at the aggregated measure of the Legislative Effectiveness Score, but at its many component parts, isolating the different stages of the lawmaking process. In particular, as detailed in Appendix 4.1, we conduct separate analyses of the number of bills each lawmaker sponsored, the number receiving action in committee, the number reaching the floor, the number passing the House, and the number becoming law. As with our explorations of members' overall Legislative Effectiveness Scores, here we seek to explain the number of bills that members sponsor that reach each of these stages, with independent variables capturing all of the personal and institutional consider-ations raised in the full model discussed in Chapter 2.[31]

Such analyses show, for example, that controlling for all these other factors, women introduce 1.89 more bills on average than do men. Given that the average number of introductions for men is 17.4 bills per Congress, women introduce about 11 percent more pieces of legislation than do men. This is consistent with the behavioral claims of women exerting higher effort than men and of women adopting a larger agenda, perhaps in their role as "surrogate representatives" for all women. Moreover, we find a difference between the introduction effects for women in the majority or minority parties. Controlling for all other considerations for which members introduce more pieces of legi-slation, women in the majority party sponsor 3.35 more bills, which is a

---

[29] A regression restricted to these early Congresses finds statistically significant evidence of enhanced legislative effectiveness among majority-party women.

[30] Consistent with this argument, Frederick (2009) suggests that female Representatives, especially Republicans, have become increasingly ideological in recent Congresses, which might inhibit compromises across the parties.

[31] These analyses (as well as the results that follow in analyzing the legislative fates of bills introduced by African Americans and Southern Democrats) are based on combining all types of bills (commemorative, substantive, and substantive and significant) together with equal weights. The results are similar if we set aside commemorative bills and confine our attention to only substantive and substantive and significant bills.

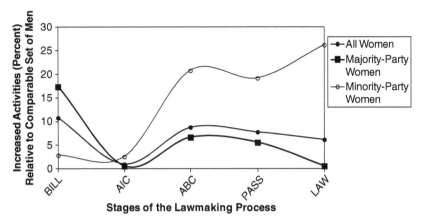

FIGURE 4.2. Minority-Party Women Excel at Consensus-Building Stages Beyond Committee

Note: The figure shows the percentage by which the activities of women exceed those of men, both overall and broken down by majority and minority party, controlling for all other factors discussed in Chapter 2, from seniority to committee leadership. For instance, while the average majority-party woman introduces about 17 percent more bills (BILL) than the average majority-party man, this advantage fades to near zero for receiving action in committee (AIC). In contrast, minority-party women are nearly identical to minority-party men through these early stages, but see a 20–25 percent boost in their bills receiving action beyond committee (ABC), passing the House (PASS), and becoming law (LAW), coinciding with the lawmaking stages in which consensus building may be most valuable for members of the minority party.

17 percent increase over majority-party men. In the minority party, this increase is only 0.44 more bills, or 3 percent more than minority-party men.

Figure 4.2 illustrates these differences, and those for each stage of the lawmaking process. Specifically, on the left of the figure are the enhanced introductions for majority-party women (shown as squares connected by the thickest line), minority-party women (shown as open circles connected by the thinnest line), and all women (shown as closed circles), based on the calculations noted immediately above. As we move to the right in the figure, we display similar enhanced activities for these groups of women for each further stage, based on separate analyses of how many members' bills reach each stage, again accounting for all other considerations.

Regarding action in committee, there is no statistically discernible difference between men and women, meaning that the additional bills sponsored by women fade away during the process of committee hearings and bill markups. However, in terms of passage out of committee and onto the floor of the House, there is a resurgence, particularly for proposals of minority-party women. Consistent with the Women's Effectiveness Hypothesis, minority-party women receive 21 percent more action beyond committee than do comparable minority-party men.[32] Such enhanced effectiveness for majority-party women is only 7 percent. These patterns are maintained for the passage of bills through the House. Consistent with our finding in Chapter 3, we note little difference in the success rate of passage on the floor of the House between the proposals of minority- or majority-party members.

In terms of the number of sponsored bills that become law, minority-party women have an enhanced lawmaking rate of 26 percent beyond that achieved by minority-party men.[33] In contrast, there is no significant difference between the overall lawmaking production of men and women in the majority party. This is not to say that women get more done when in the minority party than when they are in the majority party. Having majority-party status is greatly beneficial for both men and women. Within the majority party, there is no difference in lawmaking production by gender – despite introducing a larger portfolio, women produce no more laws than do men. However, within the minority party, perhaps due to greater consensus-building activities, women outperform men, especially in getting their bills to the floor of the House and finally into law.[34]

This finding is consistent with the Women's Effectiveness Hypothesis. In particular, these results seem to suggest that women engage in a more consensual style of lawmaking than men. Especially in terms of building the coalitional support needed to move proposals beyond the committee stage, these skills are particularly valuable when women find themselves in the institutionally disadvantaged position of being in the minority party. This argument comports well with our narrative for Marjorie Holt, at the beginning of the chapter. While not outperforming the lawmaking averages of members of the majority party, and not able to effectively substitute her budget proposal for that of the majority party, Holt continued to press her issues, build coalitions across party lines, and achieve lawmaking successes, well beyond the averages for men in the minority party. To paraphrase Marjorie Holt's sentiment, it appears that minority-party women do, indeed, believe they've got to play the game in order to win. And they do so effectively.

THE LEGISLATIVE EFFECTIVENESS OF AFRICAN AMERICANS IN CONGRESS

African Americans in Congress face many of the same limitations as women in Congress – small numbers, proposals that differ in significant ways from those of their colleagues, and possible biases that are difficult to fully discern and

---

[32] The relevant calculation involves the regression coefficient of 0.137 for minority-party women in explaining the number of bills receiving action beyond committee. Compared to the average minority-party man, who shepherds 0.66 of his sponsored bills through the committee process on average, this is a 21 percent boost (0.137/0.66).

[33] Based on regression results, women in the minority party produce an additional 0.09 laws on average. This is a 26 percent boost beyond the average of 0.33 laws produced per minority-party man.

[34] In a separate analysis, not included here in detail, we also find a significantly larger number of cosponsors gained by minority-party women over those gained by minority-party men.

document. Yet the strategy of women in Congress to reach across party lines and build consensus is perhaps less likely to be successful for African Americans. Nearly all African Americans in Congress during our time period were Democrats, typically significantly more liberal than the average Democrat and thus far more liberal than most Republicans, making coalition building difficult.[35] Moreover, while many women's issues, such as health care and education, had the possibility of resonating in nearly all legislative districts, comparable "black-interest" legislation tended to focus on the concerns of poor and minority communities, which often differed in significant ways from the constituents of other lawmakers. What legislative strategies were therefore available to African-American lawmakers, and how would such choices impact their legislative effectiveness?

Once again, the scholarly literature on the legislative behaviors of black lawmakers in Congress and in the U.S. state legislatures may be informative. Scholars are in fair agreement that African-American legislators vote consistently more liberally than white legislators, and that they also favor policies that benefit black interests more so than do their white counterparts.[36] This is wholly consistent with Congress as a representative institution. Likewise, African-American legislators vote cohesively across numerous issue areas.[37] Such cohesion may certainly be a strength. Indeed, scholars have characterized the CBC as among the most influential voting blocs in Congress.[38] However, cohesive minority groups can only produce laws by gaining broader support, which may be challenging depending on the proposal at hand.

Moreover, African Americans may face a number of biases in the lawmaking process more generally. Racial biases against African Americans have been shown to arise not only in the electoral arena but also within legislatures.[39] Fear of a white voter backlash to concentrated power by African-American lawmakers may have led Democratic leaders to spread black lawmakers across different committees and

---

[35] Throughout this section, we focus solely on African-American Democrats because, across our thirty-six-year time frame, only two black Republicans served in Congress (Gary Franks of Connecticut and J.C. Watts of Oklahoma).

[36] See Canon (1999), Cobb and Jenkins (2001), Hall (1996), Haynie (2001), Lublin (1997), Tate (2003), and Whitby and Krause (2001).

[37] See Gile and Jones (1995), Levy and Stoudinger (1976), Pinney and Serra (1999), and Singh (1998).

[38] Whitby (2002, 94) notes the widespread view of the CBC as "one of the most influential voting blocs in Congress," and Swain (1995, 234) argues that the CBC became a major policy player in the 103rd Congress (1993–94), providing a crucial margin of victory on sixteen of eighty-seven key votes during those two years. The 103rd Congress also corresponded with a substantial increase in the number of African-American Representatives in the House (from twenty-six in the 102nd to thirty-nine in the 103rd).

[39] In observing the U.S. state legislatures, Haynie (2002, 309) writes, "Even when African American candidates are able to overcome numerous race-related obstacles and win elected office, they may face additional race-based hurdles in their attempts to influence the policy process." As such, even if the legislature yields "racially neutral policies," it is possible that the institution has "racial biases at one or more stages of the decision-making process."

subcommittees.[40] Whereas Representative Louis Stokes considered the incorporation of CBC members into the most powerful committees as a lawmaking success, that strategy came at the cost of not gaining even more concentrated power on a small number of substantive committees.[41]

As is almost always the case, any legislative strategy with major benefits also features significant costs. Consistent with our narrative of the tightened and tailored agenda of Stokes at the start of the chapter, scholars have found African Americans to likewise generally concentrate their legislative portfolios around a smaller number of issues than do their white counterparts. While women tend to expand their legislative portfolios to include women's issues, African Americans tend to narrow their portfolios in order to dedicate more of their efforts to black-interest legislation.[42] Moreover, they make such proposals when the chances of success are the greatest (although still far from stellar), such as when Democrats are in the majority.[43]

How do such strategic choices as being spread broadly across committees or narrowing their legislative portfolios influence the overall legislative effectiveness of African Americans? To date, the clearest answers arise in state legislative arenas. For example, reputational rankings of members in the North Carolina state legislature reveal a perception of African-American legislators as less effective than other lawmakers.[44] Furthermore, upon disaggregating the reputational rankings into the three separate respondent categories of journalists, lobbyists, and other legislators, African-American members were consistently deemed to be less effective by lobbyists and their fellow legislators, yet not by journalists. This would be consistent with African Americans generating a common external message that nevertheless does not translate into the lawmaking success detected by interest groups and other lawmakers.

In considering more-objective indicators of legislative effectiveness, African-American state legislators have been found to be systematically less successful than white legislators at achieving bill passage in Arkansas, California, and Illinois, possibly due to making proposals that were too liberal for the mainstream of the legislature.[45] At the congressional level, studies have shown results

---

[40] Griffin and Keane (2011, 152) discuss how African Americans are spread thinly across the committees in contemporary Congresses, perhaps either for symbolic benefits for the Democratic caucus or to limit concentrated power in a small number of committees out of "fear of white voter backlash." In contrast to this perspective, Haynie (2005) points to the inclusion of African-American Representatives on every committee in the 107th Congress as evidence of political "incorporation."

[41] As noted by Swain (1995, 40), while African-American members were mostly on nonexclusive committees before 1974, by 1992 they were relatively well represented on all congressional committees and had held five committee chairmanships during that time period.

[42] See Bratton and Haynie (1999), Griffin and Keane (2011), Grose (2011), and Tate (2003).

[43] See Whitby (2002).

[44] Haynie (2002) offers details and analyses.

[45] Bratton and Haynie (1999) investigate legislative politics in six states (Arkansas, California, Illinois, Maryland, New Jersey, and North Carolina) across the years 1969, 1979, and 1989.

similar to our finding from Chapter 2 of lower Legislative Effectiveness Scores for African Americans, with noteworthy exceptions.[46]

That said, we are interested not only in the relative effectiveness of African Americans compared to their white counterparts, but more fundamentally in how the behavioral strategies of minorities interact with legislative institutions to explain patterns of legislative effectiveness. Consistent with Chapter 3 and our discussion of women in Congress previously, we are specifically interested in how African Americans navigate lawmaking considerations when in the minority party or the majority party to successfully advance their agenda items. Unsurprisingly, earlier work has found African-American lawmakers to be more successful when in the majority party than in the minority party.[47] Certainly the majority party brings institutional advantages as well as an alignment of policy preferences.

Our inquiry is somewhat different, however. We are interested in comparing black Democrats to other (non-African American) Democrats. Do African Americans outperform or underperform relative to other Democrats, and does this difference manifest itself to a greater extent when Democrats are in the majority party or in the minority party? Such a systematic comparison has not been conducted previously. Yet the scholarship discussed previously helps us generate fairly clear expectations.

Based on prior work, we expect that, when in the majority party, African Americans introduce a smaller, more focused agenda than do other Democrats. Furthermore, this focus on black-interest issues puts them out of the Democratic Party mainstream more so than are white Democrats on average. Lack of concentrated influence in committees may also be detrimental. Any further racial biases should also diminish the legislative effectiveness of African Americans, and may be detected in our examination of the stages of the lawmaking process. In sum, we expect that African Americans will be less effective than white Democrats when in the majority party.

When in the minority party, such considerations may be muted. Not only are both white and African-American Democrats expected to be less effective when Republicans control Congress, but previous scholarship suggests that African Americans further tailor their proposed legislation when in the minority party. If this is the case, and African Americans turn away from black-interest legislation toward bills with broader appeal, any hindrance they face due to their ideological differences from Republican lawmakers may be diminished, as well, on such topics. Such tactics seemed to be the case with Stokes, who was able to

---

African American and white passage rates are statistically indistinguishable from each other in Maryland, New Jersey, and North Carolina.

[46] Griffin and Keane (2011) find that minority representatives introduced fewer bills in the 101st–106th Congresses (1989–2000), and subsequently produced fewer laws. Yet Tate (2003, 79) finds that African-American Representatives in the 104th Congress (1995–96) were just as, if not more, successful than white members at getting their bills advanced through the House.

[47] See Whitby (2002), for example.

find items that appealed across party lines, even after the Republican victories in 1994. As with Democratic majorities, if there are further biases against the proposals of African Americans under a Republican majority party, we may be able to detect them with our focus across lawmaking stages. Absent such biases, however, we do not have strong expectations about a diminished effectiveness of black Democrats in comparison to other Democrats, when they are in the minority party. The combination of these expectations is summarized as follows:

African Americans' Effectiveness Hypothesis: In the majority party, African-American Democrats are less effective than other Democrats. In the minority party, African Americans and other Democrats are likely to be equally effective.

As with our examination of female legislators, our analysis here takes three parts: first an overall assessment of African Americans' Legislative Effectiveness Scores by party status across all recent Congresses combined, then an over-time comparison of each Congress separately, and finally an exploration of effectiveness by stage of the lawmaking process. In combination, these three approaches support the African Americans' Effectiveness Hypothesis, while also reaffirming the findings of earlier studies about the patterns of behavior upon which that hypothesis is built.

In Chapter 2, in explaining who scored the highest on the LES, we controlled for many institutional and individual characteristics of members of Congress. The regression coefficient that emerged for African Americans was negative and statistically significant. The size of that coefficient indicated that African-American lawmakers were about 22 percent less effective than typical white legislators, controlling for all other considerations. Separating that effect into one for African Americans in the majority party and one for African Americans in the minority party, we find a statistically significant and negative effect for African Americans in the majority party. Specifically, a regression coefficient of –0.38 emerges. Compared to the average LES of 1.48 for non-black majority-party members, this is a 26 percent reduction in effectiveness for African Americans when in the majority party. Such an effect is about double the percent reduction in effectiveness for African Americans relative to whites when in the minority party.[48] Moreover, that latter effect is not statistically discernible from zero at conventional levels of significance, providing initial evidence in support of the African Americans' Effectiveness Hypothesis.

These patterns become even starker when we look at them over time. Figure 4.3 illustrates the coefficient on a regression explaining each member's Legislative Effectiveness Score for each Congress, with all of the same control

[48] The coefficient of –0.056 for African-American minority-party members is compared to the average LES of non-black minority-party members, which is 0.399. This is a decline in effectiveness of about 14 percent for African Americans when in the minority party, when compared to others in the minority party.

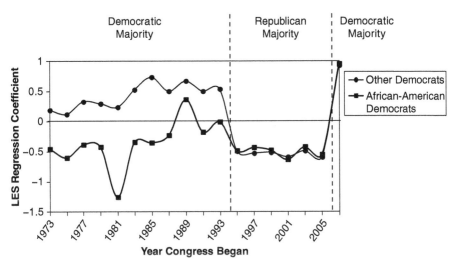

FIGURE 4.3. When Are African Americans Less Effective Than Other Democrats? When Democrats Hold the Majority

Note: The figure shows the relative effectiveness of African-American Democrats and other Democrats as compared to Republicans, controlling for all other factors discussed in Chapter 2, from seniority to committee leadership. The circles along the thin line show the boost in Legislative Effectiveness Scores (LES) for most Democrats over Republicans when in the majority party, and a deficit in the minority party. The squares along the thick line show no such LES boost for African-American Democrats when Democrats were in the majority party prior to 1994. Instead, we find a significant gap between the effectiveness of African Americans and other Democrats precisely when their majority-party status would have been expected to help produce their greatest effectiveness.

variables as in the full model of Chapter 2. Now, however, instead of including a variable for being in the majority party, we include a variable for African-American Democrats and another for Other Democrats. Consistent with the benefit that arises from being in the majority party, we expect these variables to have positive coefficients when Democrats are in the majority and are outperforming the baseline category of Republicans. And we expect negative coefficients when Republicans are in the majority party. And, indeed, that is what we find for non-black Democrats.

Startlingly, a very different pattern emerges for African-American Democrats than for other Democrats. In the first eight Congresses of our dataset (1973–87), not only do African-American Democrats underperform relative to other Democrats, but they also underperform relative to Republicans, who are in the minority party. This is not to say that the average LES of African Americans (mean = 0.98) over this time period was lower than that of minority-party Republicans (mean = 0.39). The difference between the regression coefficients and these raw scores arises because the regressions account for the benefit of being a subcommittee or committee chair, and more than half of all African

Americans served in these influential roles, while Republicans did not. However, controlling for such considerations as seniority, committee positions, and the like, African Americans did not receive the positive boost that other Democrats enjoyed above and beyond the legislative effectiveness of Republicans. Moreover, setting aside all such controls, non-black Democrats averaged an LES of 1.43 in this era, or nearly 50 percent greater than that of African-American Democrats. Whether their ineffectiveness during the 1970s and 1980s can be attributed to the small number of African Americans in Congress during this time period, to racial biases, or to other considerations is worthy of further investigation in the future; but this effect seems to have diminished in recent decades.

The gap between African-American Democrats and all other Democrats narrowed between 1987 and 1993 (during the 101st–103rd Congresses), and then disappeared altogether. This disappearance coincided with Republicans gaining majority-party control of the House. When in the minority party, no difference in LES is detected by race, upon controlling for all other factors. As of the 110th Congress (2007–08), once again no difference is found between African-American and other Democrats, despite Democrats reclaiming majority party control.[49] Except for this one Congress, the analysis illustrated in Figure 4.3 is wholly consistent with the African Americans' Effectiveness Hypothesis.

What accounts for these dramatic differences between African Americans and other Democrats? Is it related to a smaller and more tailored agenda, to some biases in the committee system, or to some other factor in the lawmaking process? By analyzing each stage of the lawmaking process separately, some insights emerge. As before, we examine each of the five major stages of the lawmaking process separately, controlling for all of the same personal and institutional factors as in our previous full specifications.[50] Here now we also account for whether the member is an African American in the majority party or an African American in the minority party. Similar to Figure 4.2 for women, we show these effects by stage of the lawmaking process for African Americans in Figure 4.4.

Consistent with the prior literature suggesting a tailored legislative portfolio advanced by African Americans when in the majority party, we find that black Democrats introduced 23 percent fewer bills when in the majority party than did other Democrats.[51] Yet this strategy did not result in greater success. Indeed, their smaller portfolios diminished further throughout the lawmaking process. Relative to comparable majority-party Democrats, African Americans received 27 percent less action in committee, 35 percent less action beyond committee, 35 percent

---

[49] This finding is consistent with Tate (2010), who analyzes the evolution of the CBC in the post-1990s era and argues that, as its membership increased, the CBC became less radical, thereby contributing to its increased aggregate effectiveness as a voting coalition.

[50] Unlike for the aggregated LES measure, this part of the analysis does not assign different weights based on bill types.

[51] Compared to an average of 22.3 bills introduced by non-black majority-party Democrats, the coefficient of –5.15 is indicative of a 23 percent smaller agenda.

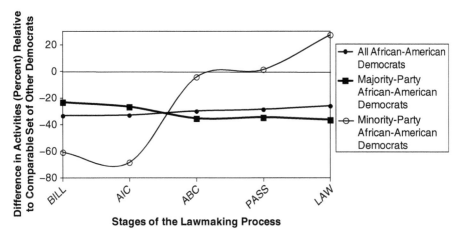

FIGURE 4.4. Proposals of African Americans Falter Under Democratic Control

Note: The figure shows the percentage by which the activities of African-American Democrats differed from those of other Democrats, both overall and broken down by majority and minority party, controlling for all other factors discussed in Chapter 2, from seniority to committee leadership. For instance, while the average majority-party African-American Democrat introduces about 23 percent fewer bills (BILL) than other majority-party Democrats, those proposals fared poorly, with this disadvantage reaching 27 percent for receiving action in committee (AIC), 35 percent for action beyond committee (ABC), 35 percent for passing the House (PASS), and 36 percent for becoming law (LAW). In contrast, the limited number of bills sponsored by African-American Democrats when in the minority party outperformed the proposals of other Democrats at the later stages of the lawmaking process.

fewer bills passing the House, and 36 percent fewer laws.[52] This is indicative of the bills sponsored by African Americans being screened out during the committee process more than those of other Democrats, despite Democrats being in the majority party (and controlling for the tightened agenda at the bill introduction stage). Those African-American-sponsored bills reaching the floor of the House passed and became law at about the same rate as bills proposed by other Democrats.[53] Thus, the diminished effectiveness of African-American Democrats when in the majority party can be traced to two factors: (1) a smaller agenda, and (2) unfavorable treatment in committees. Future scholarship exploring the

[52] All of these effects are statistically significant with $p < 0.01$. To interpret the coefficient sizes, we compared to average non-black majority-party Democrats. For example, non-black majority-party Democrats average 2.6 bills reaching the floor of the House, compared to a –0.91 coefficient for African Americans in the majority party. Similarly, the coefficient of –0.40 is compared to the average of 1.1 laws for the typical non-black majority-party Democrat to indicate a reduction of 36 percent in sponsored laws, all else equal.

[53] This can best be seen by the relatively flat line for Majority-Party African-American Democrats from the ABC stage to LAW in Figure 4.4.

legislative effectiveness of African Americans in Congress may therefore benefit from a more explicit focus on the committee stage of lawmaking.

A very different story emerges for the legislative successes of African Americans when in the minority party. Consistent with previous scholarship suggesting an even further tightened agenda, perhaps removing many black-interest proposals altogether, minority-party African-American legislators introduce nearly 60 percent fewer bills than comparable non-black minority-party members.[54] And, consistent with the experiences of African Americans when in the majority party, those bills do not receive particularly favorable treatment in committee.[55] However, in a remarkable reversal of fortune, this tightened agenda of blacks in the minority party finds its way onto the floor of the House at such a great rate that there is no discernible difference between the size of the portfolio of African Americans and that of other Democrats beyond the committee stage. This success continues through bill passage and into law. In the end, despite introducing less than half as many bills as their minority-party counterparts, controlling for seniority and other considerations, African Americans account for slightly more laws per member than do other minority-party Democrats. Thus, the strategy of African Americans when in the minority party seems to have been highly effective, as we find Republicans to have been quite receptive to their tailored proposals. That said, while many of their successes were on symbolic or commemorative bills important to their voters, the reduced number of introductions meant they were giving up on some of the key substantive interests of their constituents. From this point of view, it is unsurprising that African Americans felt more effective when in the majority party.[56]

The totality of the evidence therefore provides strong support for the African Americans' Effectiveness Hypothesis, and for the reasons behind it. Not only did African Americans advance a narrower agenda than other Democrats, but that agenda was not well received in Democrat-controlled committees. This diminished effectiveness was particularly noteworthy in the 1970s and 1980s, when the Congressional Black Caucus had less than two dozen members. As the ranks of the CBC swelled and the seniority of its members increased, their relative effectiveness grew.[57] Moreover, when in the minority party, African Americans were equally as effective (or ineffective) as their non-African-American Democratic counterparts. Despite a smaller agenda, African Americans'

---

[54] The coefficient of −6.8 indicates about a 60 percent smaller agenda than the 11.3 sponsored bills for non-black minority-party Democrats.

[55] The coefficients for introductions and action in committee are statistically significant at $p < 0.01$, whereas those for later stages are not ($p > 0.1$).

[56] In her consideration of African-American members' lawmaking activities in the 104th Congress, Tate (2003, 81) argues that "mostly symbolic legislation" made it out of the House.

[57] Related to this point, Swain (1995, 44) argues that members of the CBC became more effective lawmakers over time as they acquired knowledge and insight into the parliamentary processes that govern the House.

proposals were more likely to reach the floor and then equally likely to become law as were those of others in the minority party. Therefore, while facing clear obstacles in terms of different preferences for issues and in terms of ideology, African Americans found a strategy that worked reasonably well in the minority party, but perhaps somewhat less well (relative to other Democrats) during periods of Democratic control.

THE LEGISLATIVE EFFECTIVENESS OF SOUTHERN DEMOCRATS IN CONGRESS

Relative to women and African Americans, Southern Democrats may be more difficult to recognize as a minority group by those unfamiliar with congressional history. Rather than by their race or gender, Southern Democrats are characterized by their party and by the geographic location of their districts.[58] Yet, more so than any other geographic clustering of lawmakers, conservative Southern Democrats played a key role in lawmaking throughout the twentieth century.[59] Moreover, their declining numbers and changing ideological composition make them an interesting counterpoint to the other two legislative minorities that we study. Yet, just like women or African Americans, Southern Democrats could only truly be effective lawmakers by building a coalition with others in order to advance their legislative proposals. We offer a historical and a theoretical treatment of this minority group in order to hypothesize about their likely legislative effectiveness.

While not monolithic, for much of the twentieth century Southern Democrats were ideologically more conservative than their copartisans, therefore often finding themselves more closely aligned with Republicans than with Northern Democrats. Southern Democrats were courted by both Democrats and Republicans as their votes would be crucial to ensuring the passage (or defeat) of controversial bills that divided the parties. There is little evidence to suggest that the "conservative coalition" comprised of Republicans and Southern Democrats existed in the form of an organized institution.[60] However, this coalition played an important role in tempering some of the New Deal proposals

---

[58] As noted, we set aside African Americans in this section's study of Southern and Northern Democrats, in order not to conflate quite distinct sets of lawmakers. Our discussion of African-American Democrats is, for the most part, self-contained in the immediately preceding section of this chapter.

[59] Consider a contrast to Northeastern Republicans, who tended to be more liberal than other Republicans over the era of our study, but who had neither the history of obstruction nor the same coherent lawmaking strategy found among Southern Democrats. In some ways, Northeastern Republicans can serve as a placebo, to examine whether the findings for Southern Democrats detailed here stand out also among other regional groupings of lawmakers who diverge ideologically from the rest of their party. For such an exploration, we replicated all of the analyses in this section, instead focused on Northeastern Republicans. In stark contrast to the findings here regarding Southern Democrats, Northeastern Republicans displayed no differences from other Republicans in their effectiveness either in the majority or the minority party.

[60] For example, see Brady and Bullock (1980, 1981) and Manley (1973).

of Franklin D. Roosevelt in the 1930s and 1940s, in opposing civil rights reforms through the 1950s and 1960s, and in thwarting the most liberal of Lyndon B. Johnson's Great Society proposals of the 1960s.

Although not typically able to successfully advance its own agenda, this coalition's blocking power was well understood.[61] By creating and reinforcing barriers to policy change, Southern Democrats stood as a powerful force in Congress.[62] Southern Democrats held important committee chairs, and conservatives within the Democratic Party leadership utilized Southerners as a "deterrent to the effectiveness of liberals."[63] In response, more-liberal (typically Northern) Democrats considered various legislative strategies and reforms to overcome the conservative coalition's strength.[64]

A concrete example of the strategy choices made by liberal Democrats came in 1959, with their formation of the Democratic Study Group (DSG), which pushed for reforms in the Democratic Caucus (and ultimately, within the House as a whole). With the reelection of the founding members of the DSG over successive Congresses, and with the addition of new Northern Democrats to the House, the Democratic caucus began to have a more liberal focus than it had in the immediate postwar years. Yet their success was still limited by conservative, non-DSG Democrats, whom they calculated had been responsible for two-thirds of their defeats on key votes in the late 1960s, voting more often against Democratic proposals than for them.[65] Despite policy setbacks, the DSG developed a successful strategy to build a broader coalition for institutional reforms in the early 1970s, which ultimately limited and redirected the power of Southern Democratic committee chairs, and chipped away at the sources of institutional influence that Southern Democrats had enjoyed.[66]

Taken by themselves, institutional changes and the articulation of a liberal Democratic agenda in the form of the DSG were not necessarily sufficient to

---

[61] A notable exception to this argument is developed by Schickler and Pearson (2009), who demonstrate how between 1937 and 1952 Southern Democrats on the Rules Committee played an agenda-setting role by joining with Republicans on the committee to successfully move conservative measures onto the floor of the House that were unambiguously opposed by most Northern Democrats and the Democratic leadership.

[62] The influence of Southern Democrats thus represented a textbook example of what political theorists Bachrach and Baratz (1962, 949) refer to as the "second face of power," erecting "barriers to the public airing of policy conflicts."

[63] This point of view is effectively argued by Stevens, Miller, and Mann (1974, 669).

[64] Numerous scholars offer key insights into the causes and consequences of such congressional reforms (e.g., Manley 1973; Schickler 2001; Stevens et al. 1974; Rohde 1991).

[65] See Rohde (1991, 18–19).

[66] Adler (2002, 142–170), Rohde (1991), and Schickler (2001, 189–248) provide details of the nature and scope of the 1970s legislative reforms in Congress. Independent of these institutional changes, Manley (1973, 233) documents how Republican Party leaders, including Gerald Ford, began to question the virtues of relying on a Democrat-enabled conservative coalition, as such strategies seemed to be short-sighted efforts that undermined Republican efforts to regain control of the House.

undermine the influence of Southern Democrats. For example, given the significant Republican gains in Congress following Ronald Reagan's election in 1980, Southern Democrats felt particularly emboldened to influence the policy agenda of the Democratic Party; and thirty-three (mostly Southern) Democrats formed the Conservative Democratic Forum to press their case.[67] However, Democrats experienced significant gains in the 1982 elections, giving Northern (and other liberal-leaning) Democrats sufficient votes to push aside conservative Southern Democrats. In opposition to some of the more polarizing elements of President Reagan's policy agenda, Northern Democrats once again parted ways with conservatives in the Southern wing of their party, now with sufficient numbers to continue on without them.[68] By 1994, the Democrats' position in the South had weakened to the point that Republicans won a majority of Southern House races, ushering in the first period of Republican control in decades.[69]

Under Republican control, the votes of Southern Democrats were largely unnecessary to advance conservative agenda items. At the same time that the Democratic Party's electoral fortunes were dwindling in the South, changes were occurring in the ideological composition of elected Southern Democrats. Specifically, Southern Democrats were becoming notably more liberal than their historical predecessors.[70] By the time the Democrats retook the House in the 2006 elections, the collection of legislators that constituted Southern Democrats was quantitatively and qualitatively different from the body of legislators who had been elected from those states for much of the twentieth century. First, there were far fewer of them than in the postwar years; and second, they were less ideologically cohesive, yet more in line with the majority of the Democratic caucus, than their predecessors had been. Taken together, these factors combined to make them less of a pivotal force in congressional politics.

Based on this historical account, one might expect a mixed record for the legislative effectiveness of Southern Democrats. Our analysis throughout the

---

[67] See Rohde (1991, 45–48).
[68] As stated parsimoniously by Rohde (1991, 50), given their liberal orientation, the "class of 1982" was important in that "they were the block to further progress on Reagan's agenda and they shattered the pivotal role of the Boll Weevils [Southern Democrats]." Moreover, as noted by Rohde (1991, 58–65), President Reagan's policy agenda included several issues that induced many right-leaning Southern Democrats to find themselves more naturally aligned with Northern Democrats than they had in previous eras. Hence, they might have found themselves increasingly marginalized in the caucus, as they could not credibly side with Republicans on numerous high-profile issues.
[69] E. Black (1998, 593) denotes the 1994 electoral landscape as being representative of "the newest southern politics," which consists of a "white Republican Majority, more black Democrats, far fewer white Democrats, and the complete absence of black Republicans."
[70] See M. Black (2004), Fleisher (1993), and Whitby and Gilliam (1991). This change in the ideology of the Southern Democratic caucus is clearly demonstrated in graphical terms by McCarty, Poole, and Rosenthal (2006, 25), who show that the average Southern Democrat (in DW-NOMINATE space) became increasingly liberal beginning in the late 1960s.

book begins in the early 1970s, when Southern Democrats were still able to block liberal proposals; we seek to identify whether they were able to use this pivotal position to advance their own initiatives. By the mid-1980s, their votes were no longer needed and the historical record would suggest that they were being marginalized by liberal Democrats, likely making them less effective. Finally, when in the minority party, we might expect that Southern Democrats would be treated no differently than other Democrats, once we control for their more centrist ideological positions.

In addition to the historical narrative, further predictions may arise from a theoretical account of coalition building within a spatial model. As noted in Chapters 2 and 3, congressional scholars often rely on theoretical models built on members' locations in a liberal-to-conservative policy space. In such models, central actors near the median (such as Southern Democrats) are often found to be pivotal and influential.[71] Their proposals to alter status quo policies should secure a majority of votes, either on the left or the right. And proposals to modify policies away from their preferred alternatives can be stopped, with these centrists joining either Northern Democrats on the left or Republicans on the right. Such majoritarian spatial models would therefore predict that Southern Democrats would be even more effective in advancing their proposals than would Northern Democrats or Republicans, at least until liberal Democrats or conservative Republicans gained a majority of seats.

However, given the reforms in the House during the early 1970s that united and strengthened the majority party (at least in part), partisan theories of congressional policymaking may be more appropriate than majoritarian theories for explaining the relative effectiveness of Southern Democrats.[72] Here, such moderate members as Southern Democrats are put in a much less favorable position, often torn between the moderate positions of their districts and the more extreme positions of their parties.[73] While a partisan agenda may benefit majority-party members generally, the key beneficiaries are those toward the middle and extreme ends of the majority party, with moderates (vis-à-vis the House as a whole) actually losing out.[74] Their proposals would be eliminated from the agenda at the committee stage if they did not appeal to a majority of the majority party. Consistent with this theoretical perspective, we might expect Southern Democrats to be less effective than other Democrats when in the majority party, and to be equally ineffective when in the minority party.

---

[71] See, for example, Brady and Volden (1998, 2006) and Krehbiel (1998).

[72] In the terms of Aldrich and Rohde (2000a, 2001), the conditions of "conditional party government" were more likely to be met following these reforms.

[73] This logic follows the theory advanced by Cox and McCubbins (2005).

[74] Jenkins and Monroe (2012) establish that majority-party moderates suffer net policy losses and therefore tend to be compensated in other ways.

Given the mixed predictions under both the historical and spatial theoretical perspectives, we here offer two competing hypotheses and then turn to our empirical examinations to see which perspective finds support and why.

Southern Democrats' Ineffectiveness Hypothesis: In the majority party, Southern Democrats are less effective than other Democrats. In the minority party, Southern Democrats and other Democrats are likely to be equally effective.

Southern Democrats' Effectiveness Hypothesis: In the majority party, Southern Democrats are more effective than other Democrats. In the minority party, Southern Democrats and other Democrats are likely to be equally effective.

As with our assessments of women and African Americans, our first examination of Southern Democrats involves adding an indicator variable for Southern Democrats to the full model from Chapter 2 designed to explain members' Legislative Effectiveness Scores.[75] Upon doing so, we find a coefficient of -0.25 on this variable, indicating about a 20 percent lower effectiveness among Southern Democrats than among all other lawmakers, all else equal. When we break this effect down by Southern Democrats in the majority party and in the minority party (when Republicans controlled the House), we find that their diminished lawmaking occurs when in both the majority and minority party. Specifically, the coefficient on minority-party Southern Democrats is -0.11, while when in the majority party, the coefficient is -0.30.[76] Given the average LES of 1.51 for Northern Democrats when in the majority party, this coefficient indicates that Southern Democrats were about 20 percent less effective than other Democrats when in the majority party.

This initial finding tends to support the Southern Democrats' Ineffectiveness Hypothesis over the Southern Democrats' Effectiveness Hypothesis. That said, further insight can be gleaned by considering a historical perspective by our analysis of each Congress separately. We include indicator variables for Southern Democrats and for Northern Democrats, thus excluding the Majority-Party variable and leaving Republicans as the baseline category. Typical expectations, then, would be positive coefficients on these indicator variables when Democrats control the House and negative coefficients under Republican leadership. As illustrated in Figure 4.5, this is exactly what we see for Northern Democrats.

For Southern Democrats, the most relevant comparison is to all other Democrats. On the left of the figure, throughout the 1970s, we see little difference between Southern Democrats and other Democrats in 1973–74, and 1977–80 (corresponding to the 93rd, 95th, and 96th Congresses). In the 94th Congress (1975–76), however, Southern Democrats underperform relative both

---

[75] The analysis reported here is based on defining Southern Democrats as including the eleven states of the Confederacy plus Oklahoma and Kentucky. Alternative definitions, such as only the Confederate states, or including a broader set of border states, yield largely similar results.

[76] Both of these coefficients are statistically significant by conventional standards (minority p < 0.05, and majority p < 0.001).

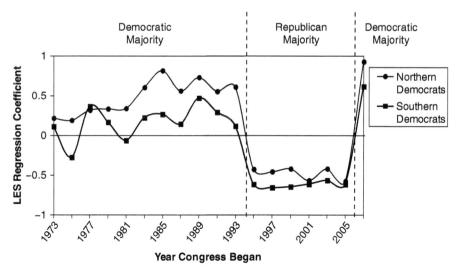

FIGURE 4.5. When Are Conservative Southern Democrats Less Effective Than Other Democrats? When Majority-Party Democrats No Longer Need Them

Note: The figure shows the relative effectiveness of Southern Democrats and other Democrats as compared to Republicans, controlling for all other factors discussed in Chapter 2, from seniority to committee leadership. African-American Democrats are excluded from the analysis, but are instead shown in Figure 4.3. The circles along the thin line show the boost in Legislative Effectiveness Scores (LES) for Northern Democrats over Republicans when in the majority party, and a deficit when in the minority party. The squares along the thick line show a smaller LES boost for Southern Democrats, especially in the late 1980s and early 1990s, when conservative Southern Democrats were no longer pivotal within the Democratic Party.

to other Democrats and to Republicans, upon controlling for their seniority and committee and subcommittee chairs, among other factors.[77] That single Congress aside, the most consistent gap between Southern Democrats and other Democrats opens up in the 1980s, beginning with the 97th Congress in 1981. This is consistent not only with partisan theories that predict a policy-making cost paid by moderates to aid the rest of the party, but also with the historical record, suggesting that liberal Democrats marginalized the conservative Southern Democrats in the 1980s upon gaining sizable enough coalitions to act without their support. Indeed, as the circles in the figure indicate, liberal Democrats were particularly effective between 1983 and 1994 (during the 98th through the 103rd Congresses).

The gap between Southern Democrats and other Democrats narrows somewhat in the late 1980s and early 1990s, perhaps due to the diminishing numbers

---

[77] The 94th Congresses saw a surge of Northern and liberal Democrats, largely in reaction to President Richard M. Nixon's Watergate Scandal and subsequent resignation.

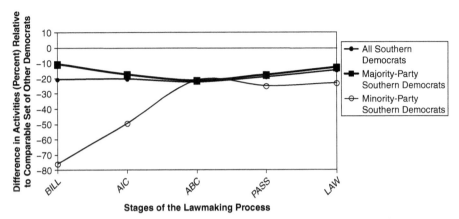

FIGURE 4.6. Southern Democrats Underperform at Each Stage of the Lawmaking Process
Note: The figure shows the percentage by which the activities of Southern Democrats differed from those of other Democrats, both overall and broken down by majority and minority party, controlling for all other factors discussed in Chapter 2, from seniority to committee leadership. African-American Democrats are excluded from the analysis, but are instead shown in Figure 4.4. When in the majority party, Southern Democrats sponsored 11 percent fewer bills (BILL) than Northern Democrats. Their bills were less successful in committee than those of other Democrats, before showing a slight resurgence late in the lawmaking process. In contrast, Southern Democrats in the minority party introduced about one-fourth the number of bills of comparable Northern Democrats. However, those bills were somewhat more favored in committee (AIC) and beyond committee (ABC), leaving Southern Democrats about 20–30 percent less active than Northern Democrats in House passage (PASS) and law production (LAW).

of Southern Democrats and to a more liberal stance among those who remain. This gap narrows further and then disappears as Democrats enter the minority party in 1995. In the 110th Congress (2007–08), the gap between Southern Democrats and other Democrats opens up again.[78] This is consistent with the overall claims of the Southern Democrats' Ineffectiveness Hypothesis, but is more difficult to explain due to the historical account in which Southern Democrats are both more liberal and more needed in the governing coalition following the 2006 elections than they were in the 1980s. Additional work into whether there continues to be a rift between Southern and non-Southern Democrats in Congress today would be welcome.

Further insights into the legislative effectiveness of Southern Democrats emerge in our assessment of these lawmakers' proposals compared to other Democrats through each stage of the lawmaking process. Similar to earlier figures for women and African Americans, Figure 4.6 illustrates the relative

---

[78] This gap also shows up in raw LES numbers, which average 1.06 for Southern Democrats and 1.53 for other Democrats in the 110th Congress.

lawmaking activities of Southern Democrats, based on regression analyses of the number of each legislator's sponsored bills that survive to the particular stage, again controlling for the full set of considerations used throughout our analyses.

The squares connected by the thick line highlight the ineffectiveness of Southern Democrats when in the majority party. In particular, perhaps recognizing that many of their proposals will not be embraced by the rest of the party and will therefore die in committee, Southern Democrats introduce about 11 percent fewer bills than do other Democrats, all else equal.[79] This projection of diminished support for their bills in committee is borne out, with majority-party Southern Democrats experiencing 17 percent less action in committee and 21 percent less action beyond committee than other Democrats.[80] Those proposals by Southern Democrats that do reach the floor of the House, however, seem to face no further decreased success rates, on average.[81] Indeed, despite having a 20 percent smaller portfolio coming out of committee, Southern Democrats have only 18 percent fewer passages through the House and 13 percent fewer laws produced than other Democrats.

When in the minority party, Southern Democrats continue to underperform relative to other Democrats. As shown by the open circles in Figure 4.6, Southern Democrats introduced far fewer bills than did other Democrats during the period of Republican control. But the Republican-controlled committees were somewhat responsive to these limited proposals, eventually sending about 21 percent fewer Southern Democratic bills to the floor in comparison to those of other Democrats. That Southern Democrats made up some ground in committees is unsurprising given that Southern Democrats' proposals were likely more conservative on average than those of other Democrats. That said, with so many fewer introductions, minority-party Southern Democrats have about 25 percent fewer bills pass the House and become law than do their Northern counterparts. However, due to the small number of minority-party successes, these differences are not statistically distinct from zero. On the whole, then, the analyses of the stages of the lawmaking process are consistent with the Southern Democrats' Ineffectiveness Hypothesis, and allow us to further dismiss the idea that these seemingly pivotal Southern Democrats received legislative deference and more lawmaking success than their non-Southern counterparts.

---

[79] The relevant calculation compares the –2.60 coefficient on Majority-Party Southern Democrats to the average of 24.4 introductions by other Democrats when in the majority party, for an approximately 11 percent smaller (–2.60/24.4) set of sponsored bills, controlling for all other considerations. Calculations for the other statistics reported in this section follow a similar form.

[80] These diminished numbers are statistically significant with p < 0.01.

[81] This is illustrated by the upward sloping line for Majority-Party Southern Democrats from the ABC stage to LAW in Figure 4.6.

THE TALE OF THREE MINORITIES

As has become clear across the course of this chapter, a legislator's success at lawmaking depends on much more than merely whether or not she is in the majority party. As we established in Chapter 3, party status is indeed important. However, an individual's decisions about how to navigate the partisan processes in Congress may be equally important. While each individual lawmaker is different, we here examined three set of members – three different legislative minorities – to highlight some of the constraints and strategic opportunities available to each. And, in each case, lawmakers' activities and choices led to enhanced or diminished legislative effectiveness, depending on whether they were in or out of the majority party.

These overall findings are summarized in the models of Table 4.1, based on the analyses presented throughout the chapter. Each model is designed to explain members' Legislative Effectiveness Scores, and each controls for all of the considerations raised in Chapter 2. Beyond those considerations we also examine each of our minority groups both in the majority party and in the minority party.

Our findings for women in Congress are quickly summarized in Model 4.1, wherein women in the minority party are found to be more effective than their male colleagues. In contrast, women and men in the majority party are equally

TABLE 4.1. *The Legislative Effectiveness of Three Minorities*

	Model 4.1	Model 4.2	Model 4.3	Model 4.4
Female × Majority Party	0.085			0.060
	(0.069)			(0.067)
Female × Minority Party	0.111***			0.092***
	(0.033)			(0.031)
African American × Majority Party		−0.377***		−0.426***
		(0.136)		(0.137)
African American × Minority Party		−0.056		−0.050
		(0.044)		(0.043)
Southern Democrat × Majority Party			−0.304***	−0.320***
			(0.060)	(0.062)
Southern Democrat × Minority Party			−0.110**	−0.095**
			(0.048)	(0.048)
Chapter 2 Controls?	Yes	Yes	Yes	Yes
N	6155	6155	6155	6155
Adjusted-R²	0.56	0.56	0.56	0.56

Notes: Ordinary least squares estimation, with Legislative Effectiveness Score as the dependent variable, robust standard errors in parentheses, and observations clustered by member. All controls from Chapter 2 are included, consistent with Model 2.3 in Table 2.5.
*p < 0.1 (two-tailed), **p < 0.05 (two-tailed), ***p < 0.01 (two-tailed).

effective. Previously, we related this finding to the consensus-building activities commonly associated with female lawmakers both in Congress and in the state legislatures. We argued that such activities should be particularly useful in reaching across party lines, which is essential for members of the minority party who wish to advance an agenda of policy change. We found this increased effectiveness of minority-party women to be robust over time, and to be linked to crucial coalition-building stages of the lawmaking process – specifically to getting their bills out of committee and to building a majority for passage by the House.

Model 4.2 summarizes our finding for African Americans, who are no more or less effective than other Democrats when in the minority party, but are much less effective than their colleagues when Democrats are in the majority. This latter finding is consistent with a prior literature emphasizing how African-American legislators have sponsored a tighter and more black-interests-focused agenda than their white colleagues. It is also linked to an argument about how African Americans have sought to act behind the scenes (such as through key positions on powerful committees) rather than to demand and force support of agenda items that do not naturally resonate with a majority of other lawmakers.[82] Indeed, when in the majority party, African-American Democrats introduced less legislation, and their agendas diminished even more rapidly than other majority-party Democrats throughout the lawmaking process. Their reduced effectiveness was particularly noteworthy in the 1970s and 1980s, when the ranks of African Americans in Congress were small and when they were limited in their seniority.

The relative effectiveness for Southern Democrats is summarized in Model 4.3, wherein (as for African Americans) their effectiveness is particularly diminished when Democrats are in the majority party.[83] This finding is linked to historical accounts in which liberal Democrats marginalized their conservative counterparts, especially in the 1980s, when their support was no longer

---

[82] Moreover, the findings of reduced African-American legislators' effectiveness is consistent with Tate (2003, 127), who argues that African-American constituents (many of whom are represented by African-American members) place a higher priority on their Representative bringing dollars back into their districts than focusing on national issues (i.e., lawmaking). In a similar vein, Griffin and Flavin (2011, 523) find that African-American constituents place a greater priority on their Representatives bringing dollars back to the district than substantively representing them in their voting behaviors. They also find (Griffin and Flavin 2007) that African-American constituents are less likely to sanction their Representatives for not representing their interests. Finally, to the extent that legislative effectiveness, as measured here, is viewed as electorally valuable, our findings are consistent with Swain's (1995, 72–73) argument about how lack of electoral competition in districts that elect African-American Representatives contributes to representation failures between African-American constituents and their members.

[83] Models including Southern Democrats as an independent variable now lead to the Distance from Median variable taking a negative and statistically significant coefficient, in line with expectations raised in Chapter 2.

essential to pass Democratic priorities. It also matches theories of how moderate party members (vis-à-vis the entire House) are less likely than extremists to benefit from strong party cohesion, which keeps items off the agenda that do not appeal to a majority of the majority party. Consistent with these accounts, we find the greatest gap in effectiveness between Southern Democrats and other Democrats during the 1980s, and that the proposals of Southern Democrats are culled out during the committee stage of the lawmaking process.

In sum, these three cases illustrate the complexities that members of Congress face in seeking to pass their agendas. Compared to others, these lawmakers either did not give in to their diminished lawmaking fates in the minority party (in the case of women) or did not fully enjoy the benefits of majority-party status (in the case of African Americans and Southern Democrats). Moreover, as illustrated in Model 4.4, all of these considerations play out in Congress simultaneously. And, just as party status alone does not dictate lawmaking success, nor does one's membership in any particular minority group. Indeed, not all women persevered and gained the successes of Marjorie Holt, nor did all African Americans advance a smaller agenda as Louis Stokes chose to do. While W.C. Daniel suffered a fate common to other Southern Democrats, he was able to secure a legislative success upon building coalitions around national defense policies that were of interest both to residents in his district and to a broader set of lawmakers.

Each lawmaker enters Congress with a daunting task. On average, any one of her sponsored bills has less than a one-in-twenty chance of surviving the process and becoming a law. Yet these members are sent to Congress with a job to do – to represent their constituents and to attempt to address the policy problems found throughout American society. While some lawmakers face greater obstacles to moving their policy agendas forward, each must choose the strategy that she feels will best serve her policymaking and electoral goals. Some of those strategic decisions are on display here, such as with the consensus-building activities of Marjorie Holt and other minority-party women, or the tightened agenda and committee work of Louis Stokes.

Such individual choices combine to produce the public policies that govern our society. Exploring such choices helps us to better understand which policy areas are addressed and which suffer from policy gridlock. In Chapter 5, we illustrate that legislative effectiveness varies not only across parties and not only across minority groups within those parties, but also across policy areas. Some policy areas are more intractable than others; for such issues, the legislative strategies that members choose become even more crucial in determining which policy proposals pass and which are abandoned.

APPENDIX 4.1: THE THREE MINORITIES AND THE STAGES
OF THE LAWMAKING PROCESS

In the analyses underpinning Figures 4.2, 4.4, and 4.6, we rely on a series of OLS
models with a dependent variable measuring the number of each member's
sponsored bills that reach each of five stages of the lawmaking process. We
include the full set of controls from Chapter 2, and focus on the coefficients on
the variables of greatest interest to us here – those for the three minorities both in
and out of the majority party.

In this appendix, we report the results of the full baseline regressions for each
stage of the process, as well as the key coefficients on the variables of greatest
interest to us, broken down by party status. We note how we make the calculations for the values reported in the figures throughout the chapter. And we
discuss some robustness considerations.

Appendix Table 4A.1 reports the results of the regressions by stage, including all
of the control variables discussed and featured in Chapter 2. We use these same
control variables throughout all analyses in this chapter. Our main variables of

APPENDIX TABLE 4A.1. *Determinants of Bill Progression in Congress*

	Model 4A.1	Model 4A.2	Model 4A.3	Model 4A.4	Model 4A.5
	Bill Introductions	Action In Committee	Action Beyond Committee	Pass House	Become Law
Seniority	0.369***	0.112***	0.100***	0.084***	0.043***
	(0.110)	(0.023)	(0.017)	(0.014)	(0.007)
State Legislative Experience	−3.003**	−0.388*	−0.223	−0.133	−0.089
	(1.328)	(0.209)	(0.154)	(0.128)	(0.071)
State Legislative Experience × Legislative Professionalism	3.358	1.352**	0.954*	0.676	0.388*
	(3.792)	(0.685)	(0.514)	(0.417)	(0.215)
Majority Party	0.2334	0.884***	0.879***	0.682***	0.253***
	(1.097)	(0.129)	(0.096)	(0.080)	(0.043)
Majority-Party Leadership	−3.055*	0.627	0.796**	0.793**	0.580**
	(1.749)	(0.390)	(0.353)	(0.326)	(0.243)
Minority-Party Leadership	−2.123	−0.308*	−0.220	−0.179	−0.093
	(2.164)	(0.162)	(0.138)	(0.122)	(0.070)
Speaker	−12.363***	−2.512***	−1.497***	−1.091**	−0.317
	(1.933)	(0.434)	(0.440)	(0.421)	(0.326)
Committee Chair	7.271***	5.154***	5.616***	4.336***	2.327***
	(1.973)	(0.531)	(0.481)	(0.377)	(0.245)
Subcommittee Chair	5.284***	1.956***	1.388***	1.098***	0.530***
	(0.940)	(0.190)	(0.158)	(0.125)	(0.066)

APPENDIX TABLE 4A.1. (*continued*)

	Model 4A.1	Model 4A.2	Model 4A.3	Model 4A.4	Model 4A.5
	Bill Introductions	Action In Committee	Action Beyond Committee	Pass House	Become Law
Power Committee	−1.042	−0.888***	−0.662***	−0.496***	−0.109**
	(1.012)	(0.135)	(0.106)	(0.084)	(0.050)
Distance from	−3.024	−0.038	0.099	0.017	−0.122
Median	(2.443)	(0.290)	(0.216)	(0.184)	(0.098)
Female	1.888*	0.022	0.158	0.114	0.047
	(1.145)	(0.124)	(0.111)	(0.102)	(0.073)
African American	−5.852***	−0.745***	−0.525***	−0.412***	−0.194**
	(1.421)	(0.178)	(0.159)	(0.139)	(0.079)
Latino	−6.130***	0.008	0.288	0.280	0.145
	(1.792)	(0.327)	(0.233)	(0.211)	(0.130)
Size of	0.044	−0.006	−0.003	−0.002	−0.002
Congressional	(0.035)	(0.005)	(0.004)	(0.003)	(0.002)
Delegation					
Vote Share	0.602***	0.071***	0.053***	0.039**	0.025**
	(0.203)	(0.025)	(0.020)	(0.017)	(0.011)
Vote Share²	−0.004***	−0.0005***	−0.0004***	−0.0003**	−0.0002**
	(0.001)	(0.0002)	(0.0001)	(0.0001)	(0.0001)
Constant	−7.822	−1.844**	−1.650**	−1.199*	−0.727*
	(7.283)	(0.877)	(0.709)	(0.624)	(0.385)
N	7641	7641	7641	7641	7641
Adjusted-R²	0.07	0.34	0.41	0.37	0.29

Notes: Ordinary least squares regressions, with robust standard errors in parentheses, and observations clustered by member.
*$p < 0.1$, **$p < 0.05$, ***$p < 0.01$ (two-tailed).

interest in this table are Female and African American, and we add Southern Democrats into later analyses. Apart from these main variables, significant findings emerge that are consistent with those of previous chapters. For instance, across the models of the table, we see more activity by senior members, those with previous legislative experience in professional legislatures, majority-party members, committee and subcommittee chairs, and those with moderately high vote shares.

Interpreting the coefficient sizes is quite straightforward. For example, the 1.888 coefficient on Female in Model 4A.1 is indicative of women introducing nearly two more bills per Congress than men, controlling for any differences that may occur in their party status, seniority, chair positions, and the like.

To make these values even more comparable, relative to one another across stages of the lawmaking process, we then divide the coefficient by a relevant denominator in constructing the figures. For instance, because the average male lawmaker introduces 17.448 bills, the additional 1.888 introductions for women amounts to a 10.8 percent increase (100 × 1.888/17.448) over the average man. Similar calculations are made for each of the values shown in the figures.

We further break down the effects for each of our three minorities by party status, using the same approach, but now including interaction variables for each set of lawmakers both in the majority party and in the minority party. The relevant coefficients on those variables are shown in Appendix Table 4A.2.

APPENDIX TABLE 4A.2. DETERMINANTS OF BILL PROGRESSION FOR THREE MINORITIES

TABLE 4A.2A. *Female House Members*

	Model 4A.6	Model 4A.7	Model 4A.8	Model 4A.9	Model 4A.10
	Bill Introductions	Action In Committee	Action Beyond Committee	Pass House	Become Law
Female × Majority Party	3.347** (1.613)	0.018 (0.206)	0.178 (0.192)	0.118 (0.181)	0.007 (0.132)
Female × Minority Party	0.442 (1.243)	0.027 (0.117)	0.137 (0.089)	0.109 (0.076)	0.087* (0.048)
Chapter 2 Controls?	Yes	Yes	Yes	Yes	Yes
N	7641	7641	7641	7641	7641
Adjusted-R^2	0.07	0.34	0.41	0.37	0.29

TABLE 4A.2B. *African-American House Members*

	Model 4A.11	Model 4A.12	Model 4A.13	Model 4A.14	Model 4A.15
	Bill Introductions	Action In Committee	Action Beyond Committee	Pass House	Become Law
African American × Majority Party	−5.148*** (1.914)	−0.911*** (0.298)	−0.912*** (0.237)	−0.732*** (0.202)	−0.399*** (0.110)
African American × Minority Party	−6.832*** (1.230)	−0.514*** (0.132)	−0.024 (0.135)	0.007 (0.121)	0.080 (0.079)
Chapter 2 Controls?	Yes	Yes	Yes	Yes	Yes
N	7641	7641	7641	7641	7641
Adjusted-R^2	0.07	0.34	0.41	0.37	0.29

TABLE 4A.2C. *Southern Democratic House Members*

	Model 4A.16	Model 4A.17	Model 4A.18	Model 4A.19	Model 4A.20
	Bill Introductions	Action In Committee	Action Beyond Committee	Pass House	Become Law
Southern Democrat	−2.595*	−0.637***	−0.580***	−0.390***	−0.146**
× Majority Party	(1.485)	(0.206)	(0.157)	(0.134)	(0.073)
Southern Democrat	−9.804***	−0.386***	−0.127	−0.120	−0.069
× Minority Party	(0.859)	(0.117)	(0.096)	(0.082)	(0.052)
Chapter 2 Controls?	Yes	Yes	Yes	Yes	Yes
N	7641	7641	7641	7641	7641
Adjusted-R²	0.07	0.34	0.41	0.37	0.29

Notes: Ordinary least squares regressions, with robust standard errors in parentheses, and observations clustered by member. All controls from Chapter 2 are included, consistent with Table 4A.1 above.
*p < 0.1, **p < 0.05, ***p < 0.01 (two-tailed).

All of these models include the same control variables found in Table 4A.1. The values from these tables are translated into comparable percentages for the figures in the same way, with the relevant nonminority group's average serving as the denominator.

Throughout these analyses, we do not weight different types of bills differently, as we had done in generating the Legislative Effectiveness Scores. One may therefore be concerned about the extent to which the results here are driven by unimportant legislation, such as some commemoratives. Therefore, we also reran the analyses reported here solely using substantive and substantive and significant bills. Doing so shows the same broad pattern of results as reported throughout the chapter. Minor differences that occur include: greater statistical significance for the positive effect of women in the minority party at the Action Beyond Committee and Pass House stages and a somewhat more negative effect for minority-party African Americans at these same stages. That said, by the Become Law stage, these results again mimic those reported in Table 4A.2, and shown in the figures throughout the chapter.

One may also be concerned about our use of ordinary least squares regressions for these stages, because the dependent variable is a count of bills, and because there are a large number of zeros, particularly for the later stages. A variety of alternatives may be used, including the negative binomial regressions suggested by Anderson et al. (2003). Therefore, we reran our stages analyses using this alternative approach. Once again the results largely mimic those reported here and throughout the chapter. Minor exceptions include: a weaker positive finding for minority-party women at the Become Law stage, as well as stronger negative effects for minority-party Southern Democrats at the Action in Committee stage and for majority-party Southern Democrats at the Become Law stage. Yet, once again, the broad interpretations and hypothesis testing throughout the chapter are robust to these alternatives. Because the same overall patterns emerge from these alternative specifications, we rely on OLS regressions here for their ease of interpretability.

5

Gridlock and Effective Lawmaking, Issue by Issue

Today, after almost a century of trying; today, after over a year of debate; today, after all the votes have been tallied – health insurance reform becomes law in the United States of America.
                                        – President Barack Obama, Signing Ceremony, March 23, 2010

In November 1992, a relative newcomer on the national political scene, Bill Clinton, was elected President of the United States. Arriving on the tail end of a significant economic downturn (so much so that one of his campaign themes was "It's the economy, stupid"), Clinton was embraced by younger and more liberal voters, and seemed to embody a new wave of optimism in America. He joined a Democratic House and Senate in bringing about the first period of unified party governance in over a decade, promising policy change after too much gridlock. While a wide range of policy items dominated his agenda, President Clinton made it well-known early into his administration that he sought dramatic changes to health care in the United States.

To institute these changes, Clinton formed a health care task force early in 1993, comprised of a wide range of health care specialists from within and outside of government and headed by then-First Lady Hillary Rodham Clinton. After holding a series of behind-closed-doors meetings for the better part of a year, the task force completed its deliberations by the end of 1993 and released its policy proposal to the public. As originally conceived, health care (meaning some form of health insurance coverage) would be made available to all Americans through a combination of Medicare, employer-based insurance, and government provisions for the unemployed and low-income workers. The costs of maintaining such a system would purportedly be covered through efficiencies that were expected to be gained from competition among insurance companies and providers, and from a broader insurance pool that included all Americans. Furthermore, revenues generated from several new taxes (such as those on alcohol and cigarettes) would be directed toward covering the program's costs. And large employers would face a mandate to provide afford-able health insurance to their employees.[1]

While the administration's plan engaged a problem that was widely consid-ered a fundamental concern for American society, and while policy experts of all ideological stripes advocated for some type of health care reform, Clinton's proposal quickly encountered obstacles. As Representatives and Senators digested the details of the Clinton plan and what it would mean for their constituencies, a wide range of policy alternatives emerged, with different legis-lative vehicles proposed to engage health care in both chambers. Each proposal sought to reform health care in a variety of ways, yet none gained the amount of attention received by the president's plan. And that plan was not well tailored to pick up sufficient votes in either the House or the Senate, despite unified Democratic control of Congress. The program's costs, coupled with aggressive lobbying and public relations campaigns against the reforms, left little support for Clinton's proposal. The reform effort was abandoned in the fall of 1994 without so much as a floor vote. Republicans characterized Clinton's proposals on health care and many other issues as far too liberal for the country, and captured control of the House for the first time in four decades.

Fast-forwarding to November of 2008, a relative newcomer on the national political scene, Barack Obama, was elected President of the United States. Entering the White House in the midst of one of the most substantial economic downturns since the Great Depression, President Obama faced a large policy agenda including conflicts in the Middle East and an economic system that was arguably on the brink of collapse. Yet similar to Clinton years earlier, Obama had been embraced by younger and more liberal voters, and seemed to embody a new optimism of hope for America – so much so that one of his campaign slogans was, "Change you can believe in." Such change seemed possible with the return of unified Democratic Party control of Congress and the presidency, unseen since Clinton's first two years. Also similar to Clinton, President Obama made it known very early in his term that he was putting health care reform on the front burner of his domestic political agenda.

Unlike the Clinton administration however, Obama chose to let the policy process begin largely in the Congress, with White House officials only working behind the scenes; the administration did not become formally engaged in the policy deliberations until a bipartisan health care "summit" in February 2010. As a result, congressional Democrats began the process of bargaining and compro-mise within, and across, the House and the Senate shortly after Obama took office

---

[1] Kingdon (2011, 217–221) provides a parsimonious description of the politics and policy proposals underlying the health care debates during the Clinton administration. More broadly considered, the Clinton proposals (and their ultimate downfall) have been studied by numerous scholars including Brady and Buckley (1995), Hacker (1997), Johnson and Broder (1996), Skocpol (1996), and Steinmo and Watts (1995).

in January 2009. Time after time, in their roles as lawmakers, pivotal members of the House and the Senate proved to be particularly influential in moving the legislation forward. For example, Speaker Pelosi insisted on the crafting of a single bill in the House, as opposed to separate bills from separate committees. On an issue-specific compromise, Representatives Bart Stupak (D-MI) and Joe Pitts (R-PA) played a key role in raising and resolving the issue of limiting federal funding for abortions. Democratic lawmakers in both the House and Senate worked to include concessions, such as greater federal funding of state Medicaid costs for Nebraska, in order to secure additional votes of support. Finally, to avoid a Senate filibuster following a mid-session seat gain by Republicans, the House leadership devised a multi-bill process to first approve Senate revisions and then immediately pass changes as a separate bill.

In its final form, the Patient Protection and Affordable Care Act (commonly known as "Obamacare") provided for: a substantial expansion of health insurance coverage for Americans, enhanced protections against denial of coverage for preexisting medical conditions, and the creation of health insurance exchanges within the states. While the law did not include many features that its proponents initially advanced (a federally funded insurance plan, denoted the "public option" had been excised from the bill late in 2009, for example), most observers agreed that the new law did, indeed, yield meaningful health care reform, for good or for ill. Democrats rejoiced, and Republicans prepared to take their battle to the courts.

In considering the experiences of the Clinton and Obama administrations, a natural question is: "Why were fundamental health care policy reforms obtained in 2010, but not in 1994?" Another way of engaging this point is to ask, "Why was legislative gridlock successfully overcome during the Obama administration, yet not during the Clinton years?" These questions have already received substantial attention and will undoubtedly be reexamined years and decades hence.[2] For our purposes, one very clear difference stands out. Clinton treated members of Congress as *voters*, whom he felt should have supported their president's well-thought-through proposal. Obama, instead, treated members of Congress as *lawmakers*, who would use their lawmaking roles to construct compromises and formulate a politically viable policy.[3]

---

[2] Early contributions to this debate can be found in Hacker (2010) and Kingdon (2011), both of whom suggest that the particular tactics taken by Obama and the nature of the agenda-setting environment distinguished the Obama administration's experiences from those of the Clinton administration. Other perspectives on the politics underlying the passage of the Affordable Care Act can be found in Brown (2011), Burgin (2012), Feder (2011), Hacker (2011), M.A. Peterson (2011), Quadango (2011), and White (2011).

[3] Our purpose here is not to examine whether the president's treatment of members of Congress as lawmakers helps overcome gridlock. Rather, we argue that members of Congress are lawmakers (whether presidents fully appreciate that or not), and that examining them as such is informative for understanding the presence or absence of policy gridlock in Congress.

Yet, if such lawmaking roles are indeed crucial to overcoming policy gridlock, their importance should not be limited merely to the instance of a single (albeit significant) policy change in health care. Instead, in policy area after policy area, and Congress after Congress, we should find that the nature of members in their lawmaking roles determines the course of American public policy. In this chapter, we seek to use what we have uncovered about members of Congress and their legislative effectiveness to explain why some policy issues are much more gridlocked than others, and how lawmakers as political entrepreneurs play a crucial role in bringing about policy change. Put simply, here we confront how individual legislative effectiveness (as considered in previous chapters) contributes to the productivity of the chamber as a whole.

To do so, we first establish that legislative gridlock in Congress varies substantially across different areas of public policy, as well as over time. We adapt the Legislative Effectiveness Scores used throughout this book thus far to be issue-specific, and create member LESs for each of nineteen broad issue areas across thirty years. We then utilize three aspects of those issue-specific scores to help explain issue-specific gridlock patterns. In particular, we argue that issues are likely to be more gridlocked when they: (1) are highly partisan, (2) require a high level of policy expertise, and (3) are characterized by a high degree of entrepreneurial politics. We analyze issue-specific Legislative Effectiveness Scores to determine whether each policy area in each Congress is high or low in partisanship, required expertise, and entrepreneurship. And we demonstrate how these characteristics influence what Congress as an institution accomplishes in different policy areas over time. Such analyses provide us with insights about the keys for overcoming legislative gridlock in the United States in different policy areas, shedding new light on public policymaking more generally.

HOW PERVASIVE IS GRIDLOCK IN CONGRESSIONAL POLICYMAKING?

Torn between fear of an overly strong ruler and the reality of a need for leadership and coordinated action across the states, the Framers of the U.S. Constitution instituted a system of separated powers. Policy change would be limited by the need to reach agreement across policymakers selected in different ways, for different terms, between the House, the Senate, and the presidency. From that point of view, policy gridlock is not new in the United States. Yet, from time to time, the distance between what the American people appear to want and what the political system offers them is substantial and difficult to comprehend.

Scholars of legislative politics have studied such gridlock in a variety of ways, and have laid blame at the feet of political parties, lawmakers with diverse preferences, tight budgets, or supermajority institutions such as the filibuster or veto, just to name a few.[4] Yet, in their analyses, scholars and public observers have largely examined national policy choices as a whole, rather than divided by the various issues to be addressed. For example, in confronting the question about whether more is accomplished under unified party government than divided government, David Mayhew identified all "landmark laws" since World War II. If lumped together by Congress, such an analysis shows little difference between the overall lawmaking output of divided governments when compared to unified governments.[5]

Such an overview is useful, and Mayhew's work definitely caught the imagination of scholars, who then sought to understand why party governance did not matter as expected. Such an overall view also allows observers among the public and the press to occasionally pin the label of "do-nothing Congress" on their political opponents.

Yet, from our perspective, such an approach suffers from at least two problems. First, it starts at the end of the lawmaking process, rather than the beginning. The concept of gridlock is based on the *gap* between public needs and political outcomes. A focus only on the outcomes misses the scope of the policy problems that citizens hope their government will address.[6] If the nation faces more crises at some times than others, a steady production of important policy changes may show a lack of response to changing policy needs rather than a steady triumph over gridlock. Second, overall lawmaking productivity disguises the fact that some policy areas are more gridlocked than others. Some issues are more intractable than others. And policymakers may often set aside the tough

---

[4] Binder and Smith (1997), for example, explore the ways that the filibuster has contributed to legislative gridlock across much of the twentieth century, while Binder (1999, 2003) builds on these points and discusses how additional features of the American political system, such as bicameralism and partisan and electoral competition, have contributed to legislative stalemate. (But see Chiou and Rothenberg 2008 for a critique of Binder's approach.) Brady and Volden (1998, 2006) and Krehbiel (1996, 1998) develop formal models that attribute gridlock to the interaction of heterogeneous preferences in the legislature and the need to generate supermajority support for any proposals to ensure that they will not be subject to veto or filibuster threats; and Callander and Krehbiel (2012) point to how these supermajoritarian institutions might prove particularly problematic for facilitating policy change in the presence of policy drift. Chiou and Rothenberg (2003, 2006, 2009) build on the analyses of Brady and Volden and of Krehbiel to explore how party discipline might interact with supermajoritarian institutions to facilitate gridlock. Howell (2003) and Moe and Howell (1999) suggest that collective action problems will generally limit the extent to which Congress can engage in meaningful policymaking (especially in comparison to the president). Diermeier and Myerson (1999) suggest that the combination of various formal parliamentary requirements and informal norms contribute to costly hurdle factors that are particularly difficult to overcome in bicameral lawmaking institutions. Stone (2013) provides a relatively novel perspective, arguing that gridlock might be due to the media environment.

[5] Mayhew's (1991) initial analysis ran through 1990, although updated versions find the same patterns.

[6] Scholars have recognized this concern in the past. For example, Binder's (2003) approach to studying gridlock overcomes this issue by first identifying the problems that receive media attention and then determining which of those problems Congress actually acted upon.

decisions to make progress on easier ones that will bring public approval and campaign contributions.

In contrast to earlier approaches, we characterize gridlock in the House of Representatives based on what percent of the bills introduced actually become law, and we do so across nineteen major policy issues from 1973 to 2002.[7] Doing so allows us to account not only for how many laws are produced, but also for how those laws compare to the demand for policy change, as captured by the number of proposals for change that are offered. This approach also allows us to characterize the issues to which Congress pays the greatest attention over time.

Clearly, there may be limitations to our approach. Members of Congress introduce bills for a large number of reasons, including position-taking or simple reactions to pleas from campaign contributors. In our view, however, the amount of pressure exerted on members, and the benefit of such position-taking, increases along with the degree to which particular policy areas feature pressing problems. Thus, the number of bills introduced serves as an appropriate proxy for public demand; the frequency with which those bills become law then serves as a valid measure of whether Congress can meet demands in particular policy areas at given points in time.[8]

In examining lawmaking by issue area and relative to bill introductions, we find significantly more variance than has been traditionally associated with congressional gridlock. Table 5.1 lists the nineteen issue areas, as well as the introductions and enactments within each policy area over our thirty-year period of examination.

The first column of Table 5.1 lists the issues, while the second column documents the percent of members of the House that sponsor bills in the given area in an average Congress. Here we see that the attention of members varies widely. Only one in five members cares enough about issues such as Civil Rights and Liberties, International Affairs, or Science and Technology to introduce even a single bill on such policies in any given Congress. In contrast, half to two-thirds

---

[7] Bills are coded into the nineteen issue areas developed by Baumgartner and Jones in their *Policy Agendas Project* (see www.policyagendas.org or Baumgartner and Jones 2002) and adapted to congressional introductions in Adler and Wilkerson's *Congressional Bills Project* (see www.congressionalbills.org or Adler and Wilkerson 2013). We end our analysis in 2002, as this is the final year of systematic coding of issues within the Congressional Bills Project at the time of our writing.

[8] When issues become prominent, many members tend to introduce bills that are very similar to one another. We consider this to be evidence of high public demand. In contrast, a disconnect between policy needs and congressional action may arise in this approach if members of Congress become so distant from the public policy problems they are elected to address that they do not even introduce bills to tackle such problems. However, given the relatively low cost of bill introduction, and given the desire of members of Congress to appear responsive to voters, we believe that our approach reasonably represents public demand for policy change. Future work linking bill introductions to public opinion surveys or other measures of public demand for policy change would be welcome.

TABLE 5.1. *Gridlock Rates Vary Substantially Across Issue Areas*

Issue Area	% Members Introducing	Bills Introduced	Laws Enacted	Success Rate (%)
Agriculture	25	4,062	126	3.10
Banking & Commerce	45	7,665	230	3.00
Civil Rights & Liberties	20	2,715	51	1.88
Defense	39	7,446	331	4.45
Education	30	4,200	98	2.33
Energy	32	5,125	129	2.52
Environment	36	5,262	197	3.74
Foreign Trade	33	5,354	124	2.32
Government Operations	63	13,658	952	6.97
Health	45	9,740	154	1.58
Housing & Community Development	23	2,800	49	1.75
International Affairs	21	2,739	177	6.46
Labor, Employment, & Immigration	43	6,987	131	1.87
Law, Crime, & Family	40	7,185	186	2.59
Macroeconomics	35	5,295	102	1.93
Public Lands	47	8,693	905	10.41
Science & Technology	18	2,126	93	4.37
Social Welfare	35	6,305	84	1.33
Transportation	38	5,746	224	3.90

Note: The table shows the aggregate numbers of bills introduced and laws produced by issue area from the 93rd through 107th Congresses (1973–2002), as well as the average percent of members offering proposals and overall success rates in each area. Success rates range from a low of 1.33 percent of Social Welfare bills becoming law to 10.41 percent for Public Lands, showing some policy areas to be much more gridlocked than others.

of all members introduce bills on Health, Public Lands, or Government Operations. Some of these differences may reflect the nature of representative governance, such as with only 25 percent of members introducing Agricultural legislation, consistent with the small number of farm-area districts. In contrast, Education is relevant in all districts, but addressed in bill introductions by only 30 percent of members. Perhaps such a low level of bill sponsorship across such policy areas reflects a high degree of issue specialization in Congress.

The next column shows the number of bills introduced across thirty years, illustrating the potential workload of Congress, in needing to sort through about 3,000–5,000 bills per year. From this point of view, it is perhaps unsurprising that bill success rates average around 4 percent of introduced legislation becoming law. Such rates come in the final two columns of the table, which show the number of laws enacted in each policy area and then calculate the success rate, defined as the percent of introduced bills that become law.

While there is substantial variation in the range of introductions across
members and issues, there is likewise substantial variation in the success rates
for the different issue areas, ranging from a low of 1.33 percent (Social Welfare)
to a high of 10.41 percent (Public Lands). In other words, in the average
Congress, only 1.33 percent of the bills that are introduced that focus on
Social Welfare policy are ultimately signed into law (which translates into
approximately six laws per Congress). In contrast, of the approximately 580
Public Lands bills that are introduced into the typical Congress, 60 of them
are signed into law on average.

It is not the case, however, that the most popular areas, in terms of number of
introductions and percent of members introducing legislation, are always those
with the greatest success rates. For instance, Health legislation has among the
lowest rates of bill success (1.58 percent), whereas International Affairs has
among the highest success rates (6.46 percent). Indeed, there is a slightly negative
(but not statistically significant) relationship between the percentage of legislators who introduce bills in a given issue area and that area's success rate. As such,
interest from more lawmakers does not necessarily result in a greater likelihood
of bill passage for any particular piece of legislation, partly because that bill is
competing with so many others.

Taken together, the results in Table 5.1 suggest that even if gridlock truly is a
pervasive feature of the contemporary Congress, not all policies are equally
gridlocked. Moreover, as demonstrated in Table 5.2, issues vary not only in
their overall success rates, but also in terms of where in the lawmaking process
they face more substantial hurdles. Consistent with the major lawmaking stages
used to construct our Legislative Effectiveness Scores, Table 5.2 focuses beyond
introduction to also account for Action in Committee, Action Beyond
Committee, Passage, and Becoming Law.

If one wishes to understand why Social Welfare policies are so gridlocked,
for example, we need not look far beyond the committee stage, where only
4.3 percent receive any attention at all, in terms of hearings, markups, or
committee and subcommittee votes. This is evident in the Percent Action in
Committee column of Table 5.2. Put simply, more than nineteen out of twenty
Social Welfare bills are dead upon arrival in committee. In contrast, bills on
Science and Technology or on International Affairs have more than four times
that rate of receiving action in committee, and nearly 30 percent of bills on Public
Lands also receive committee attention.

A similar pattern emerges for bills reaching the floor of the House. As with
those receiving Action in Committee, the most gridlocked in emerging from the
committee stage (as seen in Percent Action Beyond Committee in the table)
continue to be Social Welfare, Health, and Macroeconomics. For Social
Welfare, for example, now only one in thirty bills survives out of committee.
In contrast, the bills most likely to reach the floor of the House are on Public
Lands and on International Affairs, where one out of every five or six bills
survives the committee process.

TABLE 5.2. *Different Issues Become Gridlocked at Different Stages of Lawmaking*

Issue Area	Percent Action In Committee	Percent Action Beyond Committee	Passage Rate Upon Reaching Floor	Enactment Rate Upon Passing House
Agriculture	11.0	7.2	77	57
Banking & Commerce	14.7	9.2	77	43
Civil Rights & Liberties	8.6	6.0	75	42
Defense	12.2	8.7	89	57
Education	8.3	6.3	83	45
Energy	12.1	7.5	71	48
Environment	17.3	10.8	77	45
Foreign Trade	11.3	6.3	75	48
Government Operations	14.5	13.3	88	60
Health	7.2	4.6	77	44
Housing & Community Development	7.3	5.3	84	39
International Affairs	18.3	15.4	79	53
Labor, Employment, & Immigration	9.1	5.1	76	48
Law, Crime, & Family	14.2	7.5	80	43
Macroeconomics	6.4	4.8	78	51
Public Lands	28.4	21.9	84	57
Science & Technology	19.2	12.8	80	43
Social Welfare	4.3	3.3	77	52
Transportation	15.3	10.8	78	46

Note: The table shows significant variance across issue areas in the lawmaking stage at which policy gridlock occurs, across the 93rd through 107th Congresses (1973–2002). Percent Action in Committee reports the percent of sponsored bills receiving hearings, markups, or committee/sub-committee votes. Percent Action Beyond Committee reports the percent of sponsored bills moving beyond committee to a legislative calendar for the floor. Passage Rate Upon Reaching Floor reports the percent of bills that pass the House upon reaching the floor (i.e., upon reaching the "action beyond committee" stage). Enactment Rate Upon Passing House reports the percent of bills that become law upon passing out of the House of Representatives (i.e., upon achieving the Passage stage).

Upon running the committee gauntlet, approximately 80 percent of the remaining bills pass the House, as reported in the Passage Rate Upon Reaching Floor column of Table 5.2. That said, gridlock grabs hold of another one in five bills at the floor voting stage. And here, once again, there is considerable variation in House passage, with nine out of ten Defense bills passing the House upon reaching the floor, compared to only seven out of ten Energy bills. Finally, as is the nature of a separation of powers system, only half of the bills that pass out of the House ultimately become law, as illustrated in the final column of the table. Most of those subsequent cases of gridlock arise because the

Senate chooses to not act on the House bill. Sometimes the Senate acts, but with different language, resulting in further gridlock when House-Senate conferees are either not appointed or unsuccessful in reconciling differences. And, albeit rarely relative to the volume of legislation, bills occasionally fall to presidential vetoes (and failed override attempts) even upon passing the House and Senate. Once again, such gridlock beyond the House varies considerably by policy area, with less than 40 percent of Housing and Community Development bills becoming law upon passing the House, compared to around 60 percent for bills in Agriculture, Defense, and Government Operations.

The different stages of the process, as shown in Table 5.2 can sometimes shed light on the overall success or gridlock rates from Table 5.1. For example, Civil Rights and Liberties bills, with a success rate of only 1.88 percent, are actually in the middle of the pack in terms of committee activity and success. But they face greater difficulty passing the House and still further hardship in the Senate, resulting in the low overall success rate. In contrast, consider International Affairs and Macroeconomics bills, which perform about average in passing the House upon reaching the floor and in becoming law upon passing the House. But International Affairs legislation is so well received and likely to be acted upon in committee that its overall success rates are well above average at 6.46 percent, whereas Macroeconomics bills are three times as gridlocked in committee, resulting in just a 1.93 percent overall success rate.

In sum, while it is generally true that most bills are stopped somewhere in the legislative process, there is a good deal of variance across the different issue areas in regards to which bills, in which issue areas, are more or less likely to overcome the numerous hurdles that emerge between introduction and presidential signature.

Even further variance arises over time, from one Congress to the next. Figure 5.1 orders the issues from the most gridlocked to least, based on the averages from Table 5.1, and illustrates the highest and lowest success rates for each issue, with the middle half of the success rates noted by the black boxes. For instance, only half of one percent of Social Welfare bills became law in the 95th Congress (1977–78), whereas welfare reforms became a major issue in the early Clinton Administration, achieving success rates of 4.1 percent and 2.4 percent in the 103rd and 104th Congresses (1993–96), respectively. Yet these rates were still well below the 9.7 percent of Science and Technology bills that became law in the 100th Congress (1987–88), during the height of the Cold War. Among the greatest over-time variance is in Energy policy, which often faces success rates of less than 2 percent, but which opened up significantly to policy change with thirty-three new laws adopted in the early years of the Republican 104th and 105th Congresses (1995–98).

As these examples suggest, not only do gridlock rates vary over time, but one area's period of greatest activity could well correspond to another area's era of greatest gridlock. For instance, Figure 5.2 illustrates the success rates in Health and in Foreign Trade, as well as for all policy issues combined. For all issues, the

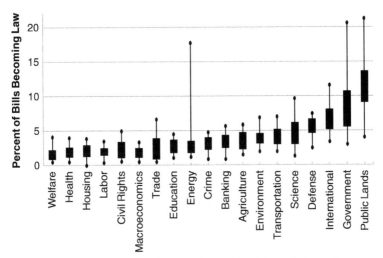

FIGURE 5.1. Gridlock Rates Vary Substantially Both Within and Across Issues
    Note: The figure shows the percent of bills that become law in each issue area, for each
of the 93rd through 107th Congresses (1973–2002). The highest and lowest success rates
are shown by the top and bottom dots for each issue, while the interquartile range of the
middle 50 percent of the data are shown by the darkened boxes.

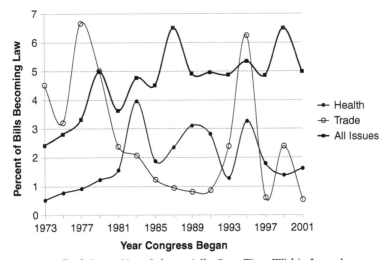

FIGURE 5.2. Gridlock Rates Vary Substantially Over Time Within Issue Areas
    Note: The figure shows the percent of bills that become law overall (squares and thick
line) and in the Health (closed circles) and Trade (open circles and thin line) issue areas,
for each of the 93rd through 107th Congresses (1973–2002), revealing substantial
variance in policy gridlock across issues over time.

policy success rate increases from around 3 percent in the mid-1970s to a steady 5 percent by the late 1980s and beyond, yet with peaks above 6 percent in the 100th (1987–88) and 106th Congresses (1999–2000). As both of those Congresses featured divided government, we might once again conclude that divided or unified government alone does not explain the overall gridlock rates in Congress. That said, overall rates mask issue-by-issue differences. The figure shows the volatility of Foreign Trade measures, with notable peaks in the 95th (1977–78) and 104th Congresses (1995–96). Health care policy also sees its highs and lows in terms of policy gridlock, yet with peaks and valleys seeming wholly independent of the overall trends or of those in distant areas such as foreign trade.

   Given such volatility and variance across issue areas over time, we suggest that scholarly and public attention should not focus around the overall gridlock rates and lawmaking activities of Congress, but should instead be more nuanced, with a focus on separate issues. Moving in that direction, we dedicate the remainder of this chapter to developing Legislative Effectiveness Scores by issue area, using patterns surrounding those scores to highlight three important explanations for gridlock across policy areas over time, demonstrating how partisan effectiveness, issue expertise, and policy entrepreneurship are each linked to policy gridlock.

LEGISLATIVE EFFECTIVENESS ACROSS ISSUE AREAS

The premise of this chapter is that viewing members of Congress in their individual lawmaking roles will help scholars and practitioners understand successful lawmaking or policy gridlock for the institution as a whole. Indeed, because the bills that individual members sponsor and attempt to move through the lawmaking process eventually become the policy changes seen at the aggregate level, "overcoming institutional gridlock" and "effective lawmaking by individuals" are naturally intertwined.

   Table 5.3 offers such an illustration of the role of legislative effectiveness in bringing about important policy changes. The table lists the House bills that became Mayhew's Landmark Laws in the 100th Congress (1987–88).[9] As shown in the final column, sponsors of these laws are among the most effective members in Congress, with Glenn Anderson (D-CA), Thomas Foley (D-WA), and Dan Rostenkowski (D-IL) all scoring above 4.2 in their Legislative Effectiveness Scores, placing them easily in the top 5 percent of all House members. Indeed, of the seven lawmakers in the table, only one is below the House average of 1.00 LES, with Harold Ford (D-TN) at 0.99. While the fact that they sponsored landmark laws certainly contributes to their LES in this Congress, it should not have been surprising that these seven were landmark law sponsors. Indeed, their average LES in the previous Congress was 4.31, and

---

[9] Analyses of landmark laws in different Congresses show similar patterns to those discussed here.

TABLE 5.3. *Most Landmark Laws Come from Highly Effective Lawmakers*

House Bill in 100th Congress	Policy	Sponsor	LES
H.R. 1	Water Quality Act of 1987	James Howard (D-NJ)	1.54
H.R. 2	Surface Transportation Act of 1987	Glenn Anderson (D-CA)	4.36
H.R. 442	Japanese-American Reparations	Thomas Foley (D-WA)	4.22
H.R. 1720	Family Support Act of 1988	Harold Ford (D-TN)	0.99
H.R. 2470	Catastrophic Health Insurance for the Aged	Fortney Stark (D-CA)	2.68
H.R. 3543	Deficit Reduction Measure	William Gray (D-PA)	1.14
H.R. 4848	Omnibus Foreign Trade Measure	Daniel Rostenkowski (D-IL)	5.40
H.R 5110	McKinney Homeless Assistance Act	Thomas Foley (D-WA)	4.22
H.R. 5210	Anti-Drug Abuse Act	Thomas Foley (D-WA)	4.22

Note: The table shows the Landmark Laws or "Important Enactments," according to David Mayhew's (1991) criteria, originating in the 100th House of Representatives (1987–88). Each bill sponsor's Legislative Effectiveness Score (LES) is listed, illustrating that they are among the most effective lawmakers in the House. These seven lawmakers were not only effective in the Congress in which their landmark laws were passed, but also previously. For example, these members averaged an LES of 4.31 in the previous Congress and 3.59 across the previous three Congresses, placing them collectively in the top 5 percent of all House members of their era.

across the previous three Congresses was 3.59, placing them collectively in the top 5 percent of all House members. Put simply, if we want a best guess for the likely sponsors of landmark laws, looking to the most effective lawmakers by our measure is a good bet.

Just as the LES is useful in addressing overall landmark laws, this approach also holds promise for explaining the variance in policy gridlock by issue area and across Congresses. However, to be most useful, we must adapt our scores to account for policy-by-policy differences. Specifically, we once again construct Legislative Effectiveness Scores for each member of the House of Representatives in each Congress; but now we do so for each of the nineteen issue areas.[10]

---

[10] The approach we offer here is quite flexible and can be extended in a variety of potentially useful directions in the future. For instance, instead of by issue area, bills could be classified by the committee(s) to which they are assigned, allowing us to score each member based on how effective she is on issues linked to certain committees. Alternatively, scores could be aggregated by subsets of members, such as in capturing which committee's (or subcommittee's) members are most effective at addressing which issue areas. Or, more generally, each committee could be given an overall score based on its members' effectiveness, to track the policymaking prowess of each

Unlike in our construction from Chapter 2, in which we found very few members of Congress who introduced no legislation whatsoever, in most issue areas most members do not introduce a single bill. We are not arguing that such members have nothing to add to policy choices in such issue areas, nor that they would be ineffective if they tried. Rather, those members are dedicating their lawmaking efforts to other issue areas. Therefore, to be consistent with the logic of issue specialization, throughout this chapter we refer to the issue-specific scores as *Interest and Legislative Effectiveness Scores* (ILES). Focusing on Health policy, for example, we see that more than half of House members have not introduced a bill in this issue area in any given Congress. Such members receive a Health ILES of zero, due as much to their lack of interest in being lawmakers in health policy as to their ineffectiveness were they to try. Such scores are consistent with our definition of legislative effectiveness from Chapter 2: "the proven ability to advance a member's agenda items through the legislative process and into law." Without introducing legislation, these lawmakers have no proven abilities in this area.

The scores are constructed following the same equation used for overall effectiveness scores in Chapter 2. Here, however, we focus only on the subset of bills that falls into each particular issue area. Specifically, we base our calculations on each policy area and each Congress separately, assigning an Interest and Legislative Effectiveness Score for each member in each Congress in each policy area. Once again, we rely on weights of $\alpha = 1$, $\beta = 5$, and $\gamma = 10$ applied to commemorative, substantive, and substantive and significant bills, respectively. Hence, similar to the calculation of the overall LES, our measure of ILES seeks to capture the difficulty in moving more substantive and more significant bills through the lawmaking process. Moreover, consistent with our earlier methodology, in calculating ILESs, we normalize the scores to ensure that for each Congress (and each issue area) the ILESs have a mean equal to one. This normalization facilitates interpersonal comparisons of ILESs across members. Finally, while the analysis presented in Chapter 2 calculated LESs for each member in the 93rd–110th Congresses, we here calculate ILESs only for the 93rd–107th Congresses, for reasons similar to those surrounding the discussion of issue-specific success rates for these same Congresses previously discussed.[11]

Having stated these points, a brief examination of the resulting ILESs reveals several interesting findings. Consider, for example, the Health ILES, wherein there is notable variation in the range of scores, from a low of zero (for those members who introduced no health-related legislation in any given Congress) to a high of 200.55, earned by Representative Paul G. Rogers (D-FL) in the 94th

committee over time (perhaps then to be shown as a function of its staff, its culture of bipartisanship, and the like).
[11] This is entirely an artifact of the coding protocol that we rely on (as developed by Adler and Wilkerson), which covers legislation only up until the 107th Congress at the time of this writing. Replications and extensions based on further data availability in the future would be welcome.

Congress (1975–76). The case of Rogers is instructive in that, during his time in Congress, he was dubbed "Mr. Health" by his colleagues, and either sponsored or played a major role in the passage of several prominent health measures, including the National Cancer Act, the Health Maintenance Organization Act, the Health Manpower Training Act, the Medical Device Amendments, the Emergency Medical Service Act, and several other substantive and significant bills. More generally, Rogers's influence in health policy is clearly detected in a consideration of his Health ILESs, which are the highest of any member of Congress.

Interestingly, upon retiring from the House in 1978, his position as health policy leader was taken up by Henry Waxman (D-CA), who subsequently had a Health ILES greater than 100 in every Congress until the Republicans gained a majority following the 1994 elections. Similar to Rogers, Waxman's high Health ILES comports with conventional wisdom. Upon replacing Rogers as chair of the Subcommittee on Health within the Energy and Commerce Committee, Waxman either sponsored or helped to ensure the passage of a wide range of prominent health measures, including the Safe Medical Devices Act, the Patent Term Restoration and Drug Competition Act, and the Orphan Drug Act. The high scores of Waxman and Rogers in the 93rd–103rd Congresses (1973–94) far exceeded the scores of similarly placed Republicans when they were in the majority party between 1995 and 2002. For those four Congresses, no member's Health ILESs averaged above 25. Hence, during those eight years of Republican rule, the most effective initiators of health policy accomplished notably less than Rogers or Waxman had accomplished in any given Congress previously. This is consistent with the democratization of effective lawmaking during the Republican era, away from the committee and subcommittee chairs, as highlighted in Chapter 3.

On its face, then, Rogers and Waxman seem to emerge naturally from the data as true health policy entrepreneurs, in that they were persistent in advancing a substantial health agenda, and (by all accounts) possessed skill at negotiating deals and tough compromises.[12] Such entrepreneurs emerge in many different issue areas at different points in time. For instance, in the area of Foreign Trade, Phil Crane (R-IL) twice scored above 100 in the Trade ILES for his role in promoting free trade policies in Republican Congresses. In contrast, in a policy area such as Government Operations, no member scored an ILES above 50, and only an average of one lawmaker per Congress scored above 25.[13]

---

[12] The legislative records of Rogers and Waxman suggest that both members represent textbook examples of "political entrepreneurs," as defined by Kingdon (2011, 180–181). They both emerge among our twenty most effective lawmakers in Chapter 6.

[13] As chair of the Government Operations Committee, Jack Brooks (D-TX) had the highest performance on this measure. He is known for helping pass the Inspector General Act of 1978, the General Accounting Office Act of 1980, and the Paperwork Reduction Act of 1980.

In Chapter 2, we estimated a series of regression models to find the determinants of members' overall LESs. Similar analyses are possible within each issue area, as illustrated in Table 5.4 for the policy areas of Health, Foreign Trade, and Government Operations.[14] More specifically, Table 5.4 presents the analysis from a regression where the dependent variable (in Model 5.2) is legislator i's Health ILES in Congress t, and the independent variables are identical to those analyzed in Table 2.5 in Chapter 2.[15] Model 5.3 presents a similar analysis for the Trade ILES, and Model 5.4 examines the Government Operations ILES.[16] As a point of comparison, Model 5.1 presents the results from an analogous model where the dependent variable is member i's overall LES for comparable years (1973–2002).

A number of similarities and differences emerge across these models. For instance, for each policy area, similar to the overall LES, a member's issue-specific ILES is strongly correlated with that member's ILES in the previous Congress, with a positive and statistically significant coefficient on Lagged Effectiveness Score. Hence, legislators who are effective at moving health policy in one Congress, for instance, continue to be relatively successful at advancing health policy in subsequent Congresses. Also similar to the overall LES, we see that holding a position of institutional influence, such as a chair or subcommittee chair, is positively related to a member's effectiveness in particular policy areas.[17] Whether because of the specialized expertise that these members possess, their role in advancing the majority party's agenda, or their powers as institutional gatekeepers, it is clear that holding these positions facilitates the advancement of a member's legislative program.[18]

There are also significant differences that emerge across policy areas, as evident in the coefficients in Table 5.4. For instance, in the area of trade policy, Seniority has a large and statistically significant effect. Each additional term in Congress boosts the average member's Trade ILES by about 10 percent, relative to the average score of 1.0. This may perhaps be due to the need to develop expertise in order to understand the intricacies of trade deals. In contrast, the coefficient on Seniority is negative for Health and Government Operations,

---

[14] Portions of this section were originally presented in: Volden, Craig, and Alan E. Wiseman. 2011a. "Breaking Gridlock: The Determinants of Health Policy Change in Congress." *Journal of Health Politics, Policy and Law* 36(2): 227–264. (Reprinted by permission of Duke University Press.)

[15] Similar to the analysis in Chapter 2, the results in Table 5.4 follow from Ordinary Least Squares regression with robust standard errors (clustered by members).

[16] It is useful to note that if we replicate the analyses in Table 5.4 and exclude those members who introduce no legislation in a particular area (i.e., all members with ILESs equal to zero), we uncover results that are substantively similar to those presented here, while the statistical significance of several variables (Majority Party, for Health and for Trade, in particular) is enhanced.

[17] While comparable in size to those for other policy areas, the coefficients on Committee Chair and Subcommittee Chair in Model 5.3 are not statistically distinct from zero, due in part to the limited overall explanatory power of Model 5.3.

[18] For more on the role of expertise in committees, see Krehbiel (1991). For the gatekeeping roles of committees, see Denzau and Mackay (1983).

TABLE 5.4. *Determinants of Legislative Effectiveness Across Policy Areas*

	Model 5.1	Model 5.2	Model 5.3	Model 5.4
	Overall LES	Health ILES	Trade ILES	GovOps ILES
Lagged Effectiveness Score	0.504***	0.755***	0.405***	0.520***
	(0.035)	(0.078)	(0.063)	(0.043)
Seniority	0.001	−0.059**	0.094**	−0.031**
	(0.008)	(0.028)	(0.047)	(0.016)
State Legislative Experience	−0.074	0.041	0.518	−0.050
	(0.068)	(0.293)	(0.363)	(0.172)
State Legislative Experience × Legislative Prof.	0.375*	0.669	−1.207	0.448
	(0.215)	(1.035)	(0.884)	(0.472)
Majority Party	0.258***	0.230	0.617*	−0.118
	(0.046)	(0.142)	(0.345)	(0.093)
Majority-Party Leadership	0.256	−0.040	0.644	0.590*
	(0.170)	(0.309)	(0.973)	(0.352)
Minority-Party Leadership	−0.047	0.126	−0.514*	−0.092
	(0.074)	(0.165)	(0.289)	(0.177)
Speaker	−0.265	2.501	−1.653	3.465**
	(0.185)	(1.970)	(1.033)	(1.662)
Committee Chair	1.898***	0.913**	1.209	2.380***
	(0.199)	(0.449)	(0.856)	(0.440)
Subcommittee Chair	0.623***	0.781***	0.470	1.129***
	(0.066)	(0.275)	(0.334)	(0.157)
Power Committee	−0.082**	−0.055	0.807***	0.364***
	(0.039)	(0.075)	(0.264)	(0.107)
Distance from Median	−0.001	0.236	0.653	−0.198
	(0.104)	(0.423)	(1.015)	(0.205)
Female	0.076*	0.178	−0.034	0.267
	(0.045)	(0.147)	(0.154)	(0.177)
African American	−0.361***	−0.497***	−0.818***	0.174
	(0.076)	(0.177)	(0.300)	(0.225)
Latino	−0.017	−0.508***	−0.225	−0.413***
	(0.110)	(0.152)	(0.324)	(0.138)
Size of Congressional Delegation	−0.001	0.002	0.005	0.002
	(0.002)	(0.003)	(0.006)	(0.003)
Vote Share	0.021*	0.003	0.080*	0.011
	(0.012)	(0.053)	(0.048)	(0.025)
Vote Share^2	−0.0001*	0.0000	−0.0006*	−0.0001
	(0.0001)	(0.0004)	(0.0003)	(0.0002)
Constant	−0.613	−0.250	−3.681	−0.231
	(0.440)	(1.903)	(2.010)	(0.937)
N	5026	5026	5026	5026
Adjusted-R^2	0.57	0.52	0.16	0.36

Notes: Ordinary least squares estimation, with overall Legislative Effectiveness Score or issue-specific Interest and Legislative Effectiveness Score as the dependent variable, robust standard errors in parentheses, and observations clustered by member.
*p < 0.1 (two-tailed), **p < 0.05 (two-tailed), ***p < 0.01 (two-tailed).

perhaps indicative of the success of junior members who bring new ideas to these policy areas.[19]

Also varying across policy areas is the effect of the Majority-Party variable. There is little difference in size between the coefficients on Majority Party for the Overall LES and for the Health ILES. But the coefficient for Trade ILES is much larger, and that for Government Operations ILES is actually negative. Of course, as highlighted in Chapter 3, the coefficient on Majority Party may only be picking up a small part of the effect from being in the majority party, with a larger indirect effect arising through variables capturing such considerations as the institutional benefits of being committee or subcommittee chairs within the majority party. Another way to think about majority party differences, then, is just to consider the raw differences in the average ILES between members of the minority party and members of the majority party. Here again, policy areas differ from one another, such as with majority-party members outperforming minority-party members by 1.2 points in their Health ILES but by less than one point in their Government Operations ILES, and by only 0.6 points in their Public Lands ILES.

Earlier in the chapter we noted that there is significant variation in the overall policy gridlock or success rates by issue area and over time. We now see that there are also significant differences across issues in the variables that are associated with individual legislative effectiveness. In our view, these two factors are inter-related. That is, the nature of different policy areas at particular points in time dictate the legislative strategies that individual lawmakers adopt to advance their policy goals, and likewise influence the overall degree of change within any given policy area. Rather than explore each and every variable from the regression in Table 5.4, we dedicate the rest of the chapter to highlighting three such relationships between issue-specific Interest and Legislative Effectiveness Scores and issue-specific policy gridlock: the roles of majority-party effectiveness, issue expertise, and political entrepreneurship. In so doing, we establish not only that

---

[19] The negative coefficients on Seniority should likely not be interpreted as implying that more senior members are not as capable at advancing health policy as more junior members. Rather, the finding might be an artifact of specialization decisions in Congress across a legislator's career path. That is, upon reaching a certain level of seniority, members have cultivated particular legislative portfolios such that those members who focus their greatest efforts on advancing health policy are most likely already in positions of institutional influence (i.e., committee and subcommittee chairs), such that no further benefits accrue from being more senior, per se. Moreover, the most effective senior members' performance may already be captured in the lagged dependent variable (therefore, in later analyses on a Congress-by-Congress basis, we set aside the lagged variable). Volden and Wiseman (2011a) estimate a slightly different regression model than Model 5.2 that controls for Seniority^2, as well as Seniority, and whether a member is the chair of a committee dealing with health policy legislation, but they do not control for whether a member is a subcommittee chair. They uncover findings that are substantively quite similar to those reported here, with one notable exception being that the estimated coefficient on Seniority is positive, while the coefficient on Seniority^2 is negative (and statistically significant), indicative of diminishing returns from expertise beyond a certain point.

gridlock arises for systematic reasons across policies and over time, but also that a focus on legislative effectiveness provides key insights into when and where such gridlock occurs and how it might be overcome.

PARTISANSHIP AND ISSUE-SPECIFIC GRIDLOCK

When members of the voting public become increasingly frustrated with the inability of Congress to deal with the pressing policy problems of the day, they look for someone to blame. And political parties serve as easy targets. Especially when one house of Congress is controlled by a different party from the other house, partisan bickering surrounds the gridlock of the Senate not acting on proposals coming out of the House, or vice versa. Likewise, when the president is from another party relative to the Congress, public discourse surrounds whose proposals will move forward, or whether gridlock will take hold of both parties' proposals.

It is in this context that scholars were surprised and challenged by Mayhew's finding of similar rates of major enactments across divided and unified government. Coupled with arguments that parties served as little more than the banding together of lawmakers with similar ideological preferences – conservatives in the Republican Party and liberals in the Democratic Party – scholars began to address more systematically what role political parties play in Congress.[20]

More than had previously been the case, scholars highlighted the roles of institutional obstacles and of members' policy preferences to explain policy gridlock.[21] For example, the filibuster in the U.S. Senate has been used with increasing frequency across recent decades, and the cloture process to end a filibuster currently requires a supermajority of sixty Senators.[22] Therefore, even a unified government might not yield sufficient votes to overcome policy gridlock, as Senate majorities rarely exceed 60 votes out of the 100 seats. In such instances, gridlock could be overcome by striking compromises with members of the minority party, highlighting the idea that parties in U.S. government are not monoliths, but are instead made up of members whose reelection fates are largely in their own hands and for whom crossing party lines may be occasionally beneficial.

In this context, strong disagreements between parties may expand policy gridlock.[23] When the parties hold their members in line (perhaps because of a

---

[20] Krehbiel's (1993) challenge to find an effect of parties that could not be as easily explained by an alignment of members' ideological preferences set the stage for a lively debate over more than a decade.

[21] See, for example, Brady and Volden (1998, 2006) and Krehbiel (1998).

[22] For important contributions to the study of the role and impact of the Senate filibuster, see Binder and Smith (1997), Koger (2010), and Wawro and Schickler (2004, 2006).

[23] See, for example, Chiou and Rothenberg (2003, 2006, 2009) and Krehbiel, Meirowitz, and Wiseman (2013) who explore the role of parties (and party polarization) in legislatures in bringing about gridlock.

high degree of polarization among party members' ideological positions), com-promise to overcome gridlock is tough to secure.[24] Whether such differences across parties are so stark and compromise so unwieldy tends to vary over time and across issue areas. Such a relationship between partisanship and policy gridlock can therefore be characterized as follows:

Partisanship and Policy Gridlock Hypothesis: Policy gridlock is more likely when the parties are more greatly divided against one another.

While there may be conditions under which a single strong majority party can ram through its policy proposals without compromise or gridlock, such circum-stances are rare, given the prevalence of divided government and institutional roadblocks to change built into the U.S. public policy process.[25] Therefore, we expect a strong relationship between party conflict and gridlock. This relation-ship should manifest itself across policy areas and over time, as the parties become more starkly divided on some issues during certain Congresses.

While there may be a number of different ways to characterize party conflict, we naturally highlight a clear measure that emerges from studying legislative effectiveness.[26] In particular, throughout Chapter 3, we focused on the differ-ence between the legislative effectiveness of members in the majority party and those in the minority party. To the extent that partisan differences are small, minority- and majority-party members should find about equal success. However, in some policy areas, and at some points in time, minority-party members' proposals are utterly ignored. Such an outright dismissal of potentially helpful policy ideas is indicative of a large degree of partisan conflict on the given issue, and should be significantly related to policy gridlock if the Partisanship and Policy Gridlock Hypothesis holds true.

To test for such a relationship, we create a variable ILES Party Difference, which measures how much the average ILES of members of the majority party exceeds that of members of the minority party.[27] We do so for each issue area

---

[24] Such an outcome could be an underappreciated consequence of conditional party government theory (i.e., Aldrich and Rohde 2000a, Rohde 1991), or other theories of endogenous party strength (e.g., Diermeier and Vlaicu 2011; Lebo, McGlynn, and Koger 2007; Patty 2008; Volden and Bergman 2006).

[25] Were one focused solely on the House of Representatives, rather than the entire lawmaking process, strong partisanship may instead enhance the ability of the majority party to act and pass policy proposals through the House.

[26] An alternative method, commonly employed in the extant literature for measuring underlying partisan conflict on particular roll calls, is to use one of several cohesion indices that measure, in various ways, how often members of one political party vote with or against members of another political party (see Krehbiel 2000 for a review and critique of various metrics). Scholars (e.g., Minozzi and Volden 2013; Snyder and Groseclose 2000) have also devised methods for identify-ing the scope of partisan influence, or pressure, on individual roll call votes, independent of the policy preferences of legislators (but see McCarty, Poole, and Rosenthal 2001; Krehbiel 2003 for critiques about certain aspects of these methodologies).

[27] We use the same approach as in Model 3.1 from Table 3.1 in Chapter 3 to generate this measure.

generally, as well as for each issue area in each Congress. At the aggregate issue level, such differences range from a 0.60 point majority party boost for the Public Lands ILES to a 1.34 point boost on the Science and Technology ILES, with a mean difference of 1.15. That Public Lands legislation is both the least gridlocked according to Table 5.1 and Figure 5.1 and the least partisan according to our measure provides the first evidence of support for the Partisanship and Policy Gridlock Hypothesis. More generally, consistent with the hypothesis, the ILES Party Difference measure correlates with issue Success Rates from Table 5.1 at a large and statistically significant level of -0.67.[28]

Put another way, we can classify each policy area as being a Highly Partisan Issue or a Low Partisan Issue based on whether it is above or below the median ILES Party Difference. Aggregating across Congresses, the Highly Partisan Issues include many of the most gridlocked policy areas, such as Health, Housing and Community Development, and Labor, Employment, and Immigration, although certainly not all of the issues with the lowest success rates. The Low Partisan Issues include Government Operations and Public Lands, both of which have the highest bill-to-law success rates. On average, the highly partisan issues feature a 2.9 percent success rate, compared to a 4.1 percent success rate for the least partisan issues according to our measure.

That said, both the success rates and the ILES Party Difference measure vary over time. For example, the ILES Party Difference was at its lowest level of 0.30 in the 97th Congress (1981–82) for the issue of Public Lands, and at its greatest level of 1.76 in the 106th Congress (1999–2000) for Macroeconomics. Consistent with the Partisanship and Policy Gridlock Hypothesis, 10.9 percent of all Public Lands bills introduced in the 97th Congress became law, compared to only 0.88 percent of Macroeconomics bills introduced in the 106th Congress. More broadly, across all fifteen Congresses and nineteen issues, the correlation between ILES Party Difference and Success Rate is highly statistically significant, at -0.30.[29]

To lend further interpretability to these results, we examined each policy area in each Congress separately, classifying them as highly partisan or low partisan issues depending on whether they were above or below the median ILES Party Difference for all issues and all Congresses. Based on these groupings, Figure 5.3 then illustrates the average success rate by Congress for the Highly Partisan Issues, compared to the Low Partisan Issues. Four noteworthy characteristics emerge from the figure. First, the success rates of the Low Partisan Issues have been rising over time, from less than 3 percent in the 94th Congress (1975–76) to nearly 8 percent in the 107th Congress (2001–02). Second, in contrast, initial rises in success rates on Highly Partisan Issues leveled out at about 4 percent throughout the 1990s, before sliding back to 3 percent at the end

---

[28] This correlation is statistically significant with $p < 0.01$.
[29] The significance level is $p < 0.001$.

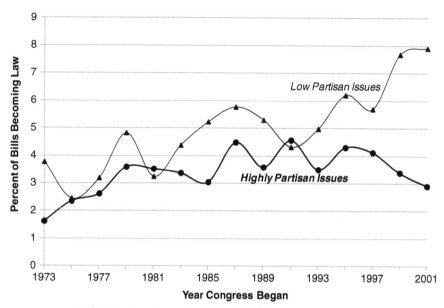

FIGURE 5.3. Highly Partisan Issues Are More Gridlocked

Note: The figure shows the percent of bills that become law, among those that are in highly partisan (thick line) and low partisan (thin line) issue areas, for each of the 93rd through 107th Congresses (1973–2002), revealing greater gridlock among highly partisan issues. Partisanship is characterized by the difference in Interest and Legislative Effectiveness Scores (ILES) between the average majority- and minority-party members. Each issue in each Congress is then labeled highly partisan if its ILES difference is above the median partisanship value for all issues and all Congresses.

of the dataset.[30] Third, in all but two Congresses, the Highly Partisan Issues were more gridlocked on average than the Low Partisan Issues, consistent with the Partisanship and Policy Gridlock Hypothesis.[31]

Fourth and finally, the largest gap between the success rates of the highly partisan and less partisan issues occurs at the end of the dataset, during a period in which Congress has grown far more polarized. Perhaps to compensate for the lack of policy movement on those issues characterized by the greatest

[30] The low success rates from the 93rd through 95th Congresses are partly a function of the much greater number of bill introductions during that period of time.

[31] The values shown in Figures 5.3, 5.4, and 5.5 are based on the averages of the aggregate success rates across the noted subset of issues in the particular Congress. These aggregate success rates are themselves based on the hundreds of bills introduced in each given issue area per Congress. At that bill level, gaps in success rates between the Highly Partisan Issues and Low Partisan Issues tend to be statistically significant (p < 0.05) for gaps above about 1.0 percent in the figure. Similar levels of statistical significance arise at the bill level for similar-sized gaps on Expertise and Entrepreneurship shown in Figures 5.4 and 5.5.

partisanship, Congress has indeed been acting upon issues with lower partisan ILES Party Differences. Most notably, an 11.6 percent success rate in International Affairs arose in the 107th Congress (2001–02) from the combined efforts of Democrats and Republicans in the wake of the 9/11 terrorist attacks of 2001. That success rate is double the rate for International Affairs in the previous Congress. While the terrorist attacks were (and hopefully will remain) rare events in American history, the patterns uncovered here hold across a wide range of policy areas and numerous Congresses. Put simply, the issues identified as partisan based on the ILES Party Difference measure face a higher degree of gridlock than do less partisan issues.

ISSUE EXPERTISE AND POLICY GRIDLOCK

Beyond partisanship, a second factor explaining issue-specific policymaking gridlock is the degree to which lawmakers gain expertise and translate that expertise into policy success. Such expertise, and its importance to the policy-making process, varies over time and across issue areas. Indeed, in some areas expertise at the disposal of senior members of Congress is needed to disentangle thorny policy puzzles, whereas the reliance on bold new initiatives is valued elsewhere.

It is innocuous to claim that some policies are inherently more complex or complicated than others. For example, devising a new policy for the processing of Social Security benefits is notably more straightforward than developing mechanisms to affect climate change. Given the underlying variance in complexity across policy areas, legislators might be relatively hesitant to adopt new policies unless they are reasonably confident that those proposals will lead to better outcomes than the situation they are currently facing.[32] In circumstances such as these, the political and policy expertise acquired by senior legislators is particularly valuable to the lawmaking process for several reasons. First, having acquired said expertise, the endorsement of a policy by a more senior lawmaker (who is deemed to be an expert) can generate enhanced support for the proposal among legislators who are less well-informed about the likely policy consequences of a given bill.[33] Moreover, independent of policy complexity, a more senior advocate, having acquired expertise through accumulated time spent in the legislature, is generally more familiar with the relevant policy stakes among his

---

[32] Such sentiments are at the heart of informational theories of legislative organization (e.g., Gilligan and Krehbiel 1987, 1990; Krehbiel 1991) as well as more recent scholarship on the impacts of policy complexity on legislative delegation decisions and collective policymaking (e.g., Callander 2008, 2011).

[33] Such a pattern of deference is consistent with Truman's (1951) discussion of the virtues of being an effective legislator. Moreover, to the extent that legislative leaders control the bill scheduling process, there are reasons to expect (i.e., Adler and Wilkerson 2013, 66–87) that proposals being advocated by legislators with expertise are most likely to be reported out of committee (thereby advancing in the legislative process).

or her colleagues on any given issue, as well as what approaches have been more-or-less successful in amassing coalitions on similar policies over time. This type of institutional memory and knowledge can be particularly valuable as legislators strive to form coalitions to pass new policies.[34] We therefore advance the following hypothesis:

Issue Expertise and Policy Gridlock Hypothesis: Policy gridlock is more likely when greater issue expertise is required to address policy needs.

Whether an issue requires political or policy expertise may be quite difficult to discern. Yet the approach that we offer here produces estimates of issue expertise quite naturally, both across issue areas and during different Congresses. Specifically, if the expertise of lawmakers is an important factor in their ability to move legislation forward, then the issue at hand is by definition one in which issue expertise is required, or at the least beneficial. Put more concretely, in Table 5.4 we offered a series of regression analyses to explain lawmakers' issue-specific ILESs. For some issues, the expertise gained through greater seniority emerged as a positive and significant determinant of legislative effectiveness. For other issues, it was not a significant factor, or even emerged as negatively related to the ILES. Although other variables, such as State Legislative Experience, might likewise tap into the concept of issue expertise, we here focus on Seniority for the sake of simplicity.[35]

We replicated the analysis from Table 5.4 for each of the nineteen issue areas, and also ran similar regressions on each of the ILES metrics by issue area and by Congress. Our key coefficient of interest is that on Seniority, which is crucial to the development of issue expertise in Congress. In looking at the aggregate issue level, we see that bills dealing with various aspects of legal policy (Civil Rights and Liberties, and Law, Crime, and Family) as well as international matters (International Affairs and Foreign Trade) all advance further when their sponsors are relatively more senior members of the House. Given that many of the bills that are covered by these policy jurisdictions deal with sophisticated issues

---

[34] Indeed, such sentiments commonly emerge in opponents' arguments against the imposition of legislative term limits. As noted by Cain and Levin (1999, 176–177), "Term limit critics argue that expertise is central to the effectiveness of a strong legislature ... experience fosters familiarity between the members, encouraging norms of collegiality and respect." In a similar vein, drawing on anecdotal evidence from the California legislature, Kousser (2005, 37) points to how term limits appear to have effectively empowered legislative staff (in lieu of experienced legislators), contributing to enhanced partisanship in the legislature, and thereby limiting the prospects for compromise and deal brokering. More generally, Kousser (2005) suggests that the implementation of term limits leads to less-well-informed policymaking. Similar points are suggested by Montcrief and Thompson (2001) and Carey et al. (2006).

[35] Other considerations, such as years of service on the relevant committee for the policy area, could likewise be used to judge a member's issue expertise. In addition, other data could be used to judge the complexity of policy issues, which may, in turn, account for the need for the development and reliance upon issue expertise.

of legal jurisprudence as well as issues that transcend narrow district-specific concerns, it seems reasonable that more senior members of the chamber would have been able to cultivate the necessary expertise across their careers to be able to engage successfully these relatively complex policy domains.

As with partisanship in the previous section, we here subdivide issues into two categories, High Expertise Issues and Low Expertise Issues, based on whether the coefficient on Seniority was above or below the median value, respectively, across issue-specific regressions for all Congresses combined. In so doing, we find initial support for the Issue Expertise and Policy Gridlock Hypothesis. Specifically, the average success rate for the High Expertise Issues is 2.9 percent, compared to a success rate of 4.1 percent for Low Expertise Issues. Put simply, issues requiring policy expertise are more gridlocked than those for which even less senior members of Congress can develop policy proposals that find success in the lawmaking process.

That said, the coefficients that arise in the issue-specific regressions across all Congresses combined may be masking the true nature of issue expertise within any given Congress. For instance, senior and effective lawmakers may be detected not only by their Seniority but also by the fact that they are effective year after year, as detected in their Lagged Effectiveness Score.[36] For this reason, and also because the expertise required to move issues forward may vary over time across issues, we next conduct similar regression analyses by issue by Congress, excluding the Lagged Effectiveness Score variable. As before, we rely on the Seniority variable's coefficient to capture issue expertise, and we use this measure of expertise in an attempt to explain the degree of policy gridlock across issues and over time. We classify each issue in each Congress as High Expertise or Low Expertise, based on whether the Seniority coefficient is above or below the median value for all issues and all Congresses.

Figure 5.4 illustrates the success rates by Congress for High Expertise Issues compared to Low Expertise Issues from 1973 to 1996. A number of patterns clearly emerge from the figure. First, during the Democratic era from 1973 to 1994, High Expertise Issues received less success than Low Expertise Issues in all Congresses except one. Second, the gap between the success rates of the High Expertise and Low Expertise Issues grew steadily over this time period. In the 103rd Congress (1993–94), in particular, about 3 percent of bills in high expertise areas became law, which is only half the rate of success for low expertise issues. It is intriguing that the expertise gridlock gap is largest at the point in time when Democrats had been in control of Congress for the greatest length of time and therefore when they had the greatest opportunity to develop and utilize their expertise. For instance, in the 103rd Congress, the average committee chair had thirteen previous terms of seniority, and the average sub-committee chair had served in nine previous Congresses.

---

[36] For this reason, it is somewhat unsurprising that the correlation between the Seniority coefficients and Success Rate by each issue area as a whole is not significantly different from zero.

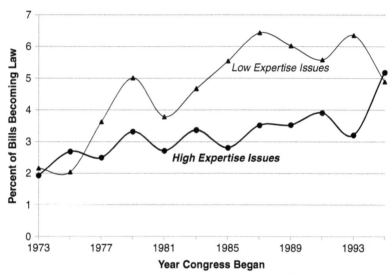

FIGURE 5.4. Issues Requiring Greater Expertise Are More Gridlocked
Note: The figure shows the percent of bills that become law, among those that are in high expertise (thick line) and low expertise (thin line) issue areas, for each of the 93rd through 104th Congresses (1973–1996), revealing greater gridlock among issues requiring greater expertise. Issue expertise is characterized by the enhanced effectiveness of senior lawmakers in their Interest and Legislative Effectiveness Scores (ILES), upon controlling for all other explanatory factors shown in Table 5.4. Each issue in each Congress is then labeled high expertise if its regression coefficient on Seniority is above the median coefficient value for all issues and all Congresses.

In contrast, when the Republicans became the majority party in 1995, their committee chairs averaged less than ten previous terms and subcommittee chairs averaged less than six. Not only had these members never served as chairs before, they had not even served in a Republican majority before. It was therefore more difficult to quickly develop the institutional capacity to translate their seniority and experience into effective lawmaking. As such, it is unsurprising that High Expertise Issues and Low Expertise Issues are blurred together in the early Republican Congresses, as illustrated on the right of Figure 5.4.[37]

In sum, issues that require a greater degree of political and policy expertise (perhaps because of their complex or technical nature) tend to be more gridlocked than those for which lawmaking depends to a lesser extent on the acquisition and utilization of expertise. Support for the Issue Expertise and Policy Gridlock Hypothesis emerges not only from the aggregate analysis of High Expertise and Low Expertise Issues, but also from examining these issues

---

[37] The prominent gap in success rates based on issue expertise found in the figure does not return for the 105th–107th Congresses.

over time. Doing so highlights that the relationship between expertise and grid-lock may be conditional on the extent to which Congress has the institutional capacity to translate expertise into policy change.[38]

POLITICAL ENTREPRENEURS AND POLICY GRIDLOCK

Beyond partisanship and expertise, a third relationship between the legislative effectiveness of individual lawmakers and aggregate patterns of policy gridlock is based on political entrepreneurship.[39] Political entrepreneurs, like entrepreneurs in business, are those who take a risk to develop a new product. In the political setting, that product could be a new way of running and winning elections, a new method of building coalitions or exerting influence, or a new public policy. To an extent, all members of Congress are political entrepreneurs, as they each need to strike out on their own in the risky business of electoral politics, and as almost all attempt to forge new public policies through the bills they sponsor. From that point of view, it is difficult to discern one political entrepreneur from another. And the link between such entrepreneurship and institutional gridlock may be difficult to detect.

The entrepreneurship that we focus on in this section is somewhat different, however. It arises from the work of James Q. Wilson, a prominent political scientist who famously identified the nature of the politics associated with different types of policy change.[40] For example, according to Wilson, when the benefits of a policy change are widely distributed across members of society and the costs are concentrated, policymaking takes the form of "entrepreneurial politics."[41] Because of the powerful concentrated interests opposed to policy change, and the difficulty in building a coalition for change among widely distributed beneficiaries, policy change is unlikely absent a political entrepreneur.[42] Such an entrepreneur faces a daunting task. She must exert all of the effort necessary to rally together a coalition based on diverse interests, all the while being vexed by the organized and concentrated forces seeking to halt policy change at every opportunity.

---

[38] Alternatively, perhaps the relationship between issue expertise and policy gridlock is robust, but the measure of issue expertise based on Seniority as constructed here does a poor job of tapping into the degree of required expertise across issues during the early years of the Republican-controlled Congresses.

[39] See Wawro (2001) for an examination of legislative entrepreneurship based largely on the sponsorship activities of members of Congress.

[40] What several scholars have come to refer to as "Wilson's Matrix" is laid out most clearly in Wilson (1980).

[41] Lowi (1964) likewise draws distinctions across policy types based on similar considerations, albeit with a different focus and different terminology. See Grossmann (2013) for a critique of the use of policy typologies more broadly.

[42] For more on the strategies needed to solve the collective action problem of mobilizing potential coalition partners with diverse interests, see Olson (1965).

If successful, such entrepreneurs become well known as the actors who can get things done in Washington. They are lawmakers such as Paul Rogers and Henry Waxman, described previously, for health policy. If such well-regarded entrepreneurs cannot bring about policy change, perhaps no one can; policy gridlock will result. In contrast, nearly any lawmaker is willing to step forward for what Wilson deems "client politics," where the benefits of policy change go to a concentrated group and the costs are widely dispersed.[43] Those paying the costs will not organize and may not even notice the policy harms on a daily basis, as the costs are disguised in the form of slightly higher prices due to regulations or subsidies, or marginally higher taxes. Those who benefit, however, receive a big payoff, part of which they are willing to share with policymakers who help advance their preferred policies, perhaps in the form of campaign contributions or other political support.

Given the relative ease of engaging in client politics and the difficulty of overcoming the hurdles of entrepreneurial politics, it is unsurprising that policy gridlock would be related to the nature of the policy changes being sought.[44] We capture such expectations in the following:

Entrepreneurial Politics and Policy Gridlock Hypothesis: Policy gridlock is more likely in policy areas and during times featuring entrepreneurial politics.

Although few scholars would disagree that entrepreneurial politics presents a significant hurdle for policy change, identifying cases of entrepreneurial politics on anything other than a policy-by-policy basis has proven difficult.[45] For instance, some health policy changes seek to benefit a large number of Americans, but at a high cost to medical providers or the insurance industry. Other changes benefit these same industries, but spread the costs broadly to all taxpayers. Is health policy therefore best characterized as facing entrepreneurial politics or client politics? And how does that compare to other policy areas at different points in time?

In our view, there are times when the nature of the political scene tends toward entrepreneurial politics in particular policy areas, such as when Congress was seeking to close tax loopholes in the mid-1980s or attempting to broaden health

---

[43] According to Wilson, "interest group politics" exists when both those who benefit and those harmed by a policy change are concentrated, while "majoritarian politics" exists when both are widely dispersed.

[44] Brady and Volden (2006) argue that gridlock under entrepreneurial politics can more easily be overcome when Congress faces few budgetary constraints than during tough budgetary times. When lawmakers cannot build coalitions with budgetary concessions and side payments, gridlock is more likely, especially in areas of entrepreneurial politics.

[45] An alternative perspective on the scope of political entrepreneurship is offered by Adler and Wilkerson (2013), who argue that much significant legislation is (effectively) must-pass, and hence, the keys to legislative success on many of the policies that are considered in a Congress involve sponsors' particular positions in the institution (e.g., whether they are chairs of committees to which bills are referred) more so than the skills or personal qualities of a sponsor, per se.

insurance coverage in 2010. In these circumstances, if policy change is to come about at all, it will be led by a political entrepreneur.[46] And our examples of Rogers and Waxman highlight one way to identify such entrepreneurs.

Specifically, we characterize issues and times of entrepreneurial politics by the existence of political entrepreneurs, those who dramatically outperform their colleagues in their Interest and Legislative Effectiveness Scores for a particular Congress and a particular policy area. The logic is simple. If policymaking is easy, such as in the case of client politics, numerous lawmakers will be competing to advance their legislative proposals, and no one will stand out dramatically over the others. In contrast, if policymaking is difficult, as in the case of entrepreneurial politics, few will pay the costs of trying to bring about policy change, and far fewer still will succeed. In such circumstances, the rare policy entrepreneurs may arise, and they will be easily recognized by their ILES far exceeding the average score of 1.0 around which our measures are centered.

To proceed, then, little is needed beyond the construction of the issue-specific ILESs described previously. We measure Entrepreneurship in each issue and each Congress based on the ILES of the highest-performing member. We begin our analysis by then aggregating these high performers up to the issue level across all Congresses, through an average of the highest ILES for that issue across all fifteen Congresses. Upon generating such an average, we find that the greatest level of entrepreneurship exists in the area of Macroeconomics, which most broadly deals with how to promote economic growth, an often widely dispersed benefit. Other policy areas with high entrepreneurship scores are Health, and Housing and Community Development, which contain many policy changes meeting Wilson's definition of entrepreneurial politics. At the other end of the spectrum are client politics areas such as Public Lands, Defense, Banking and Commerce, and Government Operations. These areas feature many policies that aim to promote the interests of concentrated groups, such as defense contractors or the banking industry. Thus, we have some confidence that our measure of entrepreneurship is indeed tapping into an underlying characteristic of entrepreneurial politics.

But does this measure also help explain policy gridlock on an issue-by-issue basis? It clearly seems so. The correlation between Entrepreneurship and Success Rate across the nineteen issues is a statistically significant -0.57.[47] This means that the most gridlocked policy areas are indeed those experiencing entrepreneurial politics. To build upon this initial result, we once again subdivide the issues at the median of the Entrepreneurship variable into Highly Entrepreneurial Issues and Low Entrepreneurial Issues. The subset of

---

[46] One form of policy entrepreneur may be those legislators whom Arnold (1990) denotes being "coalition leaders," able to articulate the electoral virtues of adopting their proposals to a sufficiently large number of legislators so as to secure passage in the House. These points will be engaged further in Chapter 6.
[47] This correlation coefficient is statistically significant with p = 0.01.

highly entrepreneurial issues average a success rate of 2.6 percent, compared to 4.3 percent for low entrepreneurial issues. This is consistent with the Entrepreneurial Politics and Policy Gridlock Hypothesis.

And these findings hold up across individual Congresses. Consider members with the highest ILES for each issue in each Congress. Among the highest scorers is Paul Rogers, with a Health ILES of 200.6 in the 94th Congress (1975–76), when he was seeking to address the shortage of health care workers and the needs of the developmentally disabled. Also noteworthy is Dan Rostenkowski's (D-IL) Macroeconomics ILES rating of 285.2 in the 100th Congress (1987–88). During this Congress, he served as chair of the Ways and Means Committee and brought about the Omnibus Budget Reconciliation Act of 1987, which took on organized interests by closing corporate loopholes and reining in large defense contractors, all for the dispersed benefit of lowering the budget deficit.

Once again, we further subdivide issue areas into Highly Entrepreneurial Issues and Low Entrepreneurial Issues, based on whether Entrepreneurship for each issue and Congress is above or below the median value. We illustrate the average success rates for each of these groupings of issues in each Congress, in Figure 5.5. As can be seen, in each Congress, Highly Entrepreneurial Issues are

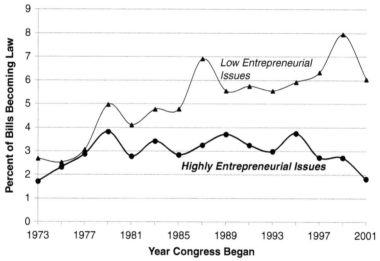

FIGURE 5.5. Issues Requiring Greater Entrepreneurship Are More Gridlocked
   Note: The figure shows the percent of bills that become law, among highly entrepreneurial (thick line) and low entrepreneurial (thin line) issue areas, for each of the 93rd through 107th Congresses (1973–2002), revealing greater gridlock among issues requiring greater entrepreneurship. Entrepreneurship is characterized by the highest Interest and Legislative Effectiveness Scores (ILES) among all lawmakers in the given issue and given Congress. Each issue in each Congress is then labeled highly entrepreneurial if its highest ILES value is above the median for all issues and all Congresses.

more gridlocked than Low Entrepreneurial Issues. And the gap between them seems to be growing over time. For instance, in the 106th Congress (1999–2000), bills in the issues characterized by entrepreneurial politics had a 2.7 percent probability of becoming law. In contrast, bills in low entrepreneurial issues had nearly triple that rate of success, at 7.9 percent. Together, these findings strongly support the Entrepreneurial Politics and Policy Gridlock Hypothesis.

OVERCOMING POLICY GRIDLOCK IN CONGRESS

In the previous sections, we established that policy gridlock in Congress varies across issue areas and over time. While accounting for such diversity in law-making success is a daunting task, in this chapter we argued that three character-istics of policies, naturally emerging from our examination of legislative effectiveness, help to explain success rates of bills becoming law. Along the way, we formulated Interest and Legislative Effectiveness Scores for each member of Congress in each of nineteen policy areas across thirty years of congres-sional history. Such scores could be used for a variety of purposes. Currently, we demonstrate their usefulness in explaining gridlock on an issue-by-issue and Congress-by-Congress basis.

Specifically, first, we measure the difference between the average ILES for members of the majority party and members of the minority party. We argue that this gap captures the degree to which the House is divided by party in each issue area and each Congress. We then show that such partisanship is associated with a much greater level of policy gridlock. Second, we run a series of regres-sions to explain the issue-specific ILESs with the same factors examined through-out the book. We detect the level of expertise that is required to advance policies by the coefficient on the Seniority variable, upon controlling for all other factors. We then show that issues requiring high expertise are more gridlocked, and that this is particularly true in the Democratic Congresses of the 1980s and early 1990s. Third, we denote as facing entrepreneurial politics those issues for which a policy entrepreneur emerges with a very high ILES relative to the average value of 1.0. We find that those highly entrepreneurial issues are also the most grid-locked in every Congress, especially recently.[48]

In some sense, these three factors – partisanship, required expertise, and entrepreneurial politics – may be tapping into related concepts. For example, if expertise is cultivated in committees, and committee chairs promote majority-party interests, then issues requiring high expertise might also be seen as highly

---

[48] To an extent, the measures constructed here may be seen as *endogenous*, arising from the same lawmaking processes that produce the success rates that we are explaining. That said, our purpose here is not to create variables that can be generated at the start of each Congress to predict its gridlock rates. Instead, we seek to illustrate how partisanship, issue expertise, and entrepreneur-ship are closely interrelated with the incidence of policy gridlock.

partisan. Such committee leaders may also emerge as the political entrepreneurs that we detect in our analysis. Indeed, there is some degree of positive association among all three of the coding schemes we use throughout this chapter.[49] For example, 58 percent of the high expertise issues are also highly partisan issues, in contrast to only 42 percent of the low expertise issues. That said, each concept is also tapping into a different element of lawmaking in Congress.

Together, these three factors help account for large swings in the success rate of bills across issues and Congresses.[50] For example, an average bill in a policy area that is low in partisanship, in requiring expertise, and in facing entrepreneurial politics has a 5.9 percent chance of becoming law.[51] This is more than two and a half times the success rate of a bill on an issue plagued by partisanship, expertise requirements, and entrepreneurial politics, of which only 2.3 percent become law.

While these results shed light on why particular topics are gridlocked at high rates, do they also point the way toward how to overcome gridlock in Congress? A simplistic reading of our results might suggest that more could be accomplished if we discourage partisanship, discourage the acquisition of expertise, and discourage the rise of political entrepreneurs. Wouldn't eliminating these factors result in more than doubling the rate of policymaking success? In our view, such suggestions get the causal processes exactly wrong. While we are reporting correlations rather than causal relationships, and while more in-depth research therefore is needed in the future, the following story seems to be more correct.

Republicans and Democrats are more starkly divided on some issues than on others. Likewise, some issues require more expertise than others. And some issues are more prone to entrepreneurial politics than others. Moreover, these considerations change over time, as issues evolve and the political landscape shifts. Nevertheless, partisanship, the need for expertise, and entrepreneurial politics all contribute to the policy gridlock detected here.

In light of such gridlock, and with a desire to nevertheless bring about policy change, what are lawmakers to do? It is instructive to revisit the case from the start of this chapter on health care reform early in the Obama administration. In that case, Democratic officials attempted to bridge the significant partisan

---

[49] The correlation coefficients across each pair of our High-Low dichotomies for partisanship, expertise, and entrepreneurship across the issues and over time range modestly from 0.10 to 0.20.

[50] Our goal here is not to fully explain the variation in success rates across issue areas and over time. Doing so would require the introduction of many new variables, such as those measuring issue salience according to the American people. Rather, we here seek to draw attention to such variance in gridlock rates and to highlight some of the many ways that a focus on legislative effectiveness sheds light on institution-level legislative success rates.

[51] A regression for the 285 issue Congress observations on the dependent variable of Success Rate, with independent variables being the dichotomous Highly Partisan Issues, High Expertise Issues, and Highly Entrepreneurial Issues, as well as a linear time trend, reveals a coefficient (and robust standard error) of -1.21 (0.36) for Party, -0.51 (0.36) for Expertise, and -1.87 (0.33) for Entrepreneurship. These results provide the estimated success rates used throughout the chapter's conclusion.

divides and incorporate ideas from Republicans. But in the end, it was a bridge too far, with Democrats unwilling to make the necessary changes to bring Republicans on board and Republicans unwilling to hand the president a major policy victory. Therefore, the final measure passed following concessions, promises, and persuasion within the Democratic Party, but without a single Republican vote. Ultimately, strong partisanship brought about the policy change.

So, too, is it with expertise and entrepreneurial politics. If policymaking requires expertise in order to secure a policy change, members seek to develop that expertise, and the source of said expertise might vary by legislator. As will be shown in Chapter 6, some members derive their expertise from their own personal or professional experiences, while others develop policy expertise that corresponds closely with the needs and priorities of their constituencies. Regardless of how such expertise is cultivated, legislators have an incentive to invest in these efforts, as doing so not only allows proposed policy changes to move forward, but also guarantees a seat at the table for the policy experts, and the chance to shape the ultimate policy choices in their favor. It is unsurprising, then, that the most effective lawmakers in one Congress are the ones sponsoring landmark laws and overcoming policy gridlock in the next. Their innate abilities and carefully cultivated skill sets may be even more important as Congress becomes more heavily gridlocked.

When political entrepreneurs are needed, effective lawmakers tend to step into such roles. As will be shown in Chapter 6, some legislators are particularly successful at leveraging their committee positions to ensure that legislation dealing with particular issues must flow through them, in order to move onward in the legislative process. These policy entrepreneurs keep pressing their issues and work on building their coalitions (sometimes actively reaching out to partners outside of the House, such as senators or allies in the White House) until the time is right to secure their long-sought policy change.

Thus, the same factors that help us explain policy gridlock point the way toward overcoming gridlock, whether it be action through key institutional positions within the majority party, the cultivation of expertise in a particular policy area over time, or the development of a reputation as the go-to political entrepreneur on a particular issue. Yet none of these tasks is easy, and they are all occurring on some of the most gridlocked policy areas in Congress. Who, then, are the individuals that take on these challenges, and what strategies do they use to advance their agenda items against all odds? These are precisely the questions we address in Chapter 6, where we identify twenty of the highest performing lawmakers according to our metrics and highlight their habits for success.

6

The Habits of Highly Effective Lawmakers

If the Founding Fathers came back and picked from our 200-year history one member of Congress to show how they intended the Congress to work, they would have selected Silvio Conte.

> – Speaker of the House Tip O'Neill (D-MA) on Silvio Conte (R-MA)[1]

He still and for always will be thought of as a legislative giant, as someone who motored around on the floor of the House like the Energizer Bunny, moving at the speed of sound from deal to deal to deal to deal as he worked his legislative magic.

> – Edward Markey (D-MA) on Edward Boland (D-MA)[2]

He was one of the great leaders in the Congress seeking health insurance for all and he worked hard to enact a decent, humane social policy for the disadvantaged.

> – Fortney "Pete" Stark (D-CA) on James Corman (D-CA)[3]

For more than a dozen years before 9/11 Jim Saxton was working for better homeland security and a more coordinated defense against terrorism. It's why he remains so effective on these issues today.... Our beaches are cleaner, our fisheries better managed, and military bases more robust because of the great work of Jim Saxton.

> – Chris Smith (R-NJ) on Jim Saxton (R-NJ)[4]

Homeless people tend not to turn out in numbers at the Polls. But Mr. Vento applied himself to the issues he cared about, did his homework, made the rounds of his colleagues, carried the water, dug the ditches, fought the good fights, made the

[1] Quoted from Parnass (2012).
[2] *Congressional Record*, 2001 (Volume 147, part 16), p. 22645.
[3] *Congressional Record*, 2001 (Volume 147, part 2), p. 2384.
[4] Quoted from Jackson, Herb. 2007. (November 9). "Tributes Pour in for Saxton." Retrieved from http://blog.northjersey.com/thepoliticalstate/526/tributes-pour-in-for-saxton/, accessed on July 2, 2013.

*compromises, and wrote landmark legislation that became law and that made a
real difference in the world.*
– Betty McCollum (D-MN) on Bruce Vento (D-MN)[5]

There are numerous ways members of Congress could fail as lawmakers. On average, 90 percent of their legislative proposals die in committee. Of those reaching the floor of the House, another 20 percent fall by the wayside without passage. And, of those passing the House, nearly half never overcome the final hurdles to becoming law. If they were baseball players, these lawmakers would be batting 0.043. If they were quarterbacks, they would be completing only 4 percent of their passes. Fans would go home. Revenues would be lost. Players would be fired.

Yet year in and year out, members of Congress battle against these odds, collectively introducing thousands of bills. They fight for the attention of committee chairs, try to persuade their colleagues of the importance of their issues, and seek to run the gauntlet of lawmaking. And some – perhaps too few – accomplish these tasks so well that their colleagues declare them to be "legislative giants," "great leaders," or "effective lawmakers."

We began this book with an effort to identify these lawmakers, generating Legislative Effectiveness Scores along the way. We illustrated how those scores revealed the choices and key roles of majority-party members, committee chairs, electorally safe lawmakers, and others. Yet by the nature of our quantitative analyses, we have focused largely on uncovering and explaining "average tendencies" in lawmaking. For example, knowing that a lawmaker is female, in the majority party, and in her fourth term gives us some expectations about what her likely effectiveness would be in comparison to her male or minority-party counterparts. Yet among such congresswomen, there remains a significant amount of variance in their effectiveness.

While therefore not fully revealing, the average effects we uncover offer some indications of how members become effective lawmakers. For instance, bills of majority-party members thrive in committees, relative to those of minority-party members (Chapter 3). Women in the minority party work to achieve consensus across party lines (Chapter 4). And senior members acquire expertise to help overcome policy gridlock (Chapter 5). Yet all of these sorts of considerations explain less than 60 percent of the variance in our LES measure.[6] For example, our analyses indicate that, controlling for a variety of factors, committee chairs are nearly 300 percent more effective in lawmaking than the average member. But this average effect masks a good deal of variation. Scores of the Democratic committee chairs in the 110th Congress ranged from a high of 18.69 for Charlie Rangel (NY-15), chair of Ways and Means, to a few chairs with scores less

---

[5] *Congressional Record*, 2000 (Volume 146, part 15), p. 22263.
[6] Specifically, the R² value of 0.56 in Model 2.3 of Table 2.5 means that 44 percent of the variance in the dependent variable remains to be explained.

than 1.00.[7] In other words, while holding a committee chair generally contributes to a legislator's effectiveness (perhaps because of the practice of the "chairman's mark," and the like, as discussed in Chapter 2), some committee chairs are still clearly more effective than others. And furthermore, as illustrated by those chairs with scores less than one, holding a committee chair is not a guarantee of lawmaking success.

Contrasting with our quantitative approach thus far, a qualitative approach could focus instead on the specific details of a small subset of lawmakers, exploring where they succeed and where they fail. Such an approach could draw lessons from such cases to flesh out the bare bones "on average" findings from quantitative research. In that way, quantitative and qualitative approaches are highly complementary. In our view, two of the greatest benefits of qualitative research are: (1) offering a lay of the land, providing the scholarly community with stylized facts and broad understandings upon which new theories could be built; and (2) filling in the details that cannot be approached fully in quantitative analyses, due to limited data availability or to subtleties that extend beyond what can be readily measured.

In this chapter, we adopt such a qualitative approach with both of these purposes in mind. Specifically, first, by drilling deeper into the strategic choices and legislative styles of highly effective lawmakers, we hope to understand better the overall patterns uncovered in earlier chapters. But also, second, we expect that the legislative habits of these members, as uncovered here, will lead to new theories and hypotheses that can be tested in a variety of ways, including in future quantitative analyses.

Put simply, in this chapter, we take a somewhat different approach to our data to investigate those members of Congress that we classify as "highly effective lawmakers." In particular, we seek to identify and study those legislators who lack clear institutional advantages and yet still outperform their peers, and those legislators who might benefit from certain institutional advantages (e.g., holding a subcommittee chair) but are notably more effective than other legislators in similar institutional positions. We seek to understand what makes these particular legislators so effective. What strategies have they engaged in, and what career paths have they chosen to ensure that they are so effective in spite of their institutional positions; or how did they utilize their institutional positions to transcend our expectations regarding their respective effectiveness? Finally, what lessons can we extract from the shared experiences of these high performers that might guide other legislators who seek to become effective lawmakers?

---

[7] Representative John Spratt (SC-5) had an LES of 0.91 (as chair of the Budget Committee), Representative Stephanie Tubbs Jones (OH-11) had an LES of 0.31 (as chair of the Standards of Official Conduct Committee), and Representative Juanita Millender-McDonald (CA-37) had an LES of 0.03 (as chair of the House Administration Committee). The scores of these latter two were undoubtedly diminished by their deaths during the 110th Congress.

EFFECTIVE LAWMAKERS AS LEADERS

The approach that we take here is, in many ways, akin to studies of "leadership" across a wide array of fields.[8] One way to study leadership is to examine highly effective leaders in order to discern their keys to success. Such an approach has been used in the business leadership literature, to understand the successes of firms like Starbucks, Zappos, Virgin Atlantic Airways, and numerous others.[9] Similarly, principles of leadership have been derived for (and from) the military, the sporting world, and beyond.[10] Leadership studies for politics often look to princes, presidents, and prime ministers.[11]

Studies of leadership in Congress tend to focus on party leaders. For example, some of these works examine the rise to power of Speakers of the House.[12] Others seek to understand the ways in which potentially idiosyncratic personality traits have influenced political careers and outcomes, and how these personality traits interacted with various institutional tools to push through a policy agenda.[13] Such works look at the constraints on party leaders that come from the disparate goals of party members, in order to determine the conditions under which party leaders are endowed with the power to push more coherent and forceful agendas.[14]

Studies of the Legislative Effectiveness Scores of party leaders in Congress could undoubtedly contribute to this venture. For instance, Figure 6.1 plots the Legislative Effectiveness Score of Nancy Pelosi (D-CA) from her freshman term to her selection as Minority Leader, relative to the average Democrat. The figure shows a steady climb in effectiveness across her first four terms, rising into the top quartile of majority-party members in the 103rd Congress (1993–94). Of her fourteen sponsored bills in that Congress, six received action in committee, five passed the House, and one became law. However, her effectiveness dropped precipitously upon her party's loss of the majority in the 1994 elections.[15] Unlike the women we highlighted in Chapter 4, Pelosi did not systematically work

---

[8] Indeed, we draw the title of this chapter from Stephen Covey's (1989) best-selling *The Seven Habits of Highly Effective People*, which blurred the boundaries between leadership studies and self-help books. A broad review of the management and organizational behavior literatures' perspectives on the social scientific study of leadership is provided by House and Aditya (1997).

[9] Naturally, as the respective leaders of these companies, Schultz (2011) focuses on Starbucks, Hsieh (2010) on Zappos, and Branson (2011) on Virgin. Some of the classic and most widely read books in this genre are Drucker (1954), Bennis (1989), Collins (2001), and Goleman, Boyatzis, and McKee (2002).

[10] Prominent examples include Carnegie (1936), Cialdini (2006), Lansing (1959), Maraniss (1999), Sun-Tzu (2011), Thaler and Sunstein (2008), and Wooden (2005).

[11] Important examples include Burns (1978), Churchill (2003), Edwards (2009), Goodwin (2005), Machiavelli (2009), and Neustadt (1990).

[12] See Jenkins and Stewart (2012).

[13] Early examples include Cooper and Brady (1981) and Jones (1968).

[14] See Rohde (1991) and Strahan (2007).

[15] Pelosi's relative effectiveness in the 104th Congress is due to the continuation of her previously sponsored bill on management of the Presidio within her district.

Volden & Wiseman

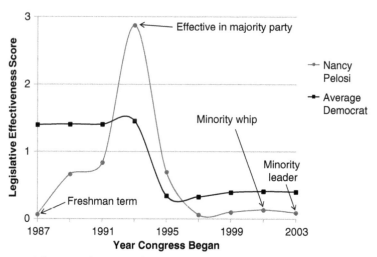

FIGURE 6.1. The Rise of Nancy Pelosi
   Note: The figure shows the Legislative Effectiveness Score (LES) of Nancy Pelosi
(D-CA) from her freshman term until she became Speaker of the House, relative to the
LES of the average Democrat. Her rapid rise among majority-party members is
noteworthy, as is her pivoting away from lawmaking toward partisan activities under
the Republican majority following the 1994 elections.

across party lines in order to keep her policy agenda alive. Instead, she fell into
the bottom quartile of Democrats, in terms of her LES.[16] With her highly liberal
district being very far away from the mainstream of the majority-party
Republicans, Pelosi turned her attentions away from promoting her own legislative agenda. She averaged only five introductions across each of the subsequent
six Republican-controlled Congresses. Instead, Pelosi set her sights on leadership
roles within the Democratic Party, such as with her fundraising and contributions to the campaigns of her partisan colleagues. Perhaps she felt that cooperat-
ing with Republicans to keep her legislative ambitions alive would have been
detrimental to this cause. Regardless, the strategy paid off, and in January of
2007, Nancy Pelosi became the first woman to serve as Speaker of the House.
   Similarly, the LES measure could be used to highlight those leaders within
congressional committees who were particularly effective at advancing legislation on behalf of themselves, their committees, and their parties. Figure 6.2, for
example, shows the Legislative Effectiveness Scores for chairs of the Natural
Resources Committee from the 93rd Congress (1973–74) through the 110th
Congress (2007–08).[17] As can be seen, the most effective leaders of this

[16] Indeed, Pelosi's score in the 106th Congress (1999–2000) placed her in the bottom decile of all
Democrats.
[17] As with many committees, this committee's name changed over our period of study, from Interior
and Insular Affairs to Natural Resources to Resources and back to Natural Resources once again.

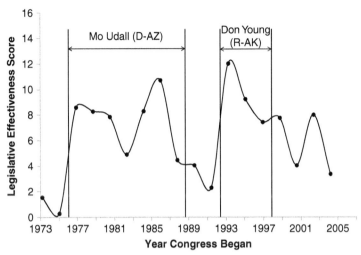

FIGURE 6.2. Identifying Effective Committee Chairs

Note: The figure shows the Legislative Effectiveness Score (LES) of the chair of the Natural Resources Committee, from the 93rd through 110th Congresses (1973–2008). As is evident from the figure, some chairs, such as Mo Udall (D-AZ) and Don Young (R-AK), are simply more effective than others, despite being endowed with the same institutional position.

committee were Mo Udall (D-AZ), who averaged an LES of 8.32 during his chairmanship, and Don Young (R-AK), who averaged an LES of 10.48 as chair.[18] In contrast, the five other Natural Resources Committee chairs during our time period averaged 4.30, leaving them less than half as effective as these two legislative giants. Identifying committee chairs through such an approach could be quite useful in finding those lawmakers who yield their institutional powers to the greatest effect.

Yet in our view, this focus on party and committee leaders is too narrow. All members of Congress are already leaders. They do not need to wait until they gain enough seniority to become committee chairs or to gain enough support within their party structures to become party leaders. Indeed, waiting to become a leader surely is a recipe to never become one. Instead, we argue that lawmakers can lead from anywhere. And their early successes pave the way to becoming great lawmaking leaders later in their careers. We therefore focus our analyses here on members of Congress who succeeded as lawmakers even absent serving as party leaders or committee chairs. Some of these members naturally rose to party and committee leadership positions in due course. But their successes as chairs or party leaders are not where we focus our attention. Rather, we seek to

---

[18] Udall is best known for his championing of environmental causes and for doubling the size of the National Park System through the Alaska Lands Act of 1980.

identify the habits that lawmakers can develop from their earliest days in Congress, habits that help explain how they have been successful well beyond the average tendencies detailed earlier in this book.[19]

IDENTIFYING HIGHLY EFFECTIVE LAWMAKERS

The first step in undertaking our analysis is to systematically identify the most highly effective lawmakers. Turning to the LES data, we applied two separate criteria, identifying: (1) members who were consistently at the top of their respective political party in effectiveness, and (2) members who were consistently among the most effective in specific policy areas. In particular, for each Congress we identified those legislators who had the top-ten highest LES scores within each party (majority and minority) but who were neither committee chairs nor party leaders. Hence, for every Congress between 1973 and 2008, we can parsimoniously classify the collection of Representatives who were unambiguously more effective at moving bills through the legislative process than their peers, despite lacking the institutional and parliamentary privileges arising from committee or party leadership.[20]

For example, Table 6.1 presents the rank-and-file legislators who had the ten highest LESs in the majority and minority parties for the 95th Congress (1977–78). Several points quickly emerge from a consideration of these lawmakers. First, among these high-fliers, there is still a good deal of variation in their scores, ranging from a low of 4.02 (Herbert Harris of Virginia) to a high of 11.45 (Paul Rogers of Florida) for majority-party members. Because LESs are normalized to an average of 1.0 within each Congress, each member in the top ten of the majority party is approximately four to eleven times more effective at moving bills through the legislative process than the average member of the House.

Second, the scope of these high scores comports with our expectations, given the reputations of some of these members. More specifically, consistent with our discussion in Chapter 5, it should be unsurprising that Paul Rogers (a.k.a.

---

[19] In many ways, our approach is a natural extension to Douglas Arnold's (1990) important contributions to the study of coalition leaders in Congress. As he eloquently notes (p. 88): "Building winning coalitions is hard work. Legislators who merely drop bills in the hopper and wait for something to happen are invariably disappointed. Nothing happens in Congress unless someone plans for it and works for it. Someone must define the problems, shape the alternatives, initiate action, mobilize support, arrange compromises, and work to see that Congress passes specific bills." Arnold explicitly sidesteps questions of "why individuals choose to become coalition leaders, invest their scarce time and precious resources in mobilizing support for proposals, or choose to attack specific problems or advance specific remedies" (p. 8). In contrast, these are precisely the types of questions that we seek to engage in this chapter.

[20] Note that in our selection process, we did not discard those legislators who held a subcommittee chair, which (as we know from our analysis in Chapter 2) also correlates with a substantial increase in legislative effectiveness, but which would have eliminated about half of the majority party from consideration, given the large number of subcommittees in the House.

TABLE 6.1. *Identifying Top-Ten Rank-and-File Lawmakers by Party*

Majority Party (Democrats)		
Name	LES	Seniority
Paul Rogers (FL-11)	11.45	12
Robert Leggett (CA-4)	7.10	8
Sonny Montgomery (MS-3)	6.15	6
Glenn Anderson (CA-32)	5.25	5
James Corman (CA-21)	4.80	9
Phillip Burton (CA-6)	4.72	7
Teno Roncalio (WY-1)	4.46	4
Robert Kastenmeier (WI-2)	4.43	10
Jonathan Bingham (NY-22)	4.24	7
Herbert Harris (VA-8)	4.02	2

Majority Party (Republicans)		
Name	LES	Seniority
Bill Frenzel (MN-3)	2.13	4
Bill Steiger (WI-6)	1.87	6
Barber Conable (NY-35)	1.79	7
John Duncan, Sr. (TN-2)	1.77	7
Jack Kemp (NY-38)	1.68	4
Manuel Lujan (NM-1)	1.64	5
Silvio Conte (MA-1)	1.47	10
Al Quie (MN-1)	1.31	10
Jim Johnson (CO-4)	1.26	3
Hamilton Fish (NY-25)	1.14	5

Note: The table lists the top-ten rank-and-file lawmakers within each party during the 95th Congress (1977–78), based on their Legislative Effectiveness Scores (LES). By setting aside committee chairs and party leaders, we are able to isolate the most effective lawmakers based on their own activities, rather than those that may be tied to their institutional positions.

"Mr. Health") was one of the highest-scoring lawmakers (indeed, the highest), who lacked a committee chair or party leadership post in the 95th Congress. His position as chair of the Subcommittee on Health within the Energy and Commerce Committee allowed him to shepherd several substantial pieces of health-related legislation through the Congress. And these legislative accomplishments, combined with his other legislative activities, contributed to his being the top-scoring member among rank-and-file Democrats.[21]

---

[21] Representative Rogers had an expansive policy portfolio during the 95th Congress, as he introduced more than 100 public bills into the U.S. House.

On the minority-party side, we see a similar pattern, in that there is a good deal of variation in the scores of the top ten minority-party legislators, ranging from a low LES of 1.14 (Hamilton Fish of New York) to a high of 2.13 (Bill Frenzel of Minnesota). While the span between these high and low scores is not as substantial as among the top ten in the majority party, it is important to remember that all of these members are still above the average LES in the 95th Congress. Furthermore, the average Republican in the 95th Congress had an LES of approximately 0.37, meaning the top minority-party lawmakers in the table are three to five times as effective as other Republicans. Similar to the majority party, several members who had reputations for being strong politicians and lawmakers appear on this list. For example, Hamilton Fish (NY-25) was known to be a moderate Republican, comfortable working across the aisle with his Democratic counterparts to facilitate legislative compromises. Jack Kemp (NY-38) ultimately went on to the Senate and ran unsuccessfully for vice president under Bob Dole in 1996. Also among these members are the future president of the World Bank (Barber Conable), future Secretary of the Interior (Manuel Lujan), and future governor of Minnesota (Al Quie).

In addition to those legislators who were among the top-ten rank-and-file members in each party, we also sought to characterize those legislators who were among the most effective in particular policy areas. More specifically, turning to the nineteen different issue areas that we considered in Chapter 5, we identified those lawmakers who had the ten-highest ILESs for each issue area across all Congresses. For example, Table 6.2 presents the top-ten legislators in Environmental Policy across all Congresses in our analyses. Despite being an issue that is conventionally associated with the Democratic Party, the top

TABLE 6.2. *Identifying Top-Ten Lawmakers by Policy Area*

Name	Congress	Environment ILES	Party	Committee Chair
Leonor Sullivan (MO-3)	93	111.74	Democrat	Yes
John Breaux (LA-7)	97	108.10	Democrat	No
John Breaux (LA-7)	98	105.61	Democrat	No
John Murphy (NY-17)	95	102.37	Democrat	Yes
John Breaux (LA-7)	99	94.80	Democrat	No
Robert Leggett (CA-4)	95	82.38	Democrat	No
John Murphy (NY-17)	96	79.59	Democrat	Yes
Jim Saxton (NJ-3)	106	78.58	Republican	No
Gerry Studds (MA-10)	102	76.33	Democrat	Yes
Jim Saxton (NJ-3)	105	75.24	Republican	No

Note: The table lists the top-ten lawmakers within environmental policy across the 93rd through 107th Congresses (1973–2002), based on their Interest and Legislative Effectiveness Scores (ILES) for this policy area. By identifying these policy leaders, we are able to isolate the most effective lawmakers in nineteen specific policy areas important to Congress.

Environmental Policy ILESs are not held exclusively by Democrats. Moreover, the highest ILES in a given Congress is not necessarily held by a legislator who chairs a committee with direct jurisdiction over environmental policy. Indeed, six of the ten highest Environment ILESs belong to legislators who did not hold the chair of any committee.[22]

Those members who lack committee chairs are of particular interest, as they were especially effective at advancing legislation in a specific policy area despite not having the extra staff, scheduling authority, and various other perks that would typically come with chairing a committee. It is especially noteworthy when a lawmaker such as John Breaux (D-LA) emerges repeatedly as a top environmental policy lawmaker despite not chairing a committee during those Congresses.[23] There is clearly something about his lawmaking style that is worth closer examination.

These same patterns emerge when we consider each of the nineteen issue areas from Chapter 5. While some policies are generally associated with one party more so than the other, members from both parties are often ranked within the top ten in any given issue area. There are also numerous instances of legislators who are ranked in the top ten despite lacking the most obvious resource that could facilitate such legislative effectiveness: a committee chair. And some members appear on these lists time and time again.

Drawing from these two lists (the overall top-ten rank-and-file members within each party and each Congress, and the top-ten ILESs in each policy area across Congresses), we identified twenty Representatives who we deemed to be the most highly effective lawmakers across the 93rd through 110th Congresses. More specifically, a lawmaker made our list by being in the overall top ten (within the majority or minority party) for four or more Congresses. Alternatively, we also included those who were among the top ten most effective legislators in a particular issue area at least twice (despite not holding a committee chair), and *also* among the overall top ten (within their respective parties) for at least two Congresses. These two criteria allow us to focus on those with outstanding overall lawmaking success, as well as those who succeed both overall and within a specific policy area.

The most highly effective rank-and-file lawmakers are listed in Table 6.3. Many features of this list are worth mentioning. First, although our criteria for selection set aside committee chairs and party leaders, many of these most effective members

---

[22] Building on this point, Representatives Studds (D-MA) and Saxton (R-NJ) are particularly interesting, as they also achieved relatively high ILESs in environmental policy in other Congresses, even when they were not committee chairs. Studds held the 12th and 16th highest ILES scores across all Congresses (68.44 in the 100th Congress, and 52.83 in the 101st Congress, respectively), while Saxton held the 17th highest ILES score across all Congresses (50.54 in the 104th Congress).
[23] Interestingly, Breaux had at least one thing in common with many other top performers in environmental policy: membership on the Merchant Marine and Fisheries Committee, out of which much influential environmental legislation arose.

TABLE 6.3. *The Twenty Most Highly Effective Rank-and-File Lawmakers*

Name	Frequency among Top 10 Overall	Top ILES Policy Areas (Appearances)
Edward Boland (D-MA)	2 in Majority	Housing (5)
John Breaux (D-LA)	3 in Majority	Environment (3)
Silvio Conte (R-MA)	4 in Minority	
James Corman (D-CA)	3 in Majority	Welfare (2)
John Duncan, Sr. (R-TN)	4 in Minority	
Hamilton Fish (R-NY)	5 in Minority	
Bill Hughes (D-NJ)	5 in Majority	Banking (1); Law, Crime, Family (1)
Robert Kastenmeier (D-WI)	7 in Majority	Banking (1); Law, Crime, Family (1)
Tom Lantos (D-CA)	3 Min, and 1 Maj	
Bill McCollum (R-FL)	1 Min, and 3 Maj	Law, Crime, Family (2)
Sonny Montgomery (D-MS)	2 in Majority	Defense (2)
Paul Rogers (D-FL)	3 in Majority	Health (3)
Jim Saxton (R-NJ)	3 in Majority	Environment (2)
Lamar Smith (R-TX)	4 in Majority	Labor (1)
Mark Udall (D-CO)	3 Min, and 1 Maj	
Tom Udall (D-NM)	4 in Minority	
Bruce Vento (D-MN)	4 in Majority	
Henry Waxman (D-CA)	8 in Majority	Health (6)
Pat Williams (D-MT)	3 in Majority	Education (2)
Don Young (R-AK)	9 in Minority	

Note: The table lists the top-twenty rank-and-file lawmakers across the 93rd through 110th Congresses (1973–2008). These members were identified by their consistent presence on the top-ten lists of overall effectiveness within their parties in each Congress, as well as on the top-ten lists by policy area across all Congresses observed. Although identified based on their success as rank-and-file members, most of these lawmakers subsequently assumed committee chairs or party leadership roles, as may be expected for effective members. These are the members studied qualitatively to uncover the five habits of highly effective lawmakers.

also served in such leadership roles at other points in their careers.[24] Second, the list contains more Democrats than Republicans. This may be due to the fact that the Democrats were in the majority for twelve of the eighteen Congresses we examine. Because most of the top scorers by issue area are from within the majority party, this naturally boosts the likelihood of Democrats on the list. Additionally, as noted in Chapter 3, when in the majority party, Republicans were less interested in

---

[24] For example, Lantos was the chair of the Committee on Foreign Affairs in the 110th Congress; Montgomery was chair of the Committee on Veterans' Affairs from the 97th to 102nd Congresses; Smith was the chair of the Committee on Standards of Official Conduct in the 106th Congress; Waxman was chair of the Committee on Oversight and Government Reform in the 110th Congress; and Young was chair of the Committee on Resources during the 104th–106th Congresses, before becoming chair of the Committee on Transportation and Infrastructure during the 107th–109th Congresses.

concentrating power among committee and subcommittee chairs, resulting in greater variety of members on the top-ten lists.

Third, the list consists entirely of men. Despite our evidence in Chapter 4 of women outperforming men in lawmaking, the small numbers of women in Congress and their lower seniority resulted in fewer women rising onto the top-ten lists repeatedly. Fourth, despite a bias toward majority-party members, there is a good variety of members who succeed repeatedly in the majority party (such as Henry Waxman's eight appearances), the minority party (such as Don Young's nine appearances), or both in the majority and minority party (Tom Lantos, Bill McCollum, and Mark Udall). Finally, while some members are particularly accomplished in a single policy area (Edward Boland in Housing, for example), others achieve great success across multiple policy areas. For instance, both Bill Hughes and Robert Kastenmeier appear on the top-ten lists both for Banking and for Law, Crime, and Family issues.

IDENTIFYING THE HABITS OF HIGHLY EFFECTIVE LAWMAKERS

Having classified twenty lawmakers as being highly effective in comparison to their peers, the questions remain: what did these members do that contributed to their high levels of effectiveness? And what lessons could an aspiring legislator glean from these Representatives' successes in seeking to become a more effective lawmaker? To answer these questions, we studied each of the lawmakers from Table 6.3 systematically and in great depth. Specifically, we closely examined the bills that each of these members sponsored and their fates, both in the Congresses in which the member rose onto our top-ten lists and also in surrounding years. Here, we relied heavily upon information from the Library of Congress THOMAS website, the *Congressional Record*, and contemporaneous media accounts. We coupled this bill-specific analysis with a broader perspective on each lawmaker's political and legislative styles, based on biographies, autobiographies, biographical sketches, and reflections upon the members as lawmakers that typically accompanied their retirements or deaths.[25] Given the extensive number of sources consulted, we limit our specific detailed references only to those instances in which we rely on a unique fact or exact quotation available only from a single source.[26]

---

[25] The most consistent source of biographical and district information across members and over time is offered in the various issues of the *Almanac of American Politics* (e.g., Barone and Ujifusa 1993; Barone, Ujifusa, and Matthews 1973).

[26] Although we rely extensively on primary sources of government documents and secondary media accounts of members and their activities, an alternative approach of interviewing members and their staffs directly has been highly beneficial to some of the best qualitative research on Congress (e.g., Fenno 1978, 1992). Given the time span that we encountered, as well as the fact that many of our subjects were long retired or deceased, our approach offered a more consistent assessment across members. That said, future qualitative work based on member interviews would be a

Emerging from this research are strong and consistent patterns of behavior that many, if not all, members shared. While there is no surefire recipe for success, a consideration of the collective experiences of these members points to five "habits" that are common across these legislators. While some lawmakers excelled based also on other idiosyncratic factors, we discerned these five to be the most regular and common. Most of the lawmakers exhibited many of these habits. Yet we do not argue that they are each either necessary or sufficient. Nor is any particular habit likely to be the most successful approach for any given lawmaker selected at random. Rather, all together, these five habits produced the opportunities that led these members to be the highly effective lawmakers that they ultimately became. While additional scholarship is clearly required before we can definitively say that a particular strategy helps *cause* a legislator to be highly effective, the patterns that we uncover here are instructive in their own right, and they should serve as the foundation for further inquiry.

We highlight each habit in turn before discussing them collectively. In so doing, we offer a lengthy vignette of an archetypal member who consistently and dramatically illustrated the habit, as well as shorter accounts of others who strongly shared the habit.

HABIT 1: DEVELOP A LEGISLATIVE AGENDA ROOTED IN PERSONAL BACKGROUND, PREVIOUS EXPERIENCES, AND POLICY EXPERTISE

Tom Lantos was elected to Congress in 1980 to represent California's 11th congressional district, and served in the House until the time of his death in February of 2008.[27] At the time of his passing, his district (then California's 12th) consisted largely of the area directly to the south of San Francisco, on the Bay Area Peninsula, the constituency of which is known to be socially progressive, yet relatively cautious toward an activist federal government. As parochial

welcome addition to the exploration of the habits we highlight. Likewise, we might also be interested in analyzing what relationships, if any, exist between these legislators' effectiveness vis-à-vis our measure, and the scope of activities that they conduct in the "public sphere" (as defined by Mayhew 2000). While we do not engage in the type of analysis that was pioneered by Mayhew in his analysis of public actions, it is interesting to note that none of the Representatives whom he identifies as "high performers" in the public sphere in the years after 1930 (i.e., Mayhew 2000, 190–191) are among those whom we identify as the top twenty most effective rank-and-file lawmakers. This lack of overlap might be because we exclude current committee chairs and party leaders from our analysis; it might also reflect a possible trade-off between engaging actions in the public sphere and lawmaking. Such topics are certainly worthy of further study.

[27] California's 11th congressional district was linked to a frightening international incident in the late 1970s. It had been represented by Democrat Leo Ryan, who was assassinated in Jonestown, Guyana, shortly before the Jonestown Massacre in 1978. There was a special election for Ryan's seat in 1979, culminating in the election of Bill Royer, a Republican. In 1980, despite being outspent by nearly 30 percent and despite Republican coattails from Ronald Reagan's victory, Lantos won by a few thousand votes.

as most congressional districts, its residents were more interested in local concerns than in foreign affairs. Yet across the nearly three decades that he served in the House, Lantos amassed a reputation as one of the foremost advocates for the protection of human rights throughout the world, and he explicitly advocated the use of American economic and (sometimes) military influence to secure these rights.

Along with Republican John Porter (IL-10), Lantos founded the bipartisan Congressional Human Rights Caucus in 1983. Evincing his profound influence, the caucus was renamed the Tom Lantos Human Rights Commission after his death. Exemplary of his legislative ambitions, Lantos sponsored the Prevention of Genocide Act of 1988 in the 100th Congress (1987–88).[28] His proposal sought to require the United States to suspend trade and oppose any international loan proposals to Iraq, in response to Iraq's treatment (under the rule of Saddam Hussein) of its Kurdish minority. This legislation was introduced nearly two years before Iraq invaded Kuwait, bringing about the first Gulf War. Lantos was clearly tuned in to matters of human rights that were outside of the mainstream focus of contemporary American political discourse. In a similar vein, in the 102nd Congress (1991–92), he introduced legislation that prohibited U.S. aid to Serbia, unless the Serbian government ceased to engage in the ethnic conflicts that were beginning to consume the country.[29] As was the case with Iraq, Lantos was at the forefront of a human rights issue that would ultimately draw worldwide attention. While neither of these measures advanced particularly far, other bills, such as a measure imposing sanctions on Burma, which Lantos introduced in the 108th Congress (2003–04), met with more success.[30]

Indeed, as shown in Table 6.3, Lantos was a particularly effective member across party lines, serving among the top-ten Democrats three times when in the minority party. Figure 6.3 shows the LES Scorecard for Lantos during these three Congresses.[31] His average LES over this period was 1.65, more than four times his party's average. He sponsored seven bills that passed the House and four that became law, a remarkable feat for any minority-party lawmaker.

Why might any individual congressman be so focused on matters of international human rights? And how might he find success in advancing such a legislative program, especially during his time in the minority party? The source

---

[28] See H.R. 5271 for details.
[29] The relevant bill was H.R. 3518, a bill "to restrict United States assistance for Serbia or any part of Yugoslavia controlled by Serbia until certain conditions are met, and for other purposes."
[30] The Burmese Freedom and Democracy Act of 2003 (H.R. 2330, Public Law 108–61) was signed into law by President Bush on July 28, 2003. Lantos had also introduced legislation that would have provided for sanctions against Burma in the 107th (H.R. 2211) and 106th (H.R. 5603) Congresses.
[31] As detailed previously, the LES Scorecard shows frequencies of sponsored bills (BILL), their action in committee (AIC), action beyond committee (ABC), passage through the House (PASS), and enactment into law (LAW), each for commemorative (C), substantive (S), and substantive and significant (SS) legislation.

```
 ┌─────────────────────────────────────┐
 │           The Lawmaker:             │
 │            Tom Lantos               │
 │            (D, CA–12)               │
 │  107th–109th Congresses (averages)  │
 ├─────────────────────────────────────┤
 │              LES: 1.65              │
 ├─────────────────────────────────────┤
```

	C	S	SS
BILL	3.33	14.67	0
AIC	0.33	3.67	0
ABC	0.33	3.33	0
PASS	0.33	2	0
LAW	0.33	1	0

FIGURE 6.3. LES Scorecard for Tom Lantos

Note: The LES Scorecard shows the average number of commemorative (C), substantive (S), and substantive and significant (SS) bills (BILL) that Tom Lantos (D-CA) introduced, as well as how many received action in committee (AIC), action beyond committee (ABC), passed the House (PASS), and became law (LAW), resulting in his Legislative Effectiveness Score (LES), across the 107th–109th Congresses (2001–06).

of Lantos's passion for human rights (and perhaps the reasons for his legislative effectiveness) can be traced back to earlier events in his personal life. Born in Budapest in 1928, Lantos was put into a Nazi forced-labor camp in 1944. He twice escaped, and then fought with the Hungarian underground against the Nazis. With the help of Swedish diplomat Raoul Wallenberg, Lantos survived the Holocaust only to learn that his mother and several other family members had all been killed by the Germans. He ultimately immigrated to the United States on an academic scholarship, where he earned his BA and MA at the University of Washington, and his PhD in economics from the University of California, Berkeley in 1953.

Lantos's career immediately after graduate school consisted largely of being an academic economist. He held a faculty position at San Francisco State University and was a television commentator on foreign policy during the late 1950s and early 1960s. He also served as a policy advisor to the U.S. Senate, and to then-Senator Joseph Biden (D-DE), in particular. Upon entering the 97th Congress as a freshman in 1981, Lantos acquired a seat on the House Foreign Affairs Committee, holding positions on the Asian and Pacific Affairs Subcommittee, as well as the Subcommittee on Europe and the Middle East.[32]

Across the next three decades in Congress, Lantos would cultivate a policy portfolio that centered on human rights and international affairs, and

---

[32] Lantos also acquired positions on the Government Operations Committee and the Select Committee on Aging.

this policy focus was reflected in his committee standing. He was the chair of the International Security, International Organizations, and Human Rights Subcommittee of the Foreign Affairs Committee in the 103rd Congress (1993–94), and he became the ranking member of that subcommittee in the 104th and 105th Congresses (1995–98), after the Democrats lost the House. He ultimately became the ranking minority member on Foreign Affairs for the 107th–109th Congresses (2001–06), from which he achieved his high levels of effectiveness.

More broadly speaking, using his position on the Foreign Affairs Committee, Lantos introduced numerous measures that flowed from his passions for protecting human rights and facilitating and maintaining democratic institutions. His activism was not limited to matters of legislation. For example, he was one of four House members arrested in 2006 for blocking the entrance to the Sudanese embassy in Washington, DC, to raise awareness of the ongoing ethnic conflicts in that region. Many observers noted how his passion for these topics was influenced by his personal background. Given his committee standing, he found himself in a position from which he could exert his influence to advance his legislative priorities.

At the time of his passing, then-Speaker Nancy Pelosi was quick to note how "wherever there was injustice or oppression, [Lantos] used his expertise and moral authority to put the United States on the side of justice and human rights."[33] President George W. Bush posthumously awarded Lantos the Presidential Medal of Freedom, "for a lifetime of leadership, for his commitment to liberty, and for his devoted service to his adopted nation."[34] Developing a legislative agenda that was fueled by personal experiences motivated Tom Lantos to exert the necessary effort to become an expert and advocate for particular policies across the partisan divide. Moreover, his expertise and advocacy efforts were widely appreciated by his colleagues in the House, who looked to him repeatedly for guidance on matters pertaining to foreign policy and human rights.

This general pattern of advocating a legislative agenda rooted in personal background, previous experiences, and policy expertise can be observed among many other highly effective lawmakers. James Corman (D-CA), in the top-ten LESs by party for the 94th through 96th Congresses (1975–80), as well as holding the fifth- and tenth-highest ILES in Welfare Policy, also illustrates this habit.[35] A dedicated lawmaker, Corman sponsored 115 public bills in the 94th Congress, many of which pertained to unemployment policy. Seven of these bills were ultimately signed into law, including the Emergency Compensation and Special Unemployment Assistance Extension Act, as well as bills that created the

---

[33] Retrieved from http://www.democraticleader.gov/issues/human-rights, accessed on June 6, 2013.
[34] Retrieved from http://georgewbush-whitehouse.archives.gov/news/releases/2008/06/20080619-9.html, accessed on June 6, 2013.
[35] Corman was also well regarded for his work on the 1964 Civil Rights Act.

National Commission on Unemployment Compensation and addressed Social Security payments, food stamp eligibility, and the provision of child care services for welfare recipients. Using his position as chairman of the Public Assistance and Unemployment Compensation Subcommittee of Ways and Means during the 95th and 96th Congresses,[36] Corman advanced several other measures that dealt with various aspects of welfare policy.[37] Beyond his legislative successes (or, perhaps, because of them), Corman was viewed as an essential go-to person for welfare policy. For example, he served as chairman of the ad hoc welfare reform committee created by Speaker Tip O'Neill in 1977 to facilitate negotiations over President Carter's proposals for welfare reform.

Such a focus on the poor, the unemployed, and child welfare may be surprising for a congressman such as Corman, who represented a district that ranked among the very top in constituency wealth and education.[38] Yet Corman's background and earlier life offer clues to his welfare lawmaking zeal. Corman's father was a silica miner who died of lung cancer when Corman was very young. As a single parent, his mother moved her family from Kansas to California in the midst of the Great Depression to find work. Being raised under such circumstances made Corman particularly sensitive to the pressing needs of the economically disadvantaged, and his legislative debates often reflected this insight. In one of his obituaries, Corman was described as openly critical of those who portrayed welfare recipients as lazy, or in other uncharitable terms, once stating, "I don't think there is anything uplifting about hunger. ... I really think you need the physical fiber to support the moral fiber."[39] Similar to Lantos, Corman's early life experiences influenced his perspective on how to evaluate and engage certain policies, which served him well as he successfully advocated for meaningful welfare reform in Congress.

Beyond Lantos and Corman, this general habit of developing expertise based on one's personal background is also seen in the legislative portfolios of other highly effective lawmakers. G. "Sonny" Montgomery (D-MS) was a military veteran of World War II and the Korean War, and built on these experiences to become one of the foremost advocates for veterans' affairs and veterans'

---

[36] The Committee on Ways and Means did not have subcommittees until the 95th Congress. At the time Corman was appointed chairman of the Public Assistance and Unemployment Compensation Subcommittee, he also acquired a seat on the Health Subcommittee of Ways and Means.

[37] Notable pieces of legislation that Corman sponsored during this time period include the Emergency Unemployment Compensation Act (H.R. 4800, Public Law 95–19), which established a thirteen-week limit for the receipt of unemployment benefits, and the Adoption Assistance and Child Welfare Act of 1980 (H.R. 3434, Public Law 96–272), which (as the title of the legislation suggests) provided for various payments to partially offset the expenses associated with the adoption and fostering of children.

[38] When Corman was first elected to Congress in 1960, his district (California's 22nd) was located in the San Fernando Valley, and ranked among the top ten for constituency wealth and average education levels (Herbers 1966).

[39] As quoted in Oliver (2001).

benefits. Bruce Vento (D-MN) was successful in pushing environmental conservation measures through Congress, and cited his childhood vacations in the Minnesota wilderness as formative to his perspective on conservation: "We depended on the parks along the St. Croix River. That was our Sunday picnic, our vacation."[40] And Pat Williams (D-MT), who focused his legislative efforts on education, including the expansion of student aid and the recruitment of high quality teachers, drew much of his inspiration from his own experiences as a public school teacher in Butte, Montana.

In each case, these legislators found a policy focus that was drawn from their own experiences, which was personally meaningful to them, and which motivated them to undertake the necessary efforts to develop expertise in these topics. Consistent with the informational theories of legislative organization that we highlight in Chapter 5, the expertise acquired by these members was ultimately recognized and rewarded by their House colleagues in that it facilitated their respective legislative successes and overall effectiveness.[41] Time and again, undertaking efforts to develop expertise rooted in one's personal background seems to arise as a clear habit of highly effective lawmakers.

HABIT 2: DEVELOP A LEGISLATIVE AGENDA
TIGHTLY FOCUSED ON DISTRICT NEEDS

Don Young (R-AK) serves as a role model for effective policymaking within the minority party. First elected to the 93rd Congress (1973–74) as the result of a special election, Young has served as the at-large representative for Alaska for four decades.[42] Prior to his election to Congress, Young had held several jobs, including being a teacher and a tugboat captain in Fort Yukon, Alaska; he had also served as the Mayor of Fort Yukon, as a state representative, and as a state senator in the Alaskan state legislature. Since the time of his first election to Congress, Young has served on the Natural Resources Committee, where he was ranking member during the 99th–103rd Congresses (1985–94), and chairman during the 104th–106th Congresses (1995–2000), following the Republican rise to being the majority party in the House. As shown in Figure 6.2, Young was a

[40] As quoted in Hamburger (1992).
[41] For in-depth theoretical work on information and legislative organization, see Gilligan and Krehbiel (1987) and Krehbiel (1991). Indeed, Krehbiel (1991, 90) points to Sonny Montgomery as an example of a "low-cost specialist" in comparison to his peers, given his prior military experience.
[42] Young had actually run for Congress in the 1972 election, losing to the Democratic incumbent Nick Begich. The details surrounding this defeat are interesting because, in the weeks before the November election, Begich disappeared in a plane (along with House Majority Leader Hale Boggs) over Alaska. Despite being missing (he had not been pronounced dead at the time of the election), Begich beat Young by almost 12,000 votes. A special election was held in March 1973, in which Young ran again; but this time he defeated the Democratic candidate, Emil Notti, with 51% of the vote.

```
┌─────────────────────────────────┐
│          The Lawmaker:          │
│          Don Young              │
│           (R, AK)               │
│  93rd–103rd Congresses (averages)│
├─────────────────────────────────┤
│          LES: 1.90              │
├─────────────────────────────────┤
```

	C	S	SS
BILL	1.82	24.73	0.82
AIC	0.36	5.18	0.55
ABC	0.18	3.45	0.55
PASS	0.18	2.91	0.36
LAW	0.18	1.36	0.27

FIGURE 6.4. LES Scorecard for Don Young

Note: The LES Scorecard shows the average number of commemorative (C), substantive (S), and substantive and significant (SS) bills (BILL) that Don Young (R-AK) introduced, as well as how many received action in committee (AIC), action beyond committee (ABC), passed the House (PASS), and became law (LAW), resulting in his Legislative Effectiveness Score (LES), across the 93rd–103rd Congresses (1973–94).

highly effective chair, above and beyond his earlier success in the minority party. He also sat on the Merchant Marine and Fisheries Committee from the time he was first elected until the committee was abolished in the 105th Congress (1997–98), and he was chair of the Transportation and Infrastructure Committee in the 107th–109th Congresses (2001–06).

From the earliest days of his congressional career, Young was a force to be reckoned with. He was designated the "freshman Congressman of the year" by his colleagues in 1973,[43] and he became one of the top ten most effective rank-and-file members of the Republican Party (as measured by his LES), beginning with his first full term in Congress. Young's LES Scorecard, averaged across his first eleven Congresses, is shown in Figure 6.4. His LES average of 1.90 over this time period is nearly five times that of his minority-party Republican colleagues. Across these 22 years, Young wrote more than 300 pieces of legislation, 20 of which became law. Of those, fifteen were substantive and another three were substantive and significant. His prolific lawmaking outpaced not only his Republican colleagues but also most members of the majority party.

So the question emerges: why was Don Young so effective? As we noted for Habit 1, there are benefits from gaining policy expertise and from issue specialization. Members such as Tom Lantos, James Corman, and Sonny Montgomery were motivated to pursue specific policy agendas because of their earlier life experiences. These experiences led them to acquire expertise about policies that

---

[43] Retrieved from http://donyoung.house.gov/Biography/, accessed on June 5, 2012.

were personally meaningful to them; their expertise ultimately won for them the respect and deference of other members of the House. Likewise, Young also engaged in a specialization strategy. But the policies that he focused on were chosen less from his formative years than from direct ties to his constituency. Bluntly stated, Young clearly pursued the legislative strategy, "All Alaska, All the Time."[44]

On matters pertaining to energy, economic development, and land use, Young used his various committee positions to advocate for, and advance, legislation that spoke to the heart of his constituency's varied needs. For example, nearly all of the bills Young introduced in his freshman term dealt with Alaska-related policy concerns, ranging from cost-of-living adjustments for Social Security payments for those living in Alaska to advocating for the creation of a Trans-Alaskan oil pipeline.[45] In the 95th Congress (1977–78) he advanced to law legislation that addressed shortcomings in the Alaska Native Claims Settlement Act that had been passed in 1971; in both the 1980s and 1990s, he subsequently advocated for further changes that were incorporated into laws.[46] He was a strong proponent of expanding oil and gas exploration in Alaska, and sponsored several bills that would have facilitated exploration in the coastal plain of the Arctic National Wildlife Refuge.

Other examples of Alaskan interests advanced by Young include subsistence use of federally protected lands in Glacier Bay National Park, and economic restitution for the losses incurred by residents of the Aleutian and Pribilof Islands during World War II.[47] In these and many other matters, Young maintained a singular focus on his constituency. He identified what issues affected them, assessed what policies could be created to address their needs, and aggressively pursued the promulgation of these policies.

Cultivating such a firm constituency-based policy portfolio clearly paid dividends for Don Young. On many of the bills that he introduced, he could credibly speak to the virtues associated with the measures in a manner that was elusive to most other members of the House. And his high level of effectiveness, particularly remarkable for those Congresses in which he was in the minority

[44] One wonders whether lawmakers from other small states (such as North Dakota) may benefit from sharing the exact same constituencies as U.S. senators from their states, thus forging perhaps a tighter bond that allows for better House-Senate coalition building, crucial to Habit 5, to be discussed.
[45] Specifically, H.R. 10279, "A bill to amend title V of the Social Security Act to provide that, in making certain allotments to States thereunder, there shall be taken into account the higher cost of living prevailing in Alaska and Hawaii," and H.R. 6756, the Trans-Alaskan Pipeline Authorization Act, addressed these issues.
[46] Specifically, his H.R. 8849 became Public Law 95–178, and he also wrote legislation that became Public Law 100–241 and Public Law 102–415.
[47] Specific introductions in these areas include: H.R. 3156, a bill "to amend the Alaska Natural Interest Lands Conservation Act to improve the management of Glacier Bay National Park, and for other purposes," in the 102nd Congress; H.R. 704, a bill "to regulate fishing in certain waters of Alaska," in the 103rd Congress; H.R. 4322, the Aleutian and Pribilof Islands Restitution Act, in the 98th Congress; and H.R. 2415, the Aleutian and Pribilof Islands Restitution Act, in the 99th Congress.

party, suggests that the House deferred to his wisdom on these matters.[48] Electorally, this legislative effectiveness on behalf of the people of Alaska seemed to benefit Young's incumbency. In the twenty general elections between 1974 and 2012, Young's Democratic opponent only came within ten percentage points on four occasions. More frequently, Young more than doubled the number of votes of his nearest opponent. Being neither uncontested nor in electoral peril placed Young in the ideal position to generate the high degree of effectiveness illustrated back in Figure 2.3 of Chapter 2.

Several other highly effective lawmakers followed a constituency-focused policy agenda strategy. Jim Saxton (R-NJ) cultivated a policy agenda that was focused largely on matters of natural resources, waterways, and fisheries, which resonated with the interests of his coastal New Jersey district (New Jersey's 13th, at the time of his retirement). Likewise, a notable portion of Saxton's legislative agenda focused on defense and armed forces matters. While most readers do not often think of military and environmental matters as walking hand in hand, such a combination makes sense when considering the composition of Saxton's district. Indeed, as he noted in 2007, "The two biggest industries in Burlington and Ocean Counties are the defense of the country and tourism ... the single biggest employer is the Department of Defense and related industries ... and without a clean environment [the tourism] industry suffers."[49] While Saxton was well-known for his influence in ensuring that South Jersey's military bases remained open in light of closure threats throughout the 1990s, his efforts to promote environmental awareness and protection were so notable as to draw accolades from a wide range of environmental groups. In fact, a conference room at the Jacques Cousteau Education Center in Tuckertown, New Jersey, was named after Saxton in honor of his retirement from Congress in 2008.[50]

Many others developed this constituency-centered habit, as well. For example, Tom Udall (D-NM) focused most of his legislative agenda on resource conservation, with an emphasis on water management, which was highly relevant for his New Mexico constituency. Robert Kastenmeier (D-WI) dedicated a substantial portion of his legislative attention to intellectual property matters,

---

[48] When the Republicans took over the House beginning with the 104th Congress, Don Young continued to be a highly effective legislator, using his position as chair of the Resources Committee (104th–106th Congresses) and Transportation and Infrastructure Committee (107th–109th) to facilitate the passage of more than fifty bills that he sponsored into law. Notoriously, one of the bills that he sponsored while chair of the Transportation and Infrastructure Committee provided for the "Bridge to Nowhere" in Ketchikan, Alaska, which would have connected Ketchikan with the island of Gravina for nearly $400 million (nearly $200 million of which would have come from congressional appropriations).

[49] As quoted in Colimore (2007).

[50] Retrieved from http://www.landtrustalliance.org/events-news/northeast-news/saxton-honored, accessed on July 8, 2013.

which was a major policy concern for the University of Wisconsin-Madison, housed in his congressional district. For each of these legislators, the overwhelming majority of their legislative attention was devoted to the needs of their constituencies. Cultivating a constituency-oriented portfolio allowed these members to acquire expertise about different policy topics at a relatively low cost. Such expertise appears to have been appreciated by their peers, leading to their enhanced effectiveness.

In contrast to such highly effective lawmakers, the easiest way to generate a low (indeed zero) Legislative Effectiveness Score is to give up entirely on the introduction of legislation. At one level, this may seem like a rational response to the repeated policy failure that members confront. Especially early in their careers, lawmakers propose dozens and dozens of bills that go nowhere, often without so much as a hearing or a vote. Yet in order to succeed, members must pick themselves up, dust themselves off, and try, try again. It is no surprise then that Habits 1 and 2 offer the formula for perseverance. For those members who came to Congress with a deep-seated burning problem or wrong in the world that they dedicated their lives to remedy, failure is not an option. And for members seeking reelection, pursuing a legislative agenda based on district interests should come naturally.

The most highly effective members serve as models of perseverance in these two ways. Many introduce the same legislation in Congress after Congress. Hamilton Fish (R-NY), for example, introduced legislation aimed at establishing a national exchange system for adoption information in five successive Congresses, despite failing to attract a single cosponsor in any Congress.[51] Many more learn from their failures and modify their bills and strategies to build broader coalitions the next time around. For example, Henry Waxman (D-CA) introduced two bills in 1981 aimed at preventing smoking through enhanced public education efforts, such as requiring health warning labels on cigarette packages. Both bills attracted more than fifty cosponsors and were the subject of subcommittee hearings, but failed to advance any further in the process.[52] In the next Congress, however, Waxman introduced legislation that provided for similar educational efforts, but had one notable change – the new bill removed a provision that gave individuals the right to bring civil suits for violations of the act.[53] Similar to earlier legislation, this new bill attracted more than fifty cosponsors and was the subject of subcommittee hearings. It went further, to ultimately pass the House and Senate (in modified form) and

[51] More specifically, A bill to establish a national adoption information exchange system was introduced by Fish as H.R. 403 in the 94th Congress, H.R. 364 in the 95th Congress, H.R. 318 in the 96th Congress, H.R. 1905 in the 97th Congress, and H.R. 572 in the 98th Congress.
[52] The bills were H.R. 4957, Comprehensive Smoking Prevention Education Act of 1981, and H.R. 5653, Comprehensive Smoking Prevention Education Act of 1982.
[53] The bill was H.R. 1824, the Comprehensive Smoking Prevention Act.

become law.[54] By continuing to introduce legislation across Congresses, and learn from failures when they arose, these legislators' hard work and perseverance paid off well beyond that of their less resolute colleagues.

HABIT 3: BE ENTREPRENEURIAL WITH POSITIONS
OF INSTITUTIONAL POWER

William "Bill" Hughes (D-NJ) was elected in 1974 to represent New Jersey's 2nd District, serving until his retirement in 1994. He was ranked among the top ten most effective rank-and-file legislators within the Democratic Party five times, comprising half of his entire career in the House. He also was among the top ten both in the Banking and in the Law, Crime, and Family policy areas. During his twenty years in Congress, Hughes was a member of the Judiciary Committee and the Merchant Marine and Fisheries Committee. His appointment to both of these committees seems appropriate, given his district's coastal location and his previous occupation as Assistant County Prosecutor in Cape May County throughout the 1960s.

In considering the broad snapshot of Hughes's legislative portfolio across his twenty years in Congress, it is clear that much of his sponsored legislation reflected his committee assignments. On matters of crime and intellectual property, he sponsored bills that addressed issues such as the use of false identification, gun crimes, government fraud, and computer-related crimes; he also sponsored measures dealing with copyright protection. On maritime matters, he introduced a wide range of legislation on ocean dumping, as well as on monitoring and cleanup policies following such dumping. It is not surprising that Hughes would cultivate a policy portfolio to reflect his committee assignments. Because members presumably have greater influence over those bills that are referred to their own committees, one would think that such a committee-focused strategy would be helpful for advancing bills through the legislative process.[55] What makes Hughes's case so distinctive, however, is how finely tailored the bulk of his legislative activities were to his positions as subcommittee chair.

More specifically, as a member of the Judiciary Committee, Hughes served as chair of the Crime Subcommittee from the 97th to 101st Congresses (1981–90), before moving on to become the chair of the Intellectual Property and Judicial Administration Subcommittee during his final two Congresses. While serving as the chair of the Crime Subcommittee, Hughes introduced a wide range of legislation that fell under the jurisdiction of that subcommittee; many of these

[54] Following subcommittee hearings on H.R. 1824, the Subcommittee on Health and the Environment of the Committee on Energy and Commerce forwarded H.R. 3979, the Comprehensive Smoking Education Act (also sponsored by Waxman) onto the full committee, which was ultimately passed by the House, Senate, and signed into law (P.L. 98–474).
[55] A formal empirical test of the hypothesis and its surrounding implications would likely be fruitful future research.

bills found their way into law. For example, his bills on fake IDs, computer fraud, child sexual abuse, and undetectable firearms all became law.[56] Each of these bills was considered by the Crime Subcommittee of the Judiciary Committee.

Upon taking over as chair of the Intellectual Property and Judicial Administration Subcommittee in the 102nd Congress (1991–92), Hughes shifted his policy focus considerably. While he continued to introduce bills that were under the purview of the Judiciary Committee, the most prominent pieces of legislation that he introduced (and those that were ultimately signed into law) were those that worked their way through his new subcommittee. Examples of such legislation include the Incarcerated Witness Fees Act of 1991 and the Copyright Royalty Tribunal Reform Act of 1993.[57] Quantitatively, of the seventy bills that Hughes introduced prior to becoming a Judiciary subcommittee chair (94th–96th Congresses), only twenty were referred to the Judiciary Committee (and none of those bills were referred to any subcommittees). In contrast, nearly 60 percent of the bills that Hughes introduced between the 97th and the 103rd Congresses were referred to the Judiciary Committee, with a strong bias toward the subcommittees that he chaired. Fully half of the bills that he introduced between the 97th and 101st Congresses that were referred to the Judiciary Committee were ultimately referred to the Crime Subcommittee; and 90 percent of the bills that he introduced into the 102nd and 103rd Congresses that were referred to the Judiciary Committee were ultimately referred to Hughes's new subcommittee. Moreover, when Hughes was chair of the Crime Subcommittee, none of the bills that he introduced engaged matters pertaining to intellectual property; a similar pattern holds once he took over as chair of the Intellectual Property and Judicial Administration Subcommittee – he effectively washed his hands of crime policy.

Figure 6.5 shows the LES Scorecard of Bill Hughes averaged across his seven terms as subcommittee chair. His overall LES averaged 6.07, more than four times that of the average majority-party member. He advanced into law twenty of his sponsored pieces of legislation, twelve of which were both substantive and significant. That Hughes used his committee power effectively is evidenced in his degree of Action in Committee (AIC). In Chapter 3, we noted that the average majority-party member receives action in committee on 11.2 percent of her bills (compared to 5.5 percent for minority-party members). In contrast, Hughes received action in committee on an astonishing 51.4 percent of his bills.

---

[56] Specifically, Hughes sponsored the False Identification Crime Control Act of 1982 (H.R. 6946, Public Law 97–398), the Contract Services for Drug Dependent Federal Officers Authorization Act of 1983 (H.R. 2173, Public Law 98–236), the Computer Fraud and Abuse Act of 1986 (H.R. 4718, Public Law 99–474), the Child Sexual Abuse and Pornography Act of 1986 (H.R. 5560, Public Law 99–628), and the Undetectable Firearms Act of 1988 (H.R. 4445, Public Law 100–649).

[57] For details, see H.R. 2324, Public Law 102–417, and H.R. 2840, Public Law 103–198.

The Lawmaker:
Bill Hughes
(D, NJ–2)
97th–103rd Congresses (averages)

LES: 6.07

	C	S	SS
BILL	0.86	25.29	8.29
AIC	0.14	9.57	8
ABC	0.14	2.29	7.71
PASS	0.14	1.57	6
LAW	0.14	1	1.71

FIGURE 6.5. LES Scorecard for Bill Hughes
Note: The LES Scorecard shows the average number of commemorative (C), substantive (S), and substantive and significant (SS) bills (BILL) that Bill Hughes (D-NJ) introduced, as well as how many received action in committee (AIC), action beyond committee (ABC), passed the House (PASS), and became law (LAW), resulting in his Legislative Effectiveness Score (LES), across the 97th–103rd Congresses (1981–94).

Without a doubt, tailoring his legislative agenda to match his institutional position yielded substantial lawmaking benefits.

In many ways, Habit 3 complements the earlier habits. The first two habits highlighted the perseverance and specialization of lawmakers, developing expertise in areas of great concern to themselves and their constituents. To the extent that Congress is well organized, members should be assigned to committees and subcommittees from which they can effectively use such expertise. When Hughes's background as a prosecutor closely matched his institutional position, it proved to be a powerful combination. That said, Hughes was also sufficiently flexible in changing the nature of his portfolio to suit his subcommittee assignments and his positions of power. This may be more difficult for other lawmakers who develop expertise in a narrower policy area.

The habit of being entrepreneurial with positions of power is not confined to majority-party members. Even members of the minority party (who therefore do not chair committees or subcommittees) can benefit from aligning their policy agendas and their institutional positions. John Duncan, Sr. (R-TN), for example, served in Congress from 1965 until 1988, and was ranked among the top ten most effective (rank-and-file) Republicans for four of those Congresses. For most of his tenure in Congress he held a seat on the Committee on Ways and Means, where he was ranking Republican for the 99th and 100th Congresses (1985–88). Many of his most prominent legislative successes are directly attributable to his sponsored bills being referred to Ways and Means. Examples include administrative improvements in the Medicare program and aid for those with black lung disease.[58] More broadly, between the 93rd and 100th Congresses, more than half of Duncan's bills were referred to Ways and Means. Given the expansive jurisdiction of Ways and Means, Duncan clearly had the opportunity to engage a wide range of policy areas, and to exercise greater influence over policy outcomes in these areas than those members who were in less-desirable committee positions.

Related to this point, the policy for which Duncan is best known serves as the exception that proves the rule. Seemingly well beyond the jurisdiction of Ways and Means was the Tellico Dam Project, a Tennessee Valley Authority project in Duncan's district impacting the habitat of the endangered snail darter fish. Construction on the project was suspended following the Supreme Court's ruling in *TVA v. Hill* (1978) that found that Tellico had violated provisions of the Endangered Species Act of 1973. Duncan attempted to reverse the Court's ruling by introducing legislation in the 95th and 96th Congresses (1977–80) that would have exempted the Tellico Dam project from the Endangered Species Act. Neither of these measures was passed, but Duncan was ultimately successful in using his institutional position to attach an amendment to an appropriations measure in 1979 that provided for an exemption for the Tellico Dam. Hence, while the policy area was effectively unrelated to Ways and Means, Duncan leveraged his institutional advantages to ensure that his policy goals were met.[59]

Many other highly effective lawmakers cultivated Habit 3. For some of these members, such as Henry Waxman (D-CA), their specific policy agendas stemmed from personal commitments to changing the status quo. For other members, such as Robert Kastenmeier (D-WI), who was discussed in Habit 2, their policy agendas had clear ties to the priorities of their constituents. Regardless of the source of these policy priorities, whether engaging matters such as immigration (Lamar Smith, R-TX), health (Paul Rogers, D-FL), or numerous others, all of these members utilized their institutional positions in ways that enhanced the scope of their policy portfolios and increased the relative probability that their bills advanced to the next step in the legislative process.

A tailored legislative agenda is by no means the only way to be entrepreneurial with positions of institutional power, however. For example, Waxman pulled out all the stops in advancing to law his Orphan Drug Act in the early 1980s. He knew that drug companies often abandoned the production of helpful pharmaceuticals that served only small populations, due to insufficient profits, and that government incentives could help. Public awareness of the problem was also on the rise, as it was featured on an episode of the wildly popular "Quincy,

---

[58] For details, see, in particular, H.R. 13501, Public Law 94–368, and H.R. 13167, Public Law 95–488.

[59] Moreover, Duncan successfully partnered with Senator Howard Baker (R-TN) to bolster support for the amendment in the U.S. Senate and subsequent conference negotiations (Cain and Kaiser 2003). His work with Baker is illustrative of Habit 5, cultivating allies beyond the House, explored later in this chapter.

M.E.," starring Jack Klugman. To capitalize on this attention, Waxman held subcommittee hearings with Klugman as a star witness, quickly winning House passage for his bill. As a deal maker, he gained the support of the pivotal Senator Orrin Hatch (R-UT) by agreeing to include an amendment for cancer screening tests of Utah residents exposed to radiation during nuclear weapons testing in the 1950s. When further objections arose in the Senate, "Quincy" aired a second episode featuring fictitious heartless politicians. Finally, to overcome a potential veto threat from President Reagan, Waxman, Klugman, and others joined in efforts that included full-page ads in major newspapers and a Christmas Eve press conference.[60]

While we highlight leaders in this chapter who were identified apart from their positions as committee chairs or party leaders, such institutional positions are also extremely valuable with respect to Habit 3. The tools of these leaders include: deciding which bills to obstruct and which to advance, tailoring a broad or narrow agenda, advertising issues and developing expertise through committee hearings, altering legislative content with amendments and markups, and restricting the institutional powers of opponents, to name a few. Effective use of the right tool at the right time helps chair and non-chair alike to become the type of policy entrepreneurs we identified in Chapter 5. In all such cases, the coupling of institutional powers with legislative priorities serves as a recipe for effective lawmaking.

HABIT 4: BE OPEN TO COMPROMISE, EVEN WITH
THOSE WHO ARE NOT NATURAL ALLIES

Hamilton Fish (R-NY) was a lawmaker who was both willing and able to reach across the party aisle to bring about broad compromises. First elected to Congress in 1968, Hamilton Fish IV represented much of the lower Hudson River Valley (New York's 28th at the time of his election).[61] He carried with him a long family tradition in the House. His father (Hamilton Fish III) had represented the same constituency from 1920 to 1944, and was a staunch opponent of the Roosevelt administration. His grandfather had also served in the House; his great-grandfather had served in the U.S. House, the Senate, as governor of New

---

[60] The details of this episode and of Waxman's entrepreneurial lawmaking are highlighted in Cohn (1981), Waxman and Green (2009), and Williams (1983).

[61] Fish's opponent in the 1968 Republican primary was G. Gordon Liddy, later infamous for organizing the Watergate burglaries, setting in motion the eventual resignation of President Nixon. After he was elected to the House, Fish actually sent a letter to the Nixon administration recommending Liddy for a job. As noted in the 1974 *Almanac of American Politics*: "[Fish] can scarcely be blamed for Liddy's subsequent activities. The now-famous man was fired from a post in the Treasury Department when he spoke out against the Administration's policy towards gun control. So the people who hired him at the White House and the Committee to Reelect the President had every reason to know what kind of nut they signed on" (Barone, Ujifusa, and Matthews 1973, 709–710).

York, and as secretary of state under President Ulysses S. Grant. After facing a relatively challenging electoral landscape early in his career, the fourth Hamilton Fish went on to serve in the House until his retirement in 1994.

While Fish had come from a long line of prominent Republicans, including his father, who had a very acrimonious relationship with Democrats (and the president, in particular), Fish established a new path for himself. In 1974, for example, he was one of the first to break from the Republican Party and vote in favor of Nixon's impeachment in the Judiciary Committee. He was consistently identified as a fiscally conservative, yet socially liberal, Republican who (in many cases) advocated for policies that found common ground with Democratic Party priorities. The majority of Fish's policy portfolio engaged topics such as housing, civil rights, energy, and conservation, which at times put him at odds with members of his own party. For example, the many bills that he introduced across his time in Congress included legislation that provided for a minimum annual income for citizens over the age of sixty-five, cost of living adjustments for government benefits, extensions of unemployment benefits, and emergency health benefits for the unemployed.[62] Figure 6.6 shows Fish's LES Scorecard for the eight Congresses that include his five appearances on our top-ten lists.

One of his more notable legislative accomplishments during this time period was facilitating the passage of the Fair Housing Act Amendments of 1988.[63] The legislation provided for enhanced enforcement of the 1968 Fair Housing Act, while also expanding its scope to prohibit discrimination of mentally or physically handicapped individuals as well as families with children. Fish's involvement on this piece of legislation is instructive regarding the virtues of compromise. Due largely to the threat of Republican opposition in the Senate, civil rights leaders had been hesitant to push for changes in the Fair Housing Act during the early years of the Reagan Administration. With the Democratic takeover of the Senate in the 1986 elections, however, civil rights advocates realized that the time was ripe for change; and legislation was introduced into the

---

[62] Prominent examples of these sorts of initiatives include: H.R. 434, "A bill to amend title II of the Social Security Act to provide that the automatic cost-of-living increases in benefits which are authorized thereunder may be made on a semiannual basis (rather than only on an annual basis as at present)," H.R. 5875, the Emergency Health Protection Act, H.R. 11976, "A bill to provide an additional 26 weeks of benefits under the emergency unemployment compensation program," and H.R. 14589, "A bill to provide an additional 26 weeks of benefits under the emergency unemployment compensation program," in the 94th Congress; H.R. 876, "A bill to amend title II of the Social Security Act to provide that the automatic cost-of-living increases in benefits which are authorized thereunder may be made on a semiannual basis (rather than only on an annual basis as at present)," and H.R. 879, "A bill to amend the Social Security Act to provide for a minimum annual income (subject to subsequent increases to reflect the cost of living) of $3,850 in the case of elderly individuals and $5,200 in the case of elderly couples," in the 95th Congress; and H.R. 329, "A bill to amend title II of the Social Security Act to provide that the automatic cost-of-living increases in benefits which are authorized thereunder may be made on a semiannual basis (rather than only on an annual basis as at present)," in the 96th Congress.

[63] For further details, see H.R. 1158, Public Law 100–430.

```
┌─────────────────────────────────────┐
│            The Lawmaker:            │
│          Hamilton Fish              │
│           (R, NY–25/21)             │
│   94th–101st Congresses (averages)  │
│ ┌─────────────────────────────────┐ │
│ │          LES: 1.18              │ │
│ └─────────────────────────────────┘ │
│        ┌──────┬───────┬──────┐      │
│        │  C   │   S   │  SS  │      │
│   BILL │ 3.13 │ 37.37 │ 0.87 │      │
│   AIC  │ 0.75 │  3.13 │ 0.63 │      │
│   ABC  │ 0.75 │  0.37 │ 0.50 │      │
│   PASS │ 0.75 │  0.37 │ 0.50 │      │
│   LAW  │ 0.50 │  0.25 │ 0.50 │      │
└─────────────────────────────────────┘
```

FIGURE 6.6. LES Scorecard for Hamilton Fish
Note: The LES Scorecard shows the average number of commemorative (C), substantive (S), and substantive and significant (SS) bills (BILL) that Hamilton Fish (R-NY) introduced, as well as how many received action in committee (AIC), action beyond committee (ABC), passed the House (PASS), and became law (LAW), resulting in his Legislative Effectiveness Score (LES), across the 94th–101st Congresses (1975–90).

House and Senate, sponsored by Representative Fish and Senator Ted Kennedy (D-MA), respectively. While both parties agreed that the existing fair housing law was too weak and that enforcement was impracticable, debates quickly emerged as to how best to strengthen the law's provisions.

At the heart of the issue was who would bear the responsibility for enforcement. Under the terms of the 1968 act, the Department of Housing and Urban Development (HUD) handled complaints, but the scope of its enforcement authority was so limited that victims of alleged bias had to file private lawsuits on their own, which could be quite expensive. The legislation that was introduced by Fish (and Kennedy) would enhance the administrative and enforcement capacity of HUD, appointing administrative law judges to deal directly with allegations of discrimination and bias. The Reagan Administration was opposed to this proposal, preferring instead to endow the Department of Justice (DoJ) with the authority to file lawsuits on behalf of alleged victims of discrimination. Proponents of the HUD option were concerned that enforcement would be very slow and costly under Reagan's proposal. In the words of Fish, the administration and the Congress "both recognize the 1968 act was toothless with respect to enforcement ... [but] judicial enforcement would be expensive and takes time ... our approach gives people a very fast remedy."[64] As a compromise, the bill that was ultimately advanced by Fish in the House and was signed into law actually provided for both methods of enforcement, offering

---

[64] As quoted in Kurtz (1987).

the prospect of both short-term remedies through HUD and long-term deterrence through DoJ, and addressing the concerns of those individuals who were hesitant to cede all enforcement authority to HUD. Fish was identified by all parties as being crucial to the passage of the legislation. Indeed, as some observers noted, Fish played "a pivotal role in reaching compromises ... neither [the Fair Housing Act Amendments nor the Americans with Disabilities Act in 1990] would have passed without Fish's work."[65]

In these and many other instances, Fish distinguished himself from many of his colleagues by being willing to reach across the aisle and find mutual ground that could serve as the foundation for legislative compromises. That this type of legislative style was becoming increasingly difficult over time was not lost on Fish. On the eve of his retirement from Congress, Fish claimed that his personality was better suited for the "less confrontational more pragmatic political style of a minority leader." In his own words, he stated, "I'm not a confrontational person so I don't know if I would have been a more successful person as a member of the majority. I doubt it."[66]

That said, compromise need not only come from those in the minority party. For example, John Breaux's (D-LA) successes on environmental policy arose from his work across party lines, an approach that he carried with him into the U.S. Senate. Breaux's record on environmental legislation put him in a distinctly conservative faction among Democratic lawmakers. Given the importance of the gas, oil, fishing, and sugar industries to his district's (and state's) economy, Breaux often advocated for policies that raised the ire of more-liberal interest groups. Indeed, during his fourteen years in the House, his average Americans for Democratic Action score was a mere 14.5 (out of 100); while his average American Conservative Union score was approximately 65. Given his conservative position among Democrats, he was often courted by Republican interests (presidents included) on crucial votes, which enhanced his ability to advance his agenda.[67]

Many other highly effective lawmakers also learned the value of being nonconfrontational in their legislative styles, even to the point of promoting policies that deviated from the mainstream of their respective parties' agendas. Silvio Conte (R-MA), for example, strongly advocated for increased spending for various social programs and reductions in defense spending. This policy agenda, of course, put him completely at odds with the dominant players in the Reagan Revolution during the 1980s. Likewise, Jim Saxton's (R-NJ) record on conservation issues placed him well outside of the Republican mainstream. Such

---

[65] As quoted in Barone and Ujifusa (1993, 909).
[66] As quoted in Henneberger (1994).
[67] One of the most quotable remarks by Breaux emerged surrounding his well-publicized support for the Reagan administration's tax cuts in exchange for favorable natural gas and sugar subsidy policies in 1981, when he quipped that his vote was not for sale, but was "available for rent" (Dowd 2001).

legislators had to find potential allies among members of the opposing party. In his recent autobiography, Henry Waxman (D-CA) argues that Paul Rogers (D-FL) was such an effective subcommittee chairman because he essentially ignored the respective party affiliations of his subcommittee members, encouraged broad feedback from all attendees during committee hearings, and did his best to incorporate said feedback into the bill before it was reported out of subcommittee.[68] As a result, whatever bills emerged from the process had significant buy-in from legislators on both sides of the aisle, helping to ensure their further progression toward law.[69] And, as we established with respect to minority-party women in Chapter 4, the benefits of consensus building extend beyond the most highly effective members. Collectively, these lawmakers' experiences speak to the value of actively seeking out potential opportunities for compromise and consensus.

One might fear, however, that Habit 4 is no longer viable for lawmakers as Congress has become a more polarized institution. We believe that drawing such a conclusion would be a mistake. Among our highly effective lawmakers in Table 6.3 are five (Tom Lantos, Lamar Smith, Mark Udall, Tom Udall, and Don Young) who were in our top-ten lists for the 109th or 110th Congresses (2005–08). Each party controlled one of these Congresses, and both were quite polarized. Despite such institutional challenges, however, these effective lawmakers continued to illustrate the value of an openness to compromise. To illustrate this point, in Table 6.4 we detail the final passage votes on the bills sponsored by these lawmakers.

Collectively, these members forged strong bipartisan compromises. On their thirty-five final-passage votes, twenty-three had sufficient support to produce passage without any member requesting a roll-call vote. Another eleven received bipartisan support, averaging merely five nay votes from members of the opposing party to the sponsor. Only one of these legislative proposals divided the two parties. Lamar Smith's (R-TX) Lawsuit Abuse Reduction Act of 2005, aimed at reducing frivolous lawsuits and limiting venue shopping, tended to be opposed by trial lawyers and attracted only sixteen House Democrats. Although the bill passed the House, it died in committee in the Senate.

While not as contentious as Smith's proposal, the thirty-four bills attracting strong bipartisan support were not aimed at trivial matters by any means. They dealt with species conservation and marine mammals. They addressed international concerns in Iran, Afghanistan, and Burma, as well as nuclear nonproliferation and promotion of the Peace Corps. They tackled water and energy

---

[68] For details, see Waxman and Green (2009, 29–30).
[69] More generally, Waxman (Waxman and Green 2009, 220) argues in the conclusion of his autobiography that one reason for his success as a lawmaker has been his practice of "seeking out members of good will with whose views I disagree"; he offers advice to potential lawmakers that echoes with some of the habits that we advance, when he argues that "patience, a knack for finding allies (especially unlikely ones), and the ability to persevere for very long stretches are the qualities that ultimately distinguish the best legislators" (Waxman and Green 2009, 223).

TABLE 6.4. *Highly Effective Lawmakers Build Broad Support, Even in Partisan Times*

Sponsor Name	Congress, Bill Number	Democratic support	Republican support
Tom Lantos (D-CA)	109th, H.R. 3858	167–1	181–23
Tom Lantos (D-CA)	110th, H.R. 390	224–0	190–1
Tom Lantos (D-CA)	110th, H.R. 885	Voice vote	Voice vote
Tom Lantos (D-CA)	110th, H.R. 1400	209–12	188–4
Tom Lantos (D-CA)	110th, H.R. 1469	Voice vote	Voice vote
Tom Lantos (D-CA)	110th, H.R. 1681	Voice vote	Voice vote
Tom Lantos (D-CA)	110th, H.R. 2446	216–5	190–5
Tom Lantos (D-CA)	110th, H.R. 3528	Voice vote	Voice vote
Tom Lantos (D-CA)	110th, H.R. 3887	222–0	183–2
Tom Lantos (D-CA)	110th, H.R. 3890	Voice vote	Voice vote
Lamar Smith (R-TX)	109th, H.R. 420	16–178	212–5
Lamar Smith (R-TX)	109th, H.R. 683	190–5	220–3
Lamar Smith (R-TX)	109th, H.R. 1036	Voice vote	Voice vote
Lamar Smith (R-TX)	109th, H.R. 4709	188–0	220–0
Lamar Smith (R-TX)	109th, H.R. 4742	Voice vote	Voice vote
Mark Udall (D-CO)	109th, H.R. 432	No objection	No objection
Mark Udall (D-CO)	109th, H.R. 1129	Voice vote	Voice vote
Mark Udall (D-CO)	109th, H.R. 2110	Voice vote	Voice vote
Mark Udall (D-CO)	109th, H.R. 5110	Voice vote	Voice vote
Mark Udall (D-CO)	110th, H.R. 49	224–0	185–0
Mark Udall (D-CO)	110th, H.R. 902	Voice vote	Voice vote
Mark Udall (D-CO)	110th, H.R. 903	Voice vote	Voice vote
Mark Udall (D-CO)	110th, H.R. 1462	Voice vote	Voice vote
Mark Udall (D-CO)	110th, H.R. 6063	228–0	181–15
Tom Udall (D-NM)	109th, H.R. 3817	Voice vote	Voice vote
Tom Udall (D-NM)	109th, H.R. 4841	Voice vote	Voice vote
Tom Udall (D-NM)	109th, H.R. 4876	Voice vote	Voice vote
Don Young (R-AK)	110th, H.R. 50	Voice vote	Voice vote
Don Young (R-AK)	110th, H.R. 830	Voice vote	Voice vote
Don Young (R-AK)	110th, H.R. 831	206–0	176–0
Don Young (R-AK)	110th, H.R. 865	Voice vote	Voice vote
Don Young (R-AK)	110th, H.R. 1006	Voice vote	Voice vote
Don Young (R-AK)	110th, H.R. 1036	Voice vote	Voice vote
Don Young (R-AK)	110th, H.R. 1114	Voice vote	Voice vote
Don Young (R-AK)	110th, H.R. 3352	196–0	112–60

Note: The table lists all final passage votes for the bills sponsored in the 109th and 110th Congresses (2005–08) by representatives on our list of the top-twenty highly effective lawmakers. In contrast to common perceptions of bitterly divided partisan lawmaking, these effective members cultivated strong bipartisan support for their legislative proposals.

policy, reauthorized NASA, and sought to modernize the American Red Cross. They confronted major issues of the information age, ranging from trademarks and copyrights to telephone records and privacy protections. In sharp contrast to the notion of majority-party proposals shoved down the throats of silenced minority-party members, these bipartisan proposals of the most effective law-makers light a different path forward. This path involves cultivating the habit of openness to compromise, even with those who are not natural allies. And it results in legislative successes time and time again.[70]

HABIT 5: CULTIVATE A BROAD SET OF ALLIES, EVEN BEYOND THE HOUSE

Mark Udall (D-CO) was elected to the House in 1998 (to represent Colorado's 2nd District). Mark was the son of prominent Arizona Congressman Mo Udall, who served in the House from 1961 to 1991, who so ably chaired the Natural Resources Committee (Figure 6.2), and who ran for president in 1976.[71] Prior to his election to Congress, Mark Udall had served as the executive director of the Colorado Outward Bound School, and was elected to the Colorado State House in 1996. Shortly thereafter, the Democratic incumbent of Colorado's 2nd (Representative David Skaggs) announced his retirement, and Udall tossed his hat into the ring. He won the Democratic primary with 44 percent of the vote, and went on to win a fiercely contested general election by less than 5,000 votes. Perhaps due to his closely divided district, Udall sought out a broad set of political allies both from within the House and beyond.

Across the ten years that he served in the House, prior to his 2008 election to the Senate, Mark Udall held seats on five different committees. Udall used these various platforms to set a legislative agenda that closely mirrored the needs and concerns of his district. Most notably, he advocated for conservation and for policies that would facilitate environmental stewardship, devoting special atten-tion to expanding the scope of wilderness protection in Colorado. Attesting to his willingness to reach across party lines, Udall was ranked within the top-ten rank-and-file Democrats as a minority-party member in the 107th through 109th Congresses (2001–06). Yet his bipartisanship did not sully his reputation among his copartisans. Indeed, Udall remained among the top ten most effective rank-and-file Democrats once his party gained majority status in 2007.

---

[70] Yet another illustration of the potential virtues of being open to compromise can be demonstrated in recent scholarship by Dietrich (2012), who identifies that legislators who engage in contentious or "angry" behaviors on the floor of the House are less likely to be centrally located on sponsorship-cosponsorship networks, which appears to be related to the scope of their legislative successes.

[71] Mark is a cousin of Tom Udall (D-NM) and also of Senator Gordon Smith (R-OR). Moreover, Tom was the son of Stewart Udall, who had served as a member of the House from 1955 to 1961, and as Secretary of the Interior in the Kennedy and Johnson administrations.

What might explain Mark Udall's notable success? Consistent with Habits 1 and 2, Udall cultivated a policy portfolio with tight ties to his constituency, as well as of personal importance to himself. An avid rock climber and outdoors enthusiast, much of his legislative portfolio engaged issues that resonated with his own interests and passions. Such specialization efforts would be expected to facilitate some degree of deference on the part of his House colleagues. And of course, there was the benefit that followed from his family's reputation. As noted by a journalist who is a close follower of Denver politics: "The magic of the Udall name is certainly one of the reasons that a junior member from the minority party has vaulted to having one of the highest profiles in the Colorado delegation. And he is gaining in national stature as an heir to his father's conservation record."[72]

Putting these obvious positives aside, several of Udall's high-profile legislative successes arose based on cultivating a further lawmaking habit – namely, reaching out to and partnering with senior allies outside of the House chamber. For example, his most prominent early success was the passage of the James Peak Wilderness and Protection Area Act in the 107th Congress (2001–02).[73] The act amended the Colorado Wilderness Act of 1993 to designate certain lands in the Arapaho and Roosevelt National Forests as the James Peak Wilderness Area, establishing them as federally protected territory. Successfully navigating the legislative waters to advance this environmental legislation was an impressive accomplishment, particularly for a second-term congressman.

At the dedication ceremony for the passage of the law, Udall was quick to credit other lawmakers, Representative Scott McInnis (R-CO) and Senator Ben Nighthorse Campbell (R-CO), as instrumental in ensuring the legislation's success. Udall openly acknowledged that he "couldn't have carried [the] legislation to fruition ... without the help of my colleagues, Congressman McInnis and Senator Campbell in particular."[74] McInnis, serving as chair of the House Subcommittee on Forests and Forest Health, helped to facilitate a compromise among Grand County Commissioners (the relevant local authority), which had been elusive for several years; Campbell ran with the ball once the legislation advanced to the Senate. As per Habit 4, Udall reached across party lines. As per Habit 3, McInnis and Campbell used their institutional positions to advance policies they favored. Perhaps most notably (and reflecting Habit 5), the coalition-building effort in support of Udall's bill stretched well beyond the House, both to the Senate and to local governments. This was crucial, as relatively local issues stand a much greater chance of success in Congress once all of the interested local actors reach an agreement.[75]

---

[72] These family connections are further discussed in Soraghan (2001).
[73] For details, refer to H.R. 1576, Public Law 107–216.
[74] As quoted in Lipsher (2002).
[75] Burns et al. (2009) demonstrate this phenomenon with respect to how states govern major cities.

This strategy of seeking allies beyond the chamber was on display again in the efforts that Udall undertook to secure the establishment of the Rocky Flats Wildlife Refuge. The Rocky Flats defense installation was located northwest of Denver and had operated from the 1950s until the late 1980s, manufacturing plutonium triggers for nuclear weapons. The plant was shut down in 1989 following an FBI raid that investigated health and environmental safety viola-tions at the facility; the area was designated as a Superfund site by the EPA shortly thereafter. Early in the 106th Congress (1999–2000), Udall introduced a bill to prohibit development within a buffer zone around Rocky Flats and to establish an advisory council to come up with a long-term management solution for the Rocky Flats site.[76] Nearly a year later, Senator Wayne Allard (R-CO) described a plan for establishing a wildlife refuge in and around the Rocky Flats site. In realizing that they had similar goals, Udall and Allard decided to intro-duce identical pieces of legislation into the House and Senate – respectively, H.R. 5264 and S. 3090 – to advance their cause. While relatively little action was taken in the 106th Congress (as these bills were not introduced until September 2000), they introduced similar bills early in the 107th Congress to greater success. More specifically, Allard used his position as a member of the Senate Armed Services Committee to attach the Rocky Flats Wildlife Refuge legislation to the 2002 defense spending bill that was working its way through his commit-tee. In Allard's words: "I saw an opportunity to move the Rocky Flats Wildlife Refuge Bill along in the legislative process and took advantage of that oppor-tunity."[77] The final bill passed through the House and the Senate in December 2001, and was signed into law by President Bush.[78]

Although he did not receive LES credit for this law, Udall benefited on policy grounds from finding a partner outside of the chamber, one who was in a position of influence, to advance his agenda. In many other instances, Udall's connections facilitated the passage of his own bills out of committee, through the House, and into law. Figure 6.7 shows Udall's LES Scorecard across the 107th through 109th Congresses (2001–06), during which he was in the minority party's top ten. His average score was 2.00, about five times the minority party average. In the majority party in the 110th Congress, Udall's LES rose further, to 2.93. And he parlayed his early effectiveness into a successful run for the U.S. Senate in 2008.

The lessons learned and habits developed by Mark Udall seemed to mirror those of his cousin, Tom Udall (D-NM). Tom entered the House with Mark in 1998 and also transitioned to the Senate in 2008. While only serving five terms in Congress, Tom Udall saw seven of his sponsored bills signed into law. Developing close working relationships with a variety of senators, Udall was also able to ultimately incorporate key aspects of his proposals into the measures

---

[76] For details of Udall's bill, see H.R. 2179.
[77] As quoted in Denver Post Washington Bureau (2001).
[78] See Public Law 107–107.

```
          The Lawmaker:
          Mark Udall
           (D, CO–2)
  107th–109th Congresses (averages)

          LES: 2.00

              C      S     SS

   BILL    0.67    32     0

   AIC       0    3.33     0

   ABC     0.33   3.67     0

   PASS    0.33   2.67     0

   LAW     0.33    1       0
```

FIGURE 6.7. LES Scorecard for Mark Udall
Note: The LES Scorecard shows the average number of commemorative (C), substantive (S), and substantive and significant (SS) bills (BILL) that Mark Udall (D-CO) introduced, as well as how many received action in committee (AIC), action beyond committee (ABC), passed the House (PASS), and became law (LAW), resulting in his Legislative Effectiveness Score (LES), across the 107th–109th Congresses (2001–06).

of other lawmakers. For example, Udall introduced legislation into the 107th Congress (2001–02) that expanded Medicaid eligibility for Native American women, which was thereafter incorporated into Senator Jeff Bingaman's (R-NM) bill, and ultimately signed into law.[79] In the 108th Congress (2003–04), he introduced public lands legislation that was incorporated into a bill introduced by Senator Pete Domenici (R-NM) and also signed into law.[80] And, reaching beyond his home state, Udall's bill on the Northern Rio Grande National Heritage Area introduced into the 109th Congress (2005–06) was incorporated into legislation that had been introduced by Senator Craig Thomas (R-WY) and was ultimately signed into law.[81]

The experiences of the Udalls illustrate the more general advantages that can be gained by cultivating allies outside of the House. To be an effective lawmaker in the U.S. separation-of-powers system, it is not enough to have a good idea and generate sufficient support among one's colleagues in the House. To see one's ideas advanced into law, it is also necessary to secure the support of pivotal players outside of the House – namely, a (potential) supermajority in the Senate (in the event of contentious policy debates), and the president. On this point, several of the highly effective lawmakers on our list, such as Silvio Conte and John Breaux, were often called upon by presidents in the case of tight votes, and

[79] For details, see H.R. 1383, Public Law 107–121.
[80] See Public Law 108–66.
[81] For details, refer to H.R. 732, Public Law 109–338.

in some cases negotiated directly with the executive branch to facilitate passage of legislative programs.[82] Breaux's interactions with the executive branch became even more notable after he moved to the Senate in 1987, where he often built bridges to Republican presidents that many of his Democratic colleagues could not.

Identifying plausible allies in these different institutional settings, either because of shared constituencies, policy goals, or governing philosophies, is a valuable skill and a necessary hurdle that must be overcome for legislators who seek to become effective in lawmaking. Whether these allies are based on race, gender, or geographic proximity, as explored in Chapter 4, or on other considerations, will depend on the specific lawmaker and the issue at hand. What does not vary, however, is the fact that a broad set of coalition partners is needed to facilitate effective lawmaking.

CONCLUSIONS AND FUTURE DIRECTIONS

Why are some members of the House of Representatives more effective at lawmaking than others? Earlier in this book, we demonstrated how a member's effectiveness was correlated with her party status, gender, race, seniority, institutional positions, and several other factors. Building on this analysis, we engaged several of these findings at a more granular level to identify the particular source of the advantage (or disadvantage) that corresponded to these factors. For example, we demonstrated that members of the majority party are generally more effective than members of the minority because of the advantages that their bills experience while in committee. This ensures that more majority-party sponsored legislation ends up being reported to the floor, benefiting majority-party members over their minority-party counterparts. Regarding gender effects, we identified that the advantage that female legislators experience is largely confined to women in the minority party. Further inspection revealed that minority-party women were more successful than their male colleagues at advancing their bills through those stages in the legislative process that relied on compromise and bargaining. Taken together, these findings suggest that male and female legislators generally engage in different types of legislative strategies, and the strategies embraced by women are particularly valuable when they are in the minority party.

Through these and other analyses, we started to develop a picture of what factors contribute to a Representative's legislative effectiveness, and why those factors matter. While such findings are clearly important in their own right, and they help inform us about the causes and consequences of legislative effectiveness, they do not explain everything. As we noted at the beginning of

---

[82] Edward Boland (D-MA), in part because of his personal ties to Tip O'Neill, was also known to have the ear of the Kennedy administration, working closely with administration officials to facilitate the passage of various legislative priorities.

TABLE 6.5. *Five Habits of Highly Effective Lawmakers*

Habit 1: *Develop a legislative agenda rooted in personal background, previous experiences, and policy expertise.*
Habit 2: *Develop a legislative agenda tightly focused on district needs.*
Habit 3: *Be entrepreneurial with positions of institutional power.*
Habit 4: *Be open to compromise, even with those who are not natural allies.*
Habit 5: *Cultivate a broad set of allies, even beyond the House.*

this chapter, there are a collection of legislators who are particularly effective at moving their proposals through Congress; and their respective strength in lawmaking does not entirely follow from those factors that we have identified as being influential for facilitating effectiveness. Bluntly stated, some lawmakers have essentially transcended their personal circumstances and institutional positions, or (alternatively) have capitalized on them in a way that is uncommon to their peers, so that they emerge as being among the most effective lawmakers in Congress. What is their secret? Why are they so effective? What makes them leaders in advancing bills through the legislative process?

To engage these questions, we took a largely *inductive* approach. That is, we let the LES data tell us who these highly effective lawmakers were and let their actions and narratives tell their own success stories. Our role was merely to piece together the common themes emerging across these narratives. More specifically, we set aside committee chairs and party leaders, focusing instead on rank-and-file lawmakers in both the minority and majority parties. We then identified those who were consistently among the most effective legislators Congress after Congress or within a particular substantive policy area. In then documenting the individual and collective experiences and histories of these twenty highly effective lawmakers, certain patterns emerged that pointed to the actions, tactics, and strategies that these legislators employed across their years in Congress to facilitate their extraordinary legislative success.

The five habits that we uncovered are listed in Table 6.5. To an extent, despite our inductive approach, these five could almost have been discerned *deductively*, based on a theory of lawmaking. That is, when we initially constructed our Legislative Effectiveness Scores, we based them on five crucial stages of the lawmaking process: bill introduction, action in committee, action beyond committee, passage through the House, and enactment into law. The five habits of highly effective lawmakers seem to reflect these stages. For instance, Habits 1 and 2 offer the reasons why members of Congress introduce the bills that they do, whether due to their personal backgrounds, previous experiences, policy expertise, or district needs. Clearly, members who are not motivated by these sorts of considerations to introduce legislation will not be as active and ultimately as effective as those who develop such habits.

Habit 3 speaks directly to the need to guide legislation through the committee process, often based on the institutional positions of highly effective members on key committees or as chairs of subcommittees most relevant to their legislative ambitions. Habit 4 reflects the need to build coalitions, for success both in committee and also on the floor. And Habit 5 relates clearly to the need to continue the lawmaking process beyond the House itself.

Put simply, although we set out on the journey of this chapter in a careful and systematic way, we did not know where it would lead. Now that we have reached the end, we see that the conclusions we have uncovered were perhaps foreshadowed by the broader legislative effectiveness project in which we are engaged, and are intimately linked to the measurement strategy we employed.[83] The highly effective lawmakers achieved their success because of the many ways in which they excelled at each of the five stages we previously identified as crucial to the lawmaking process.

That said, buried within these five habits are more-detailed keys to success. Parsimoniously stated, the most effective legislators specialize in their policy agendas; that specialization sometimes follows from their personal experiences, while other times it follows directly from their constituents' needs. Following this specialization strategy, the most effective legislators have also developed expertise and cultivated a policy portfolio that tightly corresponds to the jurisdictions of their committees. Independent of specialization efforts, many of the most effective legislators have appreciated the virtue of compromise, and have benefitted from embracing perspectives that, at times, were at odds with their party's mainstream positions. But, in reaching beyond the confines of their party and ideology, they cultivated a coalition that helped to move their bills onward through the legislative process both in the short- and long-term. The most effective lawmakers also learned that they can only push their bills so far in the House. To achieve lawmaking success, their initiatives must find support in the Senate (and ultimately in the White House), and these members proactively sought partnerships beyond the House chamber to ensure that their agendas maintained momentum after passing the House.

The five habits developed here collectively suggest lessons that other legislators might embrace if they aspire to be policymaking leaders in Congress. While some of them might seem obvious, others take practice. For example, just as young writers are told, "Write what you know," so, too, should new lawmakers develop an agenda based on personal experience and expertise, especially as it relates to their district's needs. In terms of institutional positions, lawmakers can

---

[83] These habits also speak to lawmaking activities that are not as easily measured as those used to construct our scores, such as influencing the content of other members' legislation, negotiating deals behind the scenes, or building broad coalitions. The fact that a qualitative assessment of the most effective lawmakers uncovers these factors reinforces that our measure of effectiveness, while based mainly on bill sponsorship, may well be capturing a broader set of activities crucial to legislative effectiveness.

affect the degree to which their legislative portfolio matches their committee and subcommittee assignments, from which they can exert more influence.[84] Members who do not get their preferred committee assignments thus face a choice: whether to embrace their current assignment or to develop the expertise and good favor within the party in order to strive toward a future reassignment.

Finally, lawmakers can choose their allies as well as the degree to which they are willing to compromise in order to advance their agendas. Thinking more broadly, across party lines and beyond the House, has served our highly effective lawmakers very well. Again, this implies a potential trade-off. Are a member's constituents willing to see her work outside of the party? Would they rather see legislative accomplishments coupled with compromises or ideological purity coupled with legislative gridlock? In our view, most lawmakers have the electoral leeway to choose their own path. Whether they recognize that leeway and choose to become highly effective as lawmakers, or whether they take the perhaps-safer road leading to legislative stalemate, is a choice they must make on a daily basis. Such is the nature of developing lawmaking habits.

Beyond such practical advice, the habits presented here point the way toward further scholarly research. As we noted at the beginning of this chapter, the qualitative approach we embrace here not only fleshes out the previous chapters' quantitative findings but also sets the stage for further empirical examinations. Our work here, while intriguing and suggestive, does not fully establish the value of the habits we highlight. Indeed, our approach is clearly vulnerable to the criticism that it "selects on the dependent variable." That is, by focusing only on the behaviors of the most highly effective lawmakers, we are unable to definitively characterize a recipe for legislative success for all members of Congress. It is possible, for example, that the least effective lawmakers exhibit many of the same habits as their highly effective colleagues, but with very different outcomes.[85]

Now that these habits have been identified, it would be beneficial to test their value systematically, perhaps through quantitative analyses. This could be done by using these habits as building blocks toward developing a theory of legislative leadership in Congress. Alternatively, the habits themselves could serve as the basis for more-direct empirical examinations. For example, one might assess the

---

[84] In their seminal work on committee politics, Deering and Smith (1997, 61) note that, upon arriving in Congress, "for nearly all members, appropriate committee assignments are essential to a successful stay on Capitol Hill." Moreover, their analysis reveals that newly elected members "distinguish among committees based on personal aspirations and goals" (p. 63).

[85] Indeed, many qualitative assessments of leaders, more broadly construed, face this same critique. In our view, as part of a broader scholarly endeavor, our approach is a valuable building block. It should not, however, be thought of as the definitive word on how to become an effective lawmaker. Nonetheless, given the extent to which the habits we uncover here match the stages of lawmaking central to our quantitative work, and match the insights from effective lawmakers themselves (e.g., Waxman and Green 2009), we feel confident that we are on the right path, and that future work will likely attest to the importance of these five habits.

value of Habits 1 and 2 by analyzing the relationships between the diversity of a Representative's legislative agenda and her effectiveness. If specialization truly contributes to legislative effectiveness, then one would expect that those members who focus their attentions on relatively narrow policy portfolios would have higher LESs than those who have relatively diffuse policy agendas, all else equal. Intermediate steps along the way may be useful, as well. Do members who have legislative portfolios linked more closely to their backgrounds or district needs persevere in their bill introductions more fully over time? Are they better able to attract cosponsors to such proposals? Do they seem to cultivate greater expertise in these issues areas?

Similar analyses could be employed to assess the usefulness of Habit 3, regarding the relationships between legislative portfolios and committee or subcommittee memberships. How much does targeting a legislative agenda to a member's institutional position influence her overall legislative effectiveness? Which members are best at tailoring such portfolios and why? Is this habit something that all members develop as they gain experience in Congress? Does it help minority-party members in particular, given their clear disadvantage at the committee stage of the lawmaking process? Habits 4 and 5 could be examined, perhaps, with cosponsorship networks in the House, with media accounts of close relationship between House and Senate members, or with further investigations of mechanisms for overcoming House-Senate differences. Moreover, are the five habits individually valuable, or only of use when they are brought together in particular combinations?

In addition to exploring these possibilities in a more systematic manner, this chapter also motivates other questions that are important to the overall working of Congress. For example, if the habits uncovered here are reasonably accurate predictors of legislative success, why are they not embraced by *all* legislators? Does it take time for members to learn that employing these strategies can help them advance their agendas, and is that learning process enhanced or harmed by the broader organization of Congress? Alternatively, is it the case that only particular subsets of Representatives actually seek to be effective lawmakers; hence, should we not naturally expect all members of the House to engage in these types of strategies, even if well aware of their payoffs? The answers to such questions are crucial to better understanding when, why, and how Congress as a collection of its many lawmakers might be effective at creating laws in the best interests of the American people.

7

The Future of Legislative Effectiveness

"Well, Doctor, what have we got – a Republic or a Monarchy?" "A Republic, if you can keep it."
    – An exchange with Benjamin Franklin, at the close of the Constitutional
    Convention of 1787

"The House of Representatives is very human. It is a responsive audience; it can be moved to tears and give itself up to laughter, but its mood is merely of the moment. The clamor of party bitterness can be hushed or laughed at under the magic of the skilled orator, and when his voice no longer charms or amuses, passion again rages. It is a curious assemblage, this House of ours."
    – Speaker of the House Joseph "Uncle Joe" Cannon (R-IL)[1]

The U.S. Congress is a remarkable and uncommon institution of representative democracy. Far more common are parliaments with electoral systems based on proportional representation. In many such systems, party members are placed on a list for elections. How many members off that list are selected into the parliament depends on their party's proportional vote nationwide. The parties in parliament work to form governing coalitions, appointing the prime minister and cabinet. And that government's leaders and bureaucrats then formulate the policies to be approved by the parliament, typically on party-line votes. For who would want to vote against his party and be left off the party list in the next election?

In contrast, in the U.S. Congress, each seat is won by an individual, perhaps aided by her party, but perhaps not. These legislators do not appoint the executive, nor do they serve as mere rubber stamps for policies handed down from the president. Rather, policies come from these members themselves – members who are closely linked to their constituents through a tight electoral connection. These representatives take ideas from their past experiences, from

---

[1] Quoted in Busbey (1927, 303).

their constituents, or from other interested groups and individuals, formulate them into bills, and help shepherd those bills through committees, onto the legislative calendar for the chamber, through a final passage vote, and into law. Members of the U.S. Congress are, in a word, *lawmakers*. Once elected, they are mainly limited only by the quality of their ideas and by their ability to persuade others that their vision is the right one for the nation.

While these facts are commonly understood and often taught, the crucial role of members of Congress as lawmakers has too frequently been understated or pushed aside. Explorations of political parties, representation, coalitions, and gridlock have largely neglected such a lawmaking role, instead often treating members of Congress solely in terms of their ideological positions or their party affiliations. In such a view, no ability is required to formulate better policy solutions. No skill is required to build coalitions. No member is seen as more effective than any other.

Yet without recognizing that members' lawmaking role is the keystone of American legislative behavior, we suffer from an inadequate understanding of the institutional structure of the U.S. government, and of the policies that it produces. For example, the vast bureaucratic structure of the U.S. federal government has arisen from a Congress seeking to govern a growing nation confronting increasingly complex policy problems. The size and structure of bureaucratic agencies can only be understood relative to the lawmaking capabilities of members of Congress, who are seeking to rely on the outside expertise and extensive reach of administrative agencies. Similarly, the internal structures of Congress arise from the lawmaking roles of members. For instance, the power of committees comes from their ability to block or to shape legislation. Political parties facilitate the goals of party members only to the extent that lawmakers reach compromises across the disparate goals of individually elected members. And, in terms of policy choices, once again, members of Congress as lawmakers play a central role. The policies that govern the American state come from the lawmakers themselves.

As we look across the many national governments around the world, we see a diverse set of institutional structures, but also a common set of challenges. Many countries face growing or aging populations, with rapidly rising health care costs and unsustainable social programs. Most face inevitable budgetary constraints that arise from having pushed off spending cuts or tax increases for too long; instead, they have built up significant national debts that serve as a drag on the economy, and a potential burden for future generations. Global concerns also continue to mount, whether based on extremist ideologies combined with advanced weaponry, scarce resources and climate change, or informational security in an increasingly connected world. Governments can attempt to address these issues proactively or wait until they must respond to what have become crises.

For a nation that has entrusted its path forward to elected lawmakers, the question arises as to whether members of Congress are up to the task demanded of them. Is there sufficient legislative effectiveness among the senators and representatives in key institutional positions to address these numerous policy concerns in ways that serve the best interests of the American people? The complete answer to this question is beyond the scope of the work that we have undertaken in this book. Yet in our view, this question and other key questions about American democratic governance cannot be answered adequately without refocusing our efforts toward understanding Congress as an institution comprised of lawmakers. We make such an argument throughout this book, generating scores that measure members' lawmaking effectiveness, and illustrating the usefulness of such scores in understanding political parties and committees, representation, the role of race and gender, and how to overcome policy gridlock. We also highlight the habits that members can cultivate to become highly effective legislators. In so doing, we hope to begin a new conversation about the U.S. Congress.

NEW APPROACH, NEW QUESTIONS

We believe that our approach, and a focus on the lawmaking activities of members of Congress more generally, opens a new set of questions and debates for the scholarly community. Here we highlight but a few of the questions that we hope scholars will start to address as part of a larger "legislative effectiveness project."

The Electoral Connection

It is safe to say that most members of Congress are highly motivated to seek reelection.[2] To what extent does becoming an effective lawmaker aid in such efforts? Thus far, we have only explored the opposite question: to what extent does electoral safety help determine which members are highly effective? In response to that latter question, we found that neither the members facing the toughest electoral challenges nor those going entirely unchallenged were the most effective members. Rather, lawmakers with moderately safe seats were the most effective legislators, presumably because they felt some pressure to legislate while also having the latitude to dedicate themselves to lawmaking rather than solely to electioneering.

But the opposing question is certainly an intriguing one. Surely, part of being an effective lawmaker involves addressing voters' needs and district problems. For instance, we documented how Bart Stupak (D-MI) helped tackle the growing drug use crisis among teenagers in Northern Michigan and how Don Young (R-AK) directed immense resources back to his home state. Yet, do voters reward such effective lawmaking? An exploration of whether more effective incumbents' vote shares exceed those that would otherwise be expected based on the quality of their challengers and the nature of their constituents would be a

---

[2] The successful exploration of members of Congress through the lens of reelection seeking was begun most significantly by Mayhew (1974).

welcome advance.[3] Perhaps more-effective lawmakers perform better at the polls, face fewer challenges, or are more likely to retain their seats. Or perhaps their effectiveness allows them the leeway to become even more effective in the future, granting them the freedom to reach out across party lines to forge compromises, even if such actions place them out of step with their legislative districts.[4] Disentangling the direction of causality between electoral and law-making successes may prove difficult. Moreover, the answer may be a conditional one, that effectiveness in some policy areas is more highly rewarded in the electoral arena than effectiveness in other areas. And yet, these questions are well worth exploring to the best of scholars' current ability.

However, such explorations may be a bit premature. Political science research has produced extensive evidence that voters may be insufficiently informed to detect which lawmakers should receive credit for which legislation.[5] That said, it seems highly likely that voters would be willing to consider not only the party and ideological stances of the candidates they are selecting for office, but also how effective those candidates would be as lawmakers. Political scientists have increasingly relied upon experiments to discern the extent to which changes in the information available to voters affect their likelihood of voting and their vote choices.[6] Embedding descriptions of the legislative effectiveness of lawmakers into survey-based experiments may serve as a natural extension.

Furthermore, we find it highly plausible that politicians themselves would be interested in promoting their candidacies based on their legislative effectiveness. Candidates have long relied on credit claiming, and are often inventive in the lengths to which they go to make the case that they are influential on behalf of voters.[7] It would be surprising, therefore, if the most highly effective lawmakers did not use systematic measures of effectiveness, either ours or others yet to be developed, to promote their electoral chances. Similarly, challengers to the least effective lawmakers might likewise emphasize their opponents' woeful records. While certainly not the only criterion that voters should use in their choices, the complete absence of unbiased information about lawmaking effectiveness is surely not leading to better representation. As elections become more highly contested, information about the success of campaigns emphasizing legislative

---

[3] Jacobson (1999) offers a useful overview of the politics of congressional elections.

[4] Such conjectures comport well with the rapidly developing theoretical literature on the role of valence in electoral competition (e.g., Ashworth and Bueno de Mesquita 2009; Groseclose 2001; Meirowitz 2008; Wiseman 2005, 2006). Canes-Wrone, Brady, and Cogan (2002) offer significant empirical evidence that members of Congress who deviate too far from the ideological positions of their districts suffer in the electoral arena.

[5] Delli Carpini and Keeter (1996) offer a useful overview of (and new research on) the question of Americans' political knowledge and its importance.

[6] Gerber and Green (2000) helped launch the experimental movement in the study of American politics; and a recent consideration of the field is offered by the essays found in Druckman et al. (2011).

[7] Fenno (1978) and Mayhew (1974) explore members' credit-claiming activities both in general and in specific cases.

effectiveness would be of interest to candidates, campaign managers, and scholars alike.[8]

Legislative Organization

Once elected to Congress, legislators more fully assume their roles as lawmakers seeking to navigate the norms, structures, and institutions in which they find themselves. Seniority, committee service, and party affiliation all play influential roles in the lawmaking process. For example, unsurprisingly, we found members of the majority party to be much more effective than those in the minority party. Yet rather than merely being outvoted on the floor, outmaneuvered by clever majority-party leaders, or outnumbered on their side of the ideological spectrum, minority-party members suffered the most from simple neglect. Their bills did not receive attention in committee and typically succumbed to an unceremonious death.

Yet substantial variance within the parties led to some intriguing inquiries. For example, we found that not all majority-party members performed equally well. Indeed, the Southern Democratic faction of the Democratic Party was brushed aside in the 1980s, due in no small part to its conservative stance and past obstructionism. Within the minority party, we found women substantially outperforming their male counterparts, due to their willingness to engage in consensus building across party lines. We also found that time spent in the minority party cultivating policy expertise and tailoring a legislative agenda to one's committee and subcommittee assignments was often rewarded.

Given the value of expertise, the role of seniority, and the importance of congressional committees, one is left to wonder: is Congress as a whole organized so as to be an effective institution of lawmaking? For example, are the lawmakers who would best lead key committees placed in such leadership positions, even if not the most senior member of the committee? Is the expertise of minority-party members rewarded and effectively utilized in the lawmaking process, even if such members do not share all of the end-goals desired by majority-party leaders?[9] And, are the members with the greatest policy expertise assigned to the committees and subcommittees from which they can best use their expertise to solve major policy problems?

Initial answers to such questions could be offered through a careful consideration (and perhaps reconstruction) of the Legislative Effectiveness Scores that we create here. For instance, just as we generated policy-specific scores for each of nineteen issue areas, so too could one construct committee-specific legislative effectiveness scores. With such measures in hand, scholars could explore the

---

[8] Sasha Issenberg (2012) offers a lively account of the political parties experimenting with different techniques to run effective electoral campaigns.
[9] Krehbiel (1991) offers a theoretical and empirical account of the legislative organization of Congress centered around the development of informational expertise in committees.

202 *Volden & Wiseman*

extent to which members on or off certain committees excel in lawmaking within those committees' jurisdictions. From there, it would be straightforward to ascertain whether non-committee members who are effective at lawmaking in a particular committee's jurisdiction are better able to secure a reassignment to such a committee than are those who do not excel in advancing committee-relevant legislation.[10] If so, this would provide evidence of congressional committees being constituted in ways to promote the matching of expertise and effectiveness with positions of institutional power. If not, such evidence would reaffirm the view that Congress is a "broken branch" for effective policymaking.[11]

Conditions For Policy Change

Beyond an alignment between member expertise and institutional power, another key aspect of legislative effectiveness involves coalition formation. In building coalitions, there is often no single dominant legislative strategy. For instance, we found that a variety of potential natural coalitions varied substantially in the strategies they adopted. African Americans decided to diversify their strength, seeking scattered representation across the most powerful congressional committees rather than concentrated power over issues of greatest interest to their constituents. Southern Democrats often utilized blocking coalitions, whereas minority-party women tended to reach across party lines.

In looking at the most highly effective lawmakers, we found that the development of expertise, the willingness to compromise with opponents, and the generation of allies beyond the House of Representatives were all very helpful in the coalition-building stages of the lawmaking process. With respect to policy gridlock, we found that political entrepreneurs, willing to take on the toughest issues, gained a reputation for action that attracted coalition partners. Such partners often felt that, if any policy was likely to advance through to law, it would be the policy sponsored by such entrepreneurial leaders. Thus, these entrepreneurs' bills would be the ones to which their coalition partners would try to attach their own agenda items, and the ones they would subsequently endorse and work to advance.[12]

While many of these claims follow smoothly from our analyses across the chapters, other aspects of such descriptions could be examined far more systematically. For instance, to what extent does success breed success? Are members whose bills succeed in one Congress more likely to attract more cosponsors in future Congresses, and more likely as a result to achieve further success? Put

[10] Shepsle (1978) offers a compelling assessment of the committee assignment process, quantitatively accounting for many of the well-known causes of reassignment and advancement across committees.

[11] Mann and Ornstein (2006) argue that Congress is failing the American people due to its polarization and overall dysfunction.

[12] In this view, the bills of entrepreneurs would be akin to the must-pass legislation central to Adler and Wilkerson's (2013) work or to the omnibus bills that Krutz (2001) studies.

another way, how can members build reputations as the go-to people on specific issues, apart from their institutional positions as committee or subcommittee chairs?

At the individual level, to what extent do members take stock of their own legislative achievements and learn from their early successes and failures? We found that more-effective freshmen were much more likely to generate a personal sense of progressive ambition and to seek higher office in the near future. In contrast, less-effective freshmen were more likely to abandon the whole enterprise and voluntarily retire from the House. But along the way, do members position themselves for legislative success based on their prior experiences? Here, a study of the legislative portfolios of members may be instructive.[13] For instance, if a lawmaker performs very well on environmental policymaking in one Congress, does she dedicate a larger portion of her portfolio to environmental issues in subsequent Congresses? And, is such dedication short-lived, or is it something that accumulates over time? Do new leaders in specific policy areas emerge from their earliest successes, gaining confidence with their rising issue attention and expertise, and finally peaking as the most effective members later in their careers?

Measuring Legislative Effectiveness

To reach the conclusions summarized above, we developed and utilized what we termed Legislative Effectiveness Scores. These scores focused on lawmakers' bill introductions and on the advancement of their bills in committee, to the floor, beyond the House, and into law. Commemorative bills were downgraded and significant bills were upgraded in assigning an overall score for each member in each Congress. These scores largely captured the share of all lawmaking activities in each Congress attributable to each member based on her sponsorship activities.

We believe the construction of these scores to be a significant advance over previous approaches, such as merely accounting for the percentage of a member's bills that become law.[14] They offer a more holistic view of the legislative process, and allow us to isolate the importance of different stages of lawmaking. For instance, this approach helped us identify committee action as central to the enhanced legislative success of members in the majority party. We were able to locate the success of minority-party women in the key coalition-building stages of helping their bills reach the floor and pass the House. And we found that gridlock varied substantially across particular issue areas because of their different rates of success across legislative stages.

---

[13] Such a study might build upon the approach of Sulkin (2005), who examines how members' policy portfolios reflect the issues highlighted in their electoral campaigns.
[14] However, we benefited substantially in our approach from considering numerous excellent earlier works on legislative effectiveness (e.g., Anderson et al. 2003; Cox and Terry 2008; Frantzich 1979; Matthews 1960; Moore and Thomas 1991; Padro i Miquel and Snyder 2006; Weissert 1991a).

Volden & Wiseman

The scores we construct therefore are an important breakthrough in the evolution of the study of legislative effectiveness. That said, we do not believe that such an evolution is at its end. Similar to how measures of ideological positions moved from interest group ratings based upon a few key votes to increasingly sophisticated analyses of all votes in Congress, so, too, will measures of legislative effectiveness continue to improve.[15] In our view, such measures will advance as scholars find adaptations useful for the specific questions they seek to address. For example, to address policy gridlock, we found it useful to generate separate scores by issue area. As we speculated earlier in the book, scholars may likewise wish to generate legislative effectiveness scores for each committee, in order to explore the causes and effects of committee assignments.

Our hope is that such adaptations are merely the beginning. As congressional scholars become better able to discern the direction and extent of policy changes relative to underlying status quo positions, effectiveness and ideology could be coupled, with scores then measuring each lawmaker's effectiveness in moving policy in a liberal or conservative direction. Likewise, where the budgetary consequences of particular bills have been scored by the Congressional Budget Office or others, members' effectiveness in addressing (or exacerbating) budget deficits could be measured. More broadly, for legislative proposals that are evaluated on cost-benefit grounds, members could be evaluated not only for their abilities to advance *any* legislation, but also for the extent to which the legislation they advance serves the needs of the American people.

As such measures advance, we expect that the assignment of credit to particular members of Congress will improve as well. As we discuss in Chapter 2, the scores we offer change very little if we also account for amendments offered on the floor of the House. That said, for bills offered by chairs on behalf of their committees, scholars could attempt to better track which members are responsible for which items. For amendments across the House and Senate that substitute significant amounts of language to reach bicameral consensus, scholars could trace the extent to which the language of various original bills finds its way into the final agreements.[16] In each case, the credit assigned to members could better reflect their true underlying ideas and effectiveness.

Our effectiveness scores are also biased toward the advancement of legislative initiatives, discounting the effectiveness of members in obstructing what they perceive to be the bad ideas of their political opponents. Here again, future scholarship may offer new paths forward. For instance, given the power of committee and subcommittee chairs, one could track which bills find their way out of which committees. Were the bills of Southern Democrats denied floor

---

[15] We see the key transformation in ideal-point measurement to have arisen from the work of Poole and Rosenthal (1997). Yet researchers continue to seek to improve upon such initial measures, as part of what we believe to be a constructive scientific scholarly process (e.g., Clinton, Jackman, and Rivers 2004).

[16] Wilkerson, Stramp, and Dashiell (2012) offer fruitful work in this direction.

access by particularly liberal committee and subcommittee chairs? Are different bills likely to advance through subcommittees chaired by women than by men? Do ideologically moderate chairs (based on their floor-voting patterns) act like ideological moderates in the bills they allow to move forward through their committees? Relying on such decisions, researchers could measure not only the individual effectiveness of these institutionally powerful actors in advancing legislation but also their abilities and willingness to obstruct the initiatives of opponents.

Even more broadly, the approach we offer need not stop at examinations of the U.S. House of Representatives. Most naturally, legislative effectiveness could be studied in the U.S. Senate or in the U.S. states. Although alterations to these measures would be necessary to fit specific institutional characteristics, we have no doubt that lawmakers vary in their abilities and effectiveness in such settings.[17] Our approach may also be of use in the study of legislative bodies around the world – although, here again, developing the scores with an eye to specific legislative contexts would be paramount.

Toward A Theory Of Legislative Effectiveness

Across the chapters of this book, we tested a series of hypotheses about topics ranging from political parties to policy gridlock, through the lens of the legislative effectiveness of lawmakers in Congress. In our view, the hypotheses we explored followed rather cleanly from prior scholarship and our tests shed new light on important phenomena. Moreover, our qualitative approach in Chapter 6 offered a series of insights that could be developed into testable hypotheses for future work.

While therefore theoretically grounded, this work has not relied upon an explicit theory of legislative effectiveness. In our view, such a theory, or rather a set of theories, is essential to fulfilling the promise offered by the legislative effectiveness project in its broadest sense. Indeed, a scientific approach to the study of politics demands the formulation of testable hypotheses (ideally arising from a general theory) and the subsequent rigorous testing of such hypotheses.[18] Thankfully, many existing approaches to theory building in legislative political science are amenable to the inclusion of legislative effectiveness as a core component.

One such approach would be to incorporate legislative effectiveness into the spatial models commonly used to study legislatures.[19] Although we argue that spatial ideology alone is often inadequate to accurately characterize legislative

---

[17] For example, credit across stages of the lawmaking process in the U.S. Senate may need to be altered to account for Senate rules that allow senators to bypass the committee stage and bring their proposals directly to the Senate floor.

[18] Riker (1977) lays out an early parsimonious view of a scientific approach to the study of politics.

[19] Krehbiel (1988) summarizes the value of spatial models to the study of Congress.

behavior, such approaches have thus far offered important insights. One way to incorporate effectiveness into such models is to allow lawmakers to attach some enhanced quality (or "valence") to their legislative proposals, making such proposals more attractive to other legislators, and therefore potentially improving the likelihood of their passage into law.[20] Out of such a model would arise a series of predictions about: the extent to which effective lawmakers can *pull policy* toward their preferred ideological positions, which legislators are likely to *exert the effort* necessary to move bills forward, and which legislators are likely to be *most successful* at different stages of the legislative process. Such predictions could then lead to series of additional empirical investigations.

An alternative approach for building a theory of legislative effectiveness would be to incorporate effectiveness into models of coalition building. Existing models tend to feature a legislator who serves as a proposer, seeking to modify current policy or to divide up the various valuable resources controlled by the legislature.[21] A more-effective lawmaker may then be modeled as one who is more likely to be the proposer upon entering such a bargaining game, one who brings a substantial number of coalition partners along with her if included in the coalition, or one whose support is required to secure ultimate acceptance of the proposal. Any of these alterations to standard coalition-building models would offer new hypotheses about the influence of highly effective lawmakers.

Still another approach for developing a new theory of legislative effectiveness might involve a central role of information and expertise. In informational models, some actors have more knowledge or expertise than do others, such as possessing greater information about the preferences of other actors or about how policy proposals map onto real-world outcomes.[22] If legislative effectiveness is based on such expertise or on informational advantages, opportunities and incentives to develop expertise will help determine which legislators emerge with the greatest effectiveness. Such an approach might turn scholarly attention to the role of personal and committee staffs, of informative interest groups, of issue specialization, or of relative information acquisition across political parties, offering exciting new pathways for congressional research.

These three examples (spatial, coalition building, and informational models) illustrate the potential for legislative effectiveness to play a prominent role across a wide array of theoretical studies of legislative behavior. Once again, we do not believe that researchers need to pick a single best path forward to developing new theories. Rather, those interested in the ideological consequences of legislative effectiveness might adopt a spatial approach, while those interested in coalitions or in information and expertise might turn in other directions. Collectively, both

---

[20] Hitt, Volden, and Wiseman (2014) advance a spatial theory of legislative effectiveness along these lines.

[21] Baron and Ferejohn's (1989) model is often central to such theoretical studies.

[22] For a discussion of the evolution of such models, as well as of the role of formal theories in the study of Congress, see Volden and Wiseman (2011b).

empirically and theoretically, scholars have much ground to cover, with legislative effectiveness playing a central role.

BEYOND SCHOLARSHIP

Interest in legislative effectiveness may extend well beyond students of Congress and scholars of legislative behavior. From the time of the American Revolution through securing women's suffrage in the Nineteenth Amendment through the Voting Rights Act of 1965, Americans have sought redress from inadequate representation. In a similar vein, citizens may be thought to be denied proper representation when their representatives are ineffective at articulating their concerns and advancing their interests in the legislature.

The natural recourse for ineffective representation is found at the ballot box, where voters have the right and responsibility to remove from office those who do not adequately represent them. Yet voters may suffer from an overload of information during campaigns and from the obfuscation that accompanies opposing candidates seeking to advance their competing interests.[23] Incumbents use many arguments to advance their case of being effective in Congress; how are voters to separate fact from fiction?

Just as voters take cues from the party affiliation of candidates, so, too, could they benefit from a simple summary of how effective their member of Congress has been in recent years. Voters who learn that their representative is among the most effective members of her party, or that she exceeds the level of effectiveness that would be expected given her seniority and committee leadership position, might be more likely to vote for her again. In contrast, voters may lose patience with members who are ineffective in Congress after Congress, and may wish to remove them either in the primary or in the general election.[24]

Of course, this assumes that voters value having effective lawmakers representing them. We believe that there is a larger political discussion taking place in the United States about the benefits of political compromise, and about whether parties should seek consensus and a middle ground or hold firm to their initial ideological positions. Our view on this matter arises from having studied the policies put forth across the years by the most effective lawmakers. For instance,

---

[23] Minozzi (2011) presents a theoretical argument of how opponents "jam" the messages that informed elites try to send to citizens.

[24] A recent primary challenge to long-term incumbent Mike Honda (D-CA) nicely illustrates this tendency. In late 2013, a collection of Silicon Valley entrepreneurs threw their support behind challenger Ro Khanna because they felt that Silicon Valley "hadn't been represented at the federal level," and that Honda had consistently failed to "[bring] the bacon to the Valley for the technology guy" (Quinn, Michelle and Elizabeth Titus. 2013. "Silicon Valley Takes Aim at Honda." *Politico*. September 3. Retrieved from http://www.politico.com/story/2013/09/silicon-valley-mike-honda-96201.html?hp=f2, accessed February 18, 2014).

in Chapter 6, we highlighted the environmental policy accomplishments of lawmakers such as John Breaux (D-LA) and Jim Saxton (R-NJ), and the compromises that they struck.

The core of such compromises can be understood with a stylized example of a polluting factory upstream from a small village.[25] If the interests of the business alone are taken into consideration, the pollution put into the stream will come at substantial costs to the environment, to fishing and recreation opportunities, and to a clean source of drinking water for the village. On the other hand, if environmental interests alone are considered, the factory would be shut down, leading to a pristine stream, but also producing higher-priced goods and rising unemployment. Truly effective lawmaking means taking all of these goals into consideration simultaneously, allowing pollution levels that do not overwhelm the environment or the capacity of water treatment facilities, but that also allow the factory to continue to operate at profitable and community-beneficial levels. In this view, if either side wins the political battle alone, its own interests are achieved, but with the worst effects for the other side. Such winner-take-all politics does not allow for alternatives that mitigate the most harmful effects of one-sided policymaking. And, based on our review of compromises struck by the most highly effective lawmakers, such lessons apply to myriad policy areas beyond conflicts between business and environmental groups. If voters can see the wisdom of this argument and elevate the value of compromise and legislative effectiveness over single-minded partisanship, perhaps some of the great policy problems of our day can be addressed without undue distress.

Knowledge about the effectiveness of specific lawmakers may also be of interest to those who lobby Congress. Undoubtedly, the largest and most heavily funded interest groups are already well aware of which members of Congress are most effective in the policy areas of greatest interest to them.[26] But the First Amendment right to petition government for a redress of grievances does not apply only to those who are well-financed. Individual citizens and small groups would also benefit from knowledge about which members of Congress are most effective in particular policy areas. With such information at their disposal, these interested parties can better target their proposals, making them more likely to reach the desks of key policymakers and to be considered and properly weighed in the lawmaking process.

---

[25] In the view of Coase (1960), the socially optimum solution to this sort of situation will be agreed upon through bargaining by all parties, and secured through some allocation of resources in the absence of "transactions costs." Unfortunately, transactions costs exist in nearly all such situations, and political disputes resolved in legislatures by the will of the majority can easily be biased away from a social optimum and toward the desires of one side, neglecting the concerns of opponents. In contrast, political compromise with opponents can result in policies that are undermined in their implementation and administration (e.g., Moe 1989).

[26] A future study exploring this concept, perhaps testing whether the most highly effective lawmakers are most likely to subsequently be lobbied and to receive a greater proportion of campaign contributions, would be welcome.

Finally, Representatives themselves may be interested in the extent to which they are (or are perceived to be) effective lawmakers. Indeed, members of Congress are public servants who wish to acquire and utilize political power for their constituents and for their broader political goals. And we have documented that those who see themselves as ineffectual are less likely to find the lawmaking enterprise sufficiently rewarding to continually seek reelection into Congress. Along such lines, new members of Congress may be interested in the habits they can develop in order to become more highly effective.[27] And members of Congress interested in maintaining the institutional power and prestige of the legislative branch may seek reforms to ensure that the most effective lawmakers are well positioned to use their expertise and abilities in the best interests of their beloved Congress as a whole.[28]

In so doing, lawmakers in Congress may find themselves better able to address the major problems of their time than are policymakers in other countries with different systems of democratic representation. On the other hand, by relying on a Congress comprised of *members as lawmakers*, the American system most fully experiences not only the benefits of democratic governance but all of its excesses as well. What is labeled here as "effective lawmaking" may then just take the form of members more cleverly pursuing particularistic, money-driven, electorally based self-interest, rather than seeking solutions to major public policy problems.[29]

Indeed, recent examples, such as the near default on federal government debts, the lack of bipartisanship on the most comprehensive health care reforms in decades, and a budget sequestration without sufficient discretion to mitigate its most harmful effects, do not give much reason for hope.[30] In light of such examples, it is unsurprising that the national legislature is held in low esteem by

---

[27] Indeed, former Representative Tim Roemer (D-IN) commented in a November 2012 *Politico* article on how Tip O'Neill addressed his freshman cohort in 1991 and offered tips on how to become an effective lawmaker. Roemer built on these points to offer his own advice to the freshman members of the 113th Congress, including the suggestion that they "approach committee work thoughtfully" as "it is an efficient way to become an expert on a set of serious issues . . . [which] ultimately defines your reputation and charts a career path of opportunity." Retrieved from http://www.politico.com/news/stories/1112/84197.html, accessed July 11, 2013.

[28] Mayhew (1974, 141–158) describes how reelection-seeking goals interact with institutional maintenance concerns of leaders in Congress.

[29] One fears that, if members of Congress do pay some degree of attention to measures such as the Legislative Effectiveness Scores developed here, they will find ways to game the system and obfuscate their behavior. For example, the bills that would have been sponsored and advanced by members from safe seats will instead be attributed to at-risk junior members in the party to help secure their reelection bids. Were such manipulations to become more prevalent in the future, they would make the task of assigning proper credit to members even more difficult than it has been thus far.

[30] We offer background on the passage of the 2010 Affordable Care Act at the beginning of Chapter 5. The Budget Control Act of 2011 was adopted in the summer of 2011, narrowly averting a default of the country's debts due to a failure to increase the federal debt ceiling. To address the ballooning national debt, the act put in place a sequestration procedure of automatic spending cuts that was thought to be so unattractive as to force all sides to the table for a grand budget deal. However,

the American public, with less than 20 percent expressing approval of the job Congress is doing, in poll after poll.

Yet despite such low overall approval, the vast majority of members of Congress are reelected time and time again.[31] From this point of view, we do not believe that members of Congress will substantially change their behavior without incentives from their bosses, the American voters. If voters are willing to set aside partisanship and an emphasis on ideological purity to instead focus on legislative effectiveness and the need to solve the specific problems of greatest importance, only then should we expect change. As articulated in the Declaration of Independence, the American government derives its powers from the consent of the governed. It is therefore up to the people themselves to ensure that they are effectively represented. Facilitating the election and proliferation of effective legislators is a crucial step in fulfilling the promise of American representative democracy, one that requires continual attention and a constantly renewed commitment.

politicians were unable to reach such a deal and the sequestration policy, intended to be an unfathomable threat, instead became the law of the land.
[31] This phenomenon of disliking Congress as a whole but strongly supporting one's own representative has been labeled "Fenno's Paradox," based on its description in Fenno (1978).

References

Adcock, Robert, and David Collier. 2001. "Measurement Validity: A Shared Standard for Qualitative and Quantitative Research." *American Political Science Review* 95(3): 529–546.

Adler, E. Scott. 2002. *Why Congressional Reforms Fail: Reelection and the House Committee System.* Chicago: University of Chicago Press.

Adler, E. Scott, and John Wilkerson. 2005. "The Scope and Urgency of Legislation: Reconsidering Bill Success in the House of Representatives." APSA Conference Paper.

Adler, E. Scott, and John Wilkerson. 2007. "A Governing Theory of Legislative Organization." APSA Conference Paper.

Adler, E. Scott, and John D. Wilkerson. 2013. *Congress and the Politics of Problem Solving.* New York: Cambridge University Press.

Aldrich, John H. 1995. *Why Parties? The Origin and Transformation of Political Parties in America.* Chicago: University of Chicago Press.

Aldrich, John H., and David Rohde. 2000a. "The Consequences of Party Organization in the House: The Role of the Majority and Minority Parties in Conditional Party Government." In Jon R. Bond and Richard Fleisher (eds.). *Polarized Politics: Congress and the President in a Partisan Era.* Washington, DC: CQ Press (pp. 31–72).

Aldrich, John H., and David Rohde. 2000b. "The Republican Revolution and the House Appropriations Committee." *Journal of Politics* 62(1): 1–33.

Aldrich, John H., and David Rohde. 2001. "The Logic of Conditional Party Government: Revisiting the Electoral Connection." In Lawrence C. Dodd and Bruce I. Oppenheimer (eds.). *Congress Reconsidered*, 7th Edition. Washington, DC: CQ Press (pp. 269–292).

Aldrich, John H., and David W. Rohde. 1997–1998. "The Transition to Republican Rule in the House: Implications for Theories of Congressional Politics." *Political Science Quarterly* 112(4): 541–567.

Alvarez, Lizette. 2000. "Feminine Mystique Grown in the Senate." *New York Times,* December 7, A22.

Anderson, William D., Janet M. Box-Steffensmeier, and Valeria Sinclair-Chapman. 2003. "The Keys to Legislative Success in the U.S. House of Representatives." *Legislative Studies Quarterly* 28(3): 357–386.

Anzia, Sarah, and Christopher R. Berry. 2011. "The Jackie (and Jill) Robinson Effect: Why Do Congresswomen Outperform Congressmen?" *American Journal of Political Science* 55(3): 478–493.

Anzia, Sarah F., and Molly C. Jackman. 2013. "Legislative Organization and the Second Face of Power: Evidence from U.S. State Legislatures." *Journal of Politics* 75(1): 210–224.

Arnold, R. Douglas. 1990. *The Logic of Congressional Action*. New Haven: Yale University Press.

Ashworth, Scott, and Ethan Bueno de Mesquita. 2009. "Elections and Platform with Valence Competition." *Games and Economic Behavior* 67(1): 191–216.

Bachrach, Peter, and Morton S. Baratz. 1962. "Two Faces of Power." *American Political Science Review* 56(4): 947–952.

Baker, Donald. 1978. "GOP's Holt Also Strong with Democrats; GOP's Holt Maintains Strong Tie to Democrats." *Washington Post*, October 19.

Barnello, Michelle A., and Kathleen Bratton. 2007. "Bridging the Gap in Bill Sponsorship." *Legislative Studies Quarterly* 32(3): 449–474.

Baron, David P., and John A. Ferejohn. 1989. "Bargaining in Legislatures." *American Political Science Review* 83(4): 1181–1206.

Barone, Michael, and Grant Ujifusa. 1987. *The Almanac of American Politics 1988*. Washington, DC: National Journal.

Barone, Michael, and Grant Ujifusa. 1993. *The Almanac of American Politics 1994*. Washington, DC: National Journal.

Barone, Michael, Grant Ujifusa, and Douglas Matthews. 1973. *The Almanac of American Politics 1974*. Boston: Gambit.

Barone, Michael, Grant Ujifusa, and Douglass Matthews. 1979. *The Almanac of American Politics 1980*. New York: E.P. Dutton.

Bartels, Larry M. 2008. *Unequal Democracy: The Political Economy of the New Gilded Age*. Princeton: Princeton University Press.

Baumgartner, Frank R., and Bryan D. Jones (eds.). 2002. *Policy Dynamics*. Chicago: University of Chicago Press.

Bennis, Warren. 1989. *On Becoming a Leader*. Cambridge, MA: Perseus Publishing.

Bernhard, William, and Tracy Sulkin. 2013. "Commitment and Consequences: Reneging on Cosponsorship Pledges in the U.S. House." *Legislative Studies Quarterly* 38(4): 461–487.

Binder, Sarah A. 1999. "The Dynamics of Legislative Gridlock, 1974–96." *American Political Science Review* 93(3): 519–533.

Binder, Sarah A. 2003. *Stalemate: Causes and Consequences of Legislative Gridlock*. Washington, DC: Brookings Institution Press.

Binder, Sarah A., and Steven S. Smith. 1997. *Politics or Principle? Filibustering in the United States Senate*. Washington, DC: Brookings Institution Press.

Black, Duncan. 1948. "On the Rationale of Group Decision-Making." *Journal of Political Economy* 56(1): 23–34.

Black, Duncan. 1958. *The Theory of Committee and Elections*. Cambridge: Cambridge University Press.

Black, Earl. 1998. "Presidential Address: The Newest Southern Politics." *Journal of Politics* 60(3): 591–612.

Black, Merle. 2004. "The Transformation of the Southern Democratic Party." *Journal of Politics* 66(4): 1001–1017.

Boles, Janet K. 2001. "Local Elected Women and Policy-Making: Movement Delegates or Feminist Trustees?" In Susan Carroll (ed.). *The Impact of Women In Public Office.* Bloomington: Indiana University Press (pp. 68–86).

Brady, David W., and Kara Buckley. 1995. "Health Care Reform in the 103rd Congress: A Predictable Failure." *Journal of Health Politics, Policy, and Law* 20(2): 447–454.

Brady, David W., and Charles S. Bullock, III. 1980. "Is There a Conservative Coalition in the House?" *Journal of Politics* 42(2): 549–559.

Brady, David W., and Charles S. Bullock, III. 1981. "Coalition Politics in the House of Representatives." In Lawrence C. Dodd and Bruce I. Oppenheimer (eds.). *Congress Reconsidered,* 2nd Edition. Washington, DC: CQ Press (pp. 186–203).

Brady, David W., and Craig Volden. 1998. *Revolving Gridlock: Politics and Policy from Carter to Clinton.* Boulder: Westview Press.

Brady, David W., and Craig Volden. 2006. *Revolving Gridlock: Politics and Policy from Jimmy Carter to George W. Bush,* 2nd Edition. Boulder: Westview Press.

Branson, Richard. 2011. *Losing My Virginity: How I Survived, Had Fun, and Made a Fortune Doing Business My Way,* Updated Edition. New York: Crown Business.

Bratton, Kathleen A. 2005. "Critical Mass Theory Revisited: The Behavior and Success of Token Women in State Legislatures." *Politics and Gender* 1: 97–125.

Bratton, Kathleen A., and Kerry L. Haynie. 1999. "Agenda Setting and Legislative Success in State Legislatures: The Effects of Gender and Race." *Journal of Politics* 61(3): 658–679.

Brown, Lawrence D. 2011. "The Elements of Surprise: How Health Reform Happened." *Journal of Health Politics, Policy and Law* 36(3): 420–427.

Burgin, Eileen. 2012. "Congress, Health Care Reform, and Reconciliation." *Congress & the Presidency* 39(3): 270–296.

Burns, James MacGregor. 1978. *Leadership.* New York: HarperCollins.

Burns, Nancy, Laura Evans, Gerald Gamm, and Corrine McConnaughy. 2009. "Urban Politics in the State Arena." *Studies in American Political Development* 23(1): 1–22.

Burrell, Barbara C. 1994. *A Woman's Place Is in the House: Campaigning for Congress in the Feminist Era.* Ann Arbor: University of Michigan Press.

Busbey, L. White. 1927. *Uncle Joe Cannon: The Story of a Pioneer American.* New York: Henry Holt and Company.

Cain, Bruce E., and Marc A. Levin. 1999. "Term Limits." *Annual Review of Political Science* 2(1): 163–188.

Cain, Louis P., and Brooks A. Kaiser. 2003. "Public Goods Provision: Lessons from the Tellico Dam Controversy." *Natural Resources Journal* 43(2): 979–1008.

Callander, Steven. 2008. "A Theory of Policy Expertise." *Quarterly Journal of Political Science* 3(2): 123–140.

Callander, Steven. 2011. "Searching for Good Policies." *American Political Science Review* 105(4): 643–662.

Callander, Steven, and Keith Krehbiel. 2012. "Gridlock and Delegation in a Changing World." Stanford Graduate School of Business, Research Paper No. 2100.

Calvo, Ernesto, and Inaki Sagarzazu. 2011. "Legislator Success in Committee: Gatekeeping Authority and the Loss of Majority Control." *American Journal of Political Science* 55(1): 1–15.

Canes-Wrone, Brandice, David W. Brady, and John F. Cogan. 2002. "Out of Step, Out of Office: Electoral Accountability and House Members' Voting." *American Political Science Review* 96(1): 127–140.

Canon, David T. 1999. *Race, Redistricting, and Representation: The Unintended Consequences of Black Majority Districts.* Chicago: University of Chicago Press.

Carey, John M., Richard G. Niemi, and Lynda W. Powell. 1998. "Are Women State Legislators Different?" In Susan Thomas and Clyde Wilcox (eds.). *Women and Elective Office: Past, Present, and Future.* New York: Oxford University Press (pp. 87–102).

Carey, John M., Richard G. Niemi, Lynda Powell, and Gary F. Moncrief. 2006. "The Effects of Term Limits on State Legislatures: A New Survey of the 50 States." *Legislative Studies Quarterly* 31(1): 105–34.

Carnegie, Dale. 1936. *How to Win Friends and Influence People.* New York: Simon & Schuster.

Caro, Robert. A. 1982. *The Path to Power.* New York: Alfred A. Knopf.

Carroll, Susan J. 2001. "Representing Women: Women State Legislators as Agents of Policy-Related Change." In Susan Carroll (ed.). *The Impact of Women in Public Office.* Bloomington: Indiana University Press (pp. 3–21).

Carroll, Susan J. 2002. "Representing Women: Congresswomen's Perceptions of Their Representational Roles." In Cindy Simon Rosenthal and Richard F. Fenno, Jr. (eds.). *Women Transforming Congress.* Norman: University of Oklahoma Press (pp. 50–68).

Carrubba, Clifford J., Matthew Gabel, Lacey Murrah, et al. 2006. "Off the Record: Unrecorded Legislative Votes, Selection Bias, and Roll-Call Vote Analysis." *British Journal of Political Science* 36(4): 691–704.

Carson, Jamie L., Nathan W. Monroe, and Gregory Robinson. 2011. "Unpacking Agenda Control in Congress: Individual Roll Rates and the Republican Revolution." *Political Research Quarterly* 64(1): 17–30.

Center for American Women and Politics (CAWP). 2001. "Women State Legislators: Past, Present and Future." Retrieved from http://www.cawp.rutgers.edu/research/topics/documents/StLeg2001Report.pdf, accessed January 8, 2013.

Chiou, Fang-Yi, and Lawrence S. Rothenberg. 2003. "When Pivotal Politics Meets Partisan Politics." *American Journal of Political Science* 47(3): 503–522.

Chiou, Fang-Yi, and Lawrence S. Rothenberg. 2006. "Preferences, Parties, and Legislative Productivity." *American Politics Research* 34(6): 705–731.

Chiou, Fang-Yi, and Lawrence S. Rothenberg. 2008. "Comparing Legislators and Legislatures: The Dynamics of Legislative Gridlock Reconsidered." *Political Analysis* 16(2): 197–212.

Chiou, Fang-Yi, and Lawrence S. Rothenberg. 2009. "A Unified Theory of U.S. Lawmaking: Preferences, Institutions, and Party Discipline." *Journal of Politics* 71(4): 1257–1272.

Cho, Wendy K. Tam, and James H. Fowler. 2010. "Legislative Success in a Small World: Social Network Analysis and the Dynamics of Congressional Legislation." *Journal of Politics* 72(1): 124–135.

Churchill, Winston S. 2003. *Never Give In! The Best of Winston Churchill's Speeches.* New York: Hyperion.

Cialdini, Robert B. 2006. *Influence: The Psychology of Persuasion,* Revised Edition. New York: HarperCollins.

Clinton, Joshua. 2007. "Lawmaking and Roll Calls." *Journal of Politics* 69(2): 455–467.

Clinton, Joshua D. 2012. "Using Roll Call Estimates to Test Models of Politics." *Annual Review of Political Science* 15: 79–99.

Clinton, Joshua, Simon Jackman, and Douglas Rivers. 2004. "The Statistical Analysis of Roll Call Data." *American Political Science Review* 98(2): 355–370.

Coase, Ronald H. 1960. "The Problem of Social Cost." *Journal of Law and Economics* 3(1): 1–44.

Cobb, Michael D., and Jeffery A. Jenkins. 2001. "Race and the Representation of Blacks' Interests during Reconstruction." *Political Research Quarterly* 54(1): 181–204.

Cohn, V. 1981. (March 10). "TV's 'Quincy' Tells Hill about Rare Diseases." *The Washington Post*, p. A4.

Colimore, Edward. 2007. (November 17). "Saxton Looks Back on Congressional Career." *The Philadelphia Inquirer*, p. B1.

Collie, Melissa P. 1989. "Electoral Patterns and Voting Alignments in the U.S. House, 1886–1986." *Legislative Studies Quarterly* 14: 107–128.

Collie, Melissa P., and David W. Brady. 1985. "The Decline of Partisan Voting Coalitions in the House of Representatives." In Lawrence C. Dodd and Bruce I. Oppenheimer (eds.). *Congress Reconsidered*, 3rd Edition. Washington DC: Congressional Quarterly Press (pp. 272–287).

Collins, Jim. 2001. *Good to Great: Why Some Companies Make the Leap ... and Others Don't*. New York: HarperCollins.

Cooper, Joseph, and David W. Brady. 1981. "Institutional Context and Leadership Style: The House from Cannon to Rayburn." *American Political Science Review* 75(2): 411–425.

Covey, Stephen. 1989. *The 7 Habits of Highly Effective People*. New York: The Free Press.

Cox, Gary W., and Mathew D. McCubbins. 1993. *Legislative Leviathan: Party Government in the House*. Berkeley: University of California Press.

Cox, Gary W., and Mathew D. McCubbins. 2002. "Agenda Power in the U.S. House of Representatives." In David W. Brady and Mathew D. McCubbins (eds.). *Party, Process, and Political Change in Congress*. Stanford: Stanford University Press (pp. 107–145).

Cox, Gary W., and Mathew D. McCubbins. 2005. *Setting the Agenda: Responsible Party Government in the U.S. House of Representatives*. New York: Cambridge University Press.

Cox, Gary W., and William C. Terry. 2008. "Legislative Productivity in the 93rd–105th Congresses." *Legislative Studies Quarterly* 33(4): 603–618.

Deckard, Barbara. 1972. "State Party Delegations in the U.S. House of Representatives – A Comparative Study of Group Cohesion." *Journal of Politics* 34(1): 199–222.

Deering, Christopher J., and Steven S. Smith. 1997. *Committees in Congress*, 3rd Edition. Washington, DC: CQ Press.

Delli Carpini, Michael X., and Scott Keeter. 1996. *What Americans Know about Politics and Why It Matters*. New Haven, CT: Yale University Press.

Denver Post Washington Bureau. 2001 (September 9). "Wildlife Refuge Plan for Flats Nears Passage." *The Denver Post*, p. B2.

Denzau, Arthur T., and Robert J. Mackay. 1983. "Gate-Keeping and Monopoly Power of Committees: An Analysis of Sincere and Sophisticated Behavior." *American Journal of Political Science* 27: 740–761.

Diermeier, Daniel, and Roger B. Myerson. 1999. "Bicameralism and Its Consequences for the Internal Organization of Legislatures." *American Economic Review* 89(5): 1182–1196.

Diermeier, Daniel, and Razvan Vlaicu. 2011. "Parties, Coalitions, and the Internal Organization of Legislatures." *American Political Science Review* 105(2): 359–380.

Dietrich, Bryce J. 2012. "Does John Boehner's Emotion Make Him More Likeable? The Affect of Negative Emotional Displays on an Individual's Centrality in Sponsorship-Cosponsorship Networks." Paper presented at the 2012 Annual Meetings of the Midwest Political Science Association, Chicago.

Dion, Douglas, and John D. Huber. 1996. "Procedural Choice and the House Committee on Rules." *Journal of Politics* 58(1): 25–53.

Dion, Douglas, and John D. Huber. 1997. "Sense and Sensibility: The Role of Rules." *American Journal of Political Science* 41(3): 945–957.

Dowd, Ann Reilly. 2001. (August). "Top of His Game." *Washingtonian*, p. 29.

Downs, Anthony. 1957. *An Economic Theory of Democracy*. New York: HarperCollins.

Drucker, Peter F. 1954. *The Practice of Management*. New York: Harper & Row.

Druckman, James N., Donald P. Green, James H. Kuklinski, and Arthur Lupia (eds.). 2011. *Cambridge Handbook of Experimental Political Science*. New York: Cambridge University Press.

Duerst-Lahti, Georgia. 2002a. "Knowing Congress as a Gendered Institution: Manliness and the Implications of Women in Congress." In Cindy Rosenthal (ed.). *Women Transforming Congress*. Norman: University of Oklahoma Press (pp. 20–49).

Duerst-Lahti, Georgia. 2002b. "Governing Institutions, Ideologies, and Gender: Towards the Possibility of Equal Political Representation." *Sex Roles* 47(7/8): 371–388.

Edwards, George C. 2009. *The Strategic President: Persuasion and Opportunity in Presidential Leadership*. Princeton: Princeton University Press.

Evans, C. Lawrence. 1991. *Leadership in Committee: A Comparative Analysis of Leadership Behavior in the U.S. Senate*. Ann Arbor: University of Michigan Press.

Evans, C. Lawrence. 2011. "Congressional Committees." In Eric Schickler and Frances E. Lee (eds.). *Oxford Handbook of the American Congress*. Oxford: Oxford University Press (pp. 396–425).

Evans, C. Lawrence, and Walter J. Oleszek. 1997. *Congress Under Fire: Reform Politics and the Republican Majority*. New York: Houghton Mifflin Company.

Feder, Judith. 2011. "Too Big to Fail: The Enactment of Health Care Reform." *Journal of Health Politics, Policy and Law* 36(3): 414–416.

Fenno, Richard. 2003. *Going Home: Black Representatives and Their Constituents*. Chicago: University of Chicago Press.

Fenno, Richard F., Jr. 1973. *Congressmen in Committees*. Boston: Little, Brown and Company.

Fenno, Richard F., Jr. 1978. *Home Style: House Members in Their Districts*. Boston: Little, Brown and Company.

Fenno, Richard F., Jr. 1992. *When Incumbency Fails: The Senate Career of Mark Andrews*. Washington, DC: Congressional Quarterly.

Fiorina, Morris P. 1977. *Congress: Keystone of the Washington Establishment*. New Haven: Yale University Press.

Fiorina, Morris P. 2011. "Reflections on the Study of Congress 1969–2009." In Eric Schickler and Frances E. Lee, (eds.). *Oxford Handbook of Congress*. Oxford: Oxford University Press (pp. 861–874).

Fiorina, Morris P., Samuel J. Abrams, and Jeremy C. Pope. 2006. *Culture War? The Myth of a Polarized America*, 2nd Edition. New York: Pearson Longman.

Fleisher, Richard. 1993. "Explaining the Change in Roll-Call Voting Behavior of Southern Democrats." *Journal of Politics* 55(2): 327–341.

Fowler, James H. 2006a. "Connecting the Congress: A Study of Cosponsorship Networks." *Political Analysis* 14(4); 456–487.

Fowler, James H. 2006b. "Legislative Cosponsorship Networks in the U.S. House and Senate." *Social Networks* 28(4): 454–465.

Frantzich, Stephen. 1979. "Who Makes Our Laws? The Legislative Effectiveness of Members of the U.S. Congress." *Legislative Studies Quarterly* 4(3): 409–428.

Frederick, Brian. 2009. "Are Female House Members Still More Liberal in a Polarized Era? The Conditional Nature of the Relationship between Descriptive and Substantive Representation." *Congress & the Presidency* 36(2): 181–202.

Gerber, Alan S., and Donald P. Green. 2000. "The Effects of Canvassing, Telephone Calls, and Direct Mail on Voter Turnout: A Field Experiment." *American Political Science Review* 94(3): 653–663.

Gertzog, Irwin N. 1984. *Congressional Women: Their Recruitment, Treatment, and Behavior.* New York: Praeger.

Gile, Roxanne L, and Charles E. Jones. 1995. "Congressional Racial Solidarity: Exploring Congressional Black Caucus Voting Cohesion, 1971–1990." *Journal of Black Studies* 25(5): 622–641.

Gilligan, Thomas W., and Keith Krehbiel. 1987. "Collective Decision Making and Standing Committees: An Informational Rationale for Restrictive Amendment Procedures." *Journal of Law, Economics, and Organization* 3(2): 287–335.

Gilligan, Thomas W., and Keith Krehbiel. 1990. "Organization of Informative Committees by a Rational Legislature." *American Journal of Political Science* 34(2): 531–564.

Goleman, Daniel, Richard Boyatzis, and Annie McKee. 2002. *Primal Leadership: Realizing the Power of Emotional Intelligence.* Cambridge, MA: Harvard Business Review.

Goodwin, Doris Kearns. 2005. *Team of Rivals: The Political Genius of Abraham Lincoln.* New York: Simon & Schuster.

Griffin, John D., and Patrick Flavin. 2007. "Racial Differences in Information, Expectations, and Accountability." *Journal of Politics* 69(1): 220–236.

Griffin, John D., and Patrick Flavin. 2011. "How Citizens and Their Legislators Prioritize Spheres of Representation." *Political Research Quarterly* 64(3): 520–533.

Griffin, John D., and Michael Keane. 2011. "Are African Americans Effectively Represented in Congress?" *Political Research Quarterly* 64(1): 145–156.

Grose, Christian R. 2011. *Congress in Black and White: Race and Representation in Washington and at Home.* New York: Cambridge University Press.

Groseclose, Tim. 2001. "A Model of Candidate Location When One Candidate Has a Valence Advantage." *American Journal of Political Science* 45 (4): 862–886.

Grossmann, Matt. 2013. "The Variable Politics of the Policy Process: Issue-Area Differences and Comparative Networks." *Journal of Politics* 75(1): 65–79.

Hacker, Jacob S. 1997. *The Road to Nowhere: The Genesis of President Clinton's Plan for Health Security.* Princeton: Princeton University Press.

Hacker, Jacob S. 2010. "The Road to Somewhere: Why Health Reform Happened." *Perspectives on Politics* 8(3): 861–876.

Hacker, Jacob S. 2011. "Why Reform Happened." *Journal of Health Politics, Policy and Law* 36(3): 438–441.

Hall, Richard L. 1992. "Measuring Legislative Influence." *Legislative Studies Quarterly* 17(2): 205–231.

Hall, Richard L. 1996. *Participation in Congress.* New Haven: Yale University Press.

Hamburger, Tom. 1992 (October 25). "Environmental Work Has Given Vento His Greatest Stature." *Star Tribune*, p. B1.

Hamm, Keith E., Robert Harmel, and Robert Thompson. 1983. "Ethnic and Partisan Minorities in Two Southern State Legislatures." *Legislative Studies Quarterly* 8(2): 177–189.

Harbridge, Laurel. 2013. "Is Bipartisanship Dead? Policy Agreement in the Face of Partisan Agenda-Setting in the House of Representatives." Unpublished manuscript, Northwestern University.

Hasecke, Edward B., and Jason D. Mycoff. 2007. "Party Loyalty and Legislative Success: Are Loyal Majority Party Members More Successful in the U.S. House of Representatives?" *Political Research Quarterly* 60(4): 607–617.

Haynie, Kerry L. 2001. *African American Legislators in the American States*. New York: Columbia University Press.

Haynie, Kerry L. 2002. "The Color of Their Skin or the Content of Their Behavior? Race and Perceptions of African American Legislators." *Legislative Studies Quarterly* 27(2): 295–314.

Haynie, Kerry L. 2005. "African Americans and the New Politics of Inclusion: A Representational Dilemma?" In Lawrence C. Dodd and Bruce I. Oppenheimer (eds.). *Congress Reconsidered*, 8th Edition. Washington, DC: CQ Press (pp. 395–409).

Henneberger, Melinda. 1994 (December 6). "Quiet End to a Political Dynasty; Hamilton Fish Jr. Leaves Congress and Takes 150 Years of Family History." *New York Times*, p. B4.

Herbers, John. 1966. (July 4). "Liberal on Coast Fears Rights Bills: Rep. Corman Concerned by Effect of Housing Fight." *New York Times*, p. 16.

Herron, Michael C., and Alan E. Wiseman. 2008. "Gerrymanders and Theories of Law Making: A Study of Legislative Redistricting in Illinois." *Journal of Politics* 70(1): 151–167.

Hetherington, Marc J. 2009. "Putting Polarization in Perspective." *British Journal of Political Science* 39(2): 413–448.

Hibbing, John R. 1991. *Congressional Careers: Contours of Life in the U.S. House of Representatives*. Chapel Hill: University of North Carolina Press.

Hibbing, John R. 1993. "Careerism in Congress: For Better or for Worse?" In Larry C. Dodd and Bruce I. Oppenheimer (eds.). *Congress Reconsidered*, 5th Edition. Washington, DC: CQ Press (pp. 67–88).

Hirsch, Alex V. 2011. "Theory Driven Bias in Ideal Point Estimates – A Monte Carlo Study." *Political Analysis* 19(1): 87–102.

Hirsch, Alex V., and Kenneth W. Shotts. 2012. "Policy-Specific Information and Informal Agenda Power." *American Journal of Political Science* 56(1): 67–83.

Hitt, Matthew P., Craig Volden, and Alan E. Wiseman. 2011. "A Formal Model of Legislative Effectiveness." Conference Paper. Seattle: Annual Meetings of the American Political Science Association.

Hitt, Matthew P., Craig Volden, and Alan E. Wiseman. 2014. "A Formal Model of Legislative Effectiveness." Unpublished manuscript, Vanderbilt University.

House, Robert J., and Ram N. Aditya. 1997. "The Social Scientific Study of Leadership: Quo Vadis?" *Journal of Management* 23(3): 409–473.

Howell, William G. 2003. *Power without Persuasion: The Politics of Direct Presidential Action*. Princeton: Princeton University Press.

Hsieh, Tony. 2010. *Delivering Happiness: A Path to Profits, Passion, and Purpose*. New York: Business Plus.

Humphreys, Macartan, and Jeremy M. Weinstein. 2007. "Policing Politicians: Citizen Empowerment and Political Accountability in Africa." Paper presented at American Political Science Association Annual Meetings, Chicago.

Issenberg, Sasha. 2012. *The Victory Lab: The Secret Science of Winning Campaigns*. New York: Crown Publishers.

Jackman, Molly C. 2014. "Parties, Median Legislators, and Agenda Setting: How Legislative Institutions Matter." *Journal of Politics* 76(1): 259–272.

Jacobson, Gary C. 1999. *The Politics of Congressional Elections*, 5th Edition. New York: Longman.

Jenkins, Jeffery A., Michael H. Crespin, and Jamie L. Carson. 2005. "Parties as Procedural Coalitions in Congress: An Examination of Differing Career Tracks." *Legislative Studies Quarterly* 30(3): 365–389.

Jenkins, Jeffery A., and Nathan W. Monroe. 2012. "Buying Negative Agenda Control in the U.S. House." *American Journal of Political Science* 56(4): 897–912.

Jenkins, Jeffery A., and Charles Stewart III. 2012. *Fighting for the Speakership: The House and the Rise of Party Government*. Princeton: Princeton University Press.

Jewell, Malcolm, and Marcia Whicker. 1994. *Legislative Leadership in American States*. Ann Arbor: University of Michigan Press.

Jeydel, Alana, and Andrew Taylor. 2003. "Are Women Legislators Less Effective? Evidence from the U.S. House in the 103rd–105th Congress." *Political Research Quarterly* 56(1): 19–27.

Johnson, Haynes, and David S. Broder. 1996. *The System: The American Way of Politics at the Breaking Point*. Boston: Little, Brown and Company.

Jones, Charles O. 1968. "Joseph G. Cannon and Howard W. Smith: An Essay on the Limits of Leadership in the House of Representatives." *Journal of Politics* 30: 617–646.

Kathlene, Lyn. 1994. "Power and Influence in State Legislative Policymaking: The Interactions of Gender and Position in Committee Hearing Debates." *American Political Science Review* 88(3): 560–576.

Kathlene, Lyn. 1995. "Position Power versus Gender Power." In Georgia Duerst-Lahti and Rita Mae Kelly (eds.). *Gender Power, Leadership, and Governance*. Ann Arbor: University of Michigan Press.

Kennedy, Carole. 2003. "Gender Differences in Committee Decision-Making: Process and Outputs in an Experimental Setting." *Women and Politics* 25(3): 27–45.

Kessel, John H. 1964. "The Washington Congressional Delegation." *Midwest Journal of Political Science* 8(1): 1–21.

Kessler, Daniel, and Keith Krehbiel. 1996. "Dynamics of Cosponsorship." *American Political Science Review* 90(3): 555–566.

Kingdon, John W. 2011. *Agendas, Alternatives, and Public Policies*, updated 2nd Edition. Boston: Longman.

Kirkland, Justin H. 2011. "The Relational Determinants of Legislative Outcomes: Strong and Weak Ties between Legislators." *Journal of Politics* 73(3): 887–898.

Koger, Gregory. 2010. *Filibustering: A Political History of Obstruction in the House and Senate*. Chicago: University of Chicago Press.

Kousser, Thad. 2005. *Term Limits and the Dismantling of State Legislative Professionalism*. New York: Cambridge University Press.

Krehbiel, Keith. 1988. "Spatial Models of Legislative Choice." *Legislative Studies Quarterly* 13(3): 259–319.

Krehbiel, Keith. 1991. *Information and Legislative Organization*. Ann Arbor: University of Michigan Press.

Krehbiel, Keith. 1993. "Where's the Party?" *British Journal of Political Science* 23: 235–266.

Krehbiel, Keith. 1996. "Institutional and Partisan Sources of Gridlock: A Theory of Divided and Unified Government." *Journal of Theoretical Politics* 8(1): 7–40.

Krehbiel, Keith. 1997. "Restrictive Rules Reconsidered." *American Journal of Political Science* 41(4): 919–944.

Krehbiel, Keith. 1998. *Pivotal Politics: A Theory of U.S. Lawmaking*. Chicago: University of Chicago Press.

Krehbiel, Keith. 1999. "The Party Effect from A to Z and Beyond." *Journal of Politics* 61: 832–840.

Krehbiel, Keith. 2000. "Party Discipline and Measures of Partisanship." *American Journal of Political Science* 44(2): 212–227.

Krehbiel, Keith. 2003. "The Coefficient of Party Influence." *Political Analysis* 11(1): 95–103.

Krehbiel, Keith. 2007. "Partisan Roll Rates in a Nonpartisan Legislature." *Journal of Law, Economics, and Organization* 23(1): 1–23.

Krehbiel, Keith, Adam Meirowitz, and Alan E. Wiseman. 2013. "A Theory of Competitive Partisan Lawmaking." CSDI working paper 10–2013, Vanderbilt University.

Krutz, Glen. 2001. *Hitching a Ride: Omnibus Legislating in the U.S. Congress*. Columbus: Ohio State University Press.

Krutz, Glen S. 2005. "Issues and Institutions: 'Winnowing' in the U.S. Congress." *American Journal of Political Science* 49(2): 313–326.

Kurtz, Howard. 1987 (February 15). "100th Congress Promises Fair Housing Bill a New Lease on Life." *Washington Post*, p. 4.

Lansing, Alfred. 1959. *Endurance: Shackleton's Incredible Voyage*. New York: McGraw-Hill.

Lawless, Jennifer L., and Richard L. Fox. 1995. *It Takes a Candidate: Why Women Don't Run for Political Office*. New York: Cambridge University Press.

Lazarus, Jeffrey, and Amy Steigerwalt. 2011. "Politics or Policy: How Female Legislators are Forced to Choose." Unpublished manuscript, Georgia State University.

Leader, Shela G. 1977. "The Policy Impact of Elected Women Officials." In Louis Sandy Maisel and Joseph Cooper (eds.). *The Impact of the Electoral Process*. Beverly Hills: Sage (pp. 265–284).

Lebo, Matthew J., Adam J. McGlynn, and Gregory Koger. 2007. "Strategic Party Government: Party Influence in Congress, 1789–2000." *American Journal of Political Science* 51(3): 464–481.

Levy, Arthur B., and Susan Stoudinger. 1976. "Sources of Voting Cues for the Congressional Black Caucus." *Journal of Black Studies* 7(1): 29–45.

Lipsher, Steve. 2002 (August 27). "New Wilderness Dedicated after 5 Years of Effort; James Peak 'Stunning Beauty' Saved." *Denver Post*, p. B3.

Lowi, Theodore J. 1964. "American Business, Public Policy, Case-Studies, and Political Theory." *World Politics* 16(4): 677–715.

Lublin, David. 1997. *The Paradox of Representation*. Princeton: Princeton University Press.

Machiavelli, Niccolo. 2009. *The Prince, English translation*. New York: Penguin.

Manley, John F. 1973. "The Conservative Coalition in Congress." *American Behavioral Scientist* 17(2): 223–247.

Mann, Thomas E., and Norman J. Ornstein. 2006. *The Broken Branch: How Congress Is Failing America and How to Get It Back on Track*. New York: Oxford University Press.

Mann, Thomas E., and Norman J. Ornstein. 2012. *It's Even Worse Than It Looks: How the American Constitutional System Collided with the New Politics of Extremism*. New York: Oxford University Press.

Mansbridge, Jane. 2003. "Rethinking Representation." *American Political Science Review* 97(4): 515–528.

Maraniss, David. 1999. *When Pride Still Mattered: A Life of Vince Lombardi*. New York: Simon and Schuster.

Maraniss, David, and Michael Weisskopf. 1996. *Tell Newt to Shut Up*. New York: Simon & Schuster.

Matthews, Donald R. 1960. *U.S. Senators and Their World*. Chapel Hill: University of North Carolina Press.

Mayhew, David R. 1974. *Congress: The Electoral Connection*. New Haven: Yale University Press.

Mayhew, David R. 1991. *Divided We Govern: Party Control, Lawmaking, and Investigations 1946–1990*. New Haven: Yale University Press.

Mayhew, David R. 2000. *America's Congress: Actions in the Public Sphere, James Madison through Newt Gingrich*. New Haven: Yale University Press.

Mayhew, David R. 2004. *Congress: The Electoral Connection*, 2nd Edition. New Haven: Yale University Press.

Mayhew, David R. 2011. "Theorizing about Congress." In Eric Schickler and Frances E. Lee (eds.). *Oxford Handbook of Congress*. Oxford: Oxford University Press (pp. 875–893).

McCarty, Nolan, Keith T. Poole, and Howard Rosenthal. 2001. "The Hunt for Party Discipline in Congress." *American Political Science Review* 95(3): 673–687.

McCarty, Nolan, Keith T. Poole, and Howard Rosenthal. 2006. *Polarized America: The Dance of Ideology and Unequal Riches*. Cambridge, MA: MIT Press.

Meirowitz, Adam. 2008. "Electoral Contests, Incumbency Advantages, and Campaign Finance." *Journal of Politics* 70(3): 681–699.

Meyer, Katherine. 1980. "Legislative Influence: Toward Theory Development through Causal Analysis." *Legislative Studies Quarterly* 5(4): 563–585.

Mezey, Susan Gluck. 1978. "Women and Representation: The Case of Hawaii." *Journal of Politics* 40: 369–385.

Minozzi, William. 2011. "A Jamming Theory of Politics." *Journal of Politics* 73(2): 301–315.

Minozzi, William, and Craig Volden. 2013. "Who Heeds the Call of the Party in Congress?" *Journal of Politics* 75 (3): 787–802.

Moe, Terry M. 1989. "The Politics of Bureaucratic Structure." In John E. Chubb and Paul E. Peterson (eds.). *Can the Government Govern?* Washington, DC: Brookings Institution Press (pp. 267–329).

Moe, Terry, and William Howell. 1999. "The Presidential Power of Unilateral Action." *Journal of Law, Economics, and Organization* 15(1): 132–179.

Moncrief, Gary, and Joel A. Thompson. 2001. "On the Outside Looking In: Lobbyists' Perceptions of the Effects of State Legislative Term Limits." *State Politics and Policy Quarterly* 1(4): 394–411.

Moore, Michael K., and Sue Thomas. 1991. "Explaining Legislative Success in the U.S. Senate: The Role of the Majority and Minority Parties." *Western Political Quarterly* 44 (4): 959–970.

Nelson, Garrison. 1992. *Committees in the U.S. Congress, 1947–1992*, data. Retrieved from http://web.mit.edu/17.251/www/data_page.html, accessed May 23, 2014.

Neustadt, Richard E. 1990. *Presidential Power and the Modern Presidents: The Politics of Leadership from Roosevelt to Reagan*. New York: The Free Press.

O'Connor, Patrick. 2009 (July 20). "Moderates Bedevil Waxman – Again." Retrieved from POLITICO: http://www.politico.com/news/stories/0709/25142.html, accessed May 23, 2014.

Oliver, Myrna. 2001 (January 3). "James C. Corman; 10-Term Valley Congressman Championed Civil Rights, Welfare Legislation." *Los Angeles Times*, p. B7.

Olson, Mancur. 1965. *The Logic of Collective Action: Public Goods and the Theory of Groups*. Cambridge, MA: Harvard University Press.

Oppenheimer, Bruce I. 2013. "It's Hard to Get Mileage Out of Congress: Struggling over CAFÉ Standards, 1973–2013." Paper presented for delivery at the Conference on Congress and Public Policy Making in the 21st Century at the University of Virginia, June 3–4.

Padro i Miquel, Gerard, and James M. Snyder, Jr. 2006. "Legislative Effectiveness and Legislative Careers." *Legislative Studies Quarterly* 31(3): 347–381.

Parnass, Larry. 2012 (February 17). "Hampshire Life: U.S. Rep. Silvio O. Conte's Legacy as Republican Moderate." *Daily Hampshire Gazette*. Retrieved from http://www.mlbre search.com/extmedia/Sil_Conte-Hampshire%20Life.pdf, accessed May 29, 2013.

Patty, John W. 2008. "Equilibrium Party Government." *American Journal of Political Science* 52(3): 636–655.

Peterson, Mark A. 2011. "It Was a Different Time: Obama and the Unique Opportunity for Health Care Reform." *Journal of Health Politics, Policy and Law* 36(3): 430–436.

Peterson, Paul E. 1995. *The Price of Federalism*. Washington, DC: The Brookings Institution.

Pinney, Neil, and George Serra. 1999. "The Congressional Black Caucus and Vote Cohesion: Placing the Caucus Within House Voting Patterns." *Political Research Quarterly* 52(3): 583–608.

Poggione, Sarah. 2004. "Exploring Gender Differences in States Legislators' Policy Preferences." *Political Research Quarterly* 57(2): 305–314.

Poole, Keith T., and Howard Rosenthal. 1997. *Congress: A Political-Economic History of Roll Call Voting*. Oxford: Oxford University Press.

Quadango, Jill. 2011. "Interest-Group Influence on the Patient Protection and Affordability Act of 2010: Winners and Losers in the Health Care Reform Debate." *Journal of Health Politics, Policy and Law* 36(3): 450–453.

Reingold, Beth. 1992. "Concepts of Representation among Female and Male State Legislators." *Legislative Studies Quarterly* 17(4): 509–537.

Reingold, Beth. 1996. "Conflict and Cooperation: Legislative Strategies and Concepts of Power among Female and Male State Legislators." *Journal of Politics* 58(2): 464–485.

Richardson, Lilliard E., and Patricia K. Freeman. 1995. "Gender Differences in Constituency Service among State Legislators." *Political Research Quarterly* 48(1): 166–179.

Riker, William H. 1977. "The Future of a Science of Politics." *American Behavioral Scientist* 21(1): 11–38.

Rinehart, Sue Tolleson. 1991. "Do Women Leaders Make a Difference? Substance, Style and Perceptions." In D. L. Dodson (ed.). *Gender and Policymaking: Studies of Women in Office*. New Brunswick, NJ: Center for the American Woman and Politics, Rutgers University (pp. 149–165).

Roberts, Jason M. 2005. "Minority Rights and Majority Power: Conditional Party Government and the Motion to Recommit in the House." *Legislative Studies Quarterly* 30(2): 219–234.

Roberts, Jason M., and Steven S. Smith. 2003. "Procedural Contexts, Party Strategy, and Conditional Party Voting in the U.S. House of Representatives, 1971–2000." *American Journal of Political Science* 47(2): 305–317.

Rohde, David W. 1991. *Parties and Leaders in the Postreform House*. Chicago: University of Chicago Press.

Rosenbaum, David E. 1994 (June 1). "Indictment of a Congressman: A Giant Void in Congress." *New York Times*, p. A1.

Rosenthal, Cindy Simon. 1998. *When Women Lead: Integrative Leadership in State Legislatures*. New York: Oxford University Press.

Rowe, James. 1977. "'78 Budget Passed by House with Republicans' Support; GOP Aids House Budget Vote." *Washington Post*, May 18.

Royko, Mike. 1994 (May 26). "Big Fish Shouldn't Be Fried This Time." *Chicago Tribune*, p. 3.

Saint-Germain, Michelle A. 1989. "Does Their Difference Make a Difference? The Impact of Women on Public Policy in the Arizona Legislature." *Social Science Quarterly* 70(4): 956–968.

Sanbonmatsu, Kira. 2003. "Gender-Related Political Knowledge and the Descriptive Representation of Women." *Political Behavior* 25(4): 367–388.

Sanbonmatsu, Kira, Susan J. Carroll, and Debbie Walsh. 2009. *Poised to Run: Women's Pathways to the State Legislatures*. New Brunswick, NJ: Center for American Women and Politics.

Schickler, Eric. 2001. *Disjointed Pluralism: Institutional Innovation and the Development of the U.S. Congress*. Princeton, NJ: Princeton University Press.

Schickler, Eric, and Kathryn Pearson. 2009. "Agenda Control, Majority Party Power, and the House Committee on Rules, 1937–1952." *Legislative Studies Quarterly* 34(4): 455–491.

Schiller, Wendy J. 1995. "Senators and Political Entrepreneurs: Using Bill Sponsorship to Shape Legislative Agendas." *American Journal of Political Science* 39(1): 186–203.

Schultz, Howard. 2011. *Onward: How Starbucks Fought for Its Life without Losing Its Soul*. New York: Rodale Books.

Shaffer, Robert. 1981. "Major Changes to Ethics Committee Introduced at Start of Stokes' Tenure." *Washington Post*, January 13.

Shepsle, Kenneth A. 1978. *The Giant Jigsaw Puzzle: Democratic Committee Assignments in the Modern House*. Chicago: University of Chicago Press.

Shepsle, Kenneth A., and Barry R. Weingast. 1987. "The Institutional Foundations of Committee Power." *American Political Science Review* 81(1): 85–104.

Shor, Boris, and Nolan McCarty. 2011. "The Ideological Mapping of American Legislatures." *American Political Science Review* 105(3): 530–551.

Sinclair, Barbara. 1978. "From Party Voting to Regional Fragmentation, 1933–1956." *American Politics Quarterly* 6: 125–146.

Singh, Robert. 1998. *Congressional Black Caucus: Racial Politics in the U.S. Congress.* London: Sage.

Skocpol, Theda. 1996. *Boomerang: Clinton's Health Security Effort and the Turn Against Government in U.S. Politics.* New York: Norton.

Smith, Steven S. 1989. *Call to Order: Floor Politics in the House and Senate.* Washington, DC: Brookings Institution Press.

Smith, Steven S. 2007. *Party Influence in Congress.* Cambridge: Cambridge University Press.

Snyder, James M., and Tim Groseclose. 2000. "Estimating Party Influence in Congressional Roll Call Voting." *American Journal of Political Science* 44(2): 193–211.

Snyder, James M., Jr., and Tim Groseclose. 2001. "Estimating Party Influence in Congressional Roll-Call Voting: Regression Coefficients versus Classification Success." *American Political Science Review* 95(3): 689–698.

Soraghan, Mike. 2001. (July 22). "Udall Walks Carefully as He Follows Dad's Path." *Denver Post*, p. B5.

Squire, Peverill. 1992. "Legislative Professionalism and Membership Diversity in State Legislatures." *Legislative Studies Quarterly* 17(1): 69–79.

Stein, Robert M., and Kenneth N. Bickers. 1994. "Congressional Elections and the Pork Barrel." *Journal of Politics* 56(2): 377–399.

Steinmo, Sven, and Jon Watts. 1995. "It's the Institutions, Stupid! Why Comprehensive National Health Insurance Always Fails in America." *Journal of Health Politics, Policy, and Law* 20(2): 329–372.

Stevens, Arthur G., Arthur H. Miller, and Thomas E. Mann. 1974. "Mobilization of Liberal Strength in the House, 1955–1970: The Democratic Study Group." *American Political Science Review* 68(2): 667–681.

Stewart, Charles III, and Jonathan Woon. 2005. *Congressional Committee Assignments, 103rd to 110th Congresses, 1993–2007*, data. Retrieved from http://web.mit.edu/17.251/www/data_page.html, accessed May 23, 2014.

Stiglitz, Edward H., and Barry R. Weingast. 2010. "Agenda Control in Congress: Evidence from Cutpoint Estimates and Ideal Point Uncertainty." *Legislative Studies Quarterly* 35(2): 157–189.

Stone, Daniel. 2013. "Media and Gridlock." *Journal of Public Economics* 101: 94–104.

Strahan, Randall W. 2007. *Leading Representatives: The Agency of Leaders in the Politics of the U.S. House.* Baltimore: Johns Hopkins University Press.

Sulkin, Tracy. 2005. *Issue Politics in Congress.* New York: Cambridge University Press.

Sun-Tzu. 2011. *The Art of War,* English translation. New York: Simon & Brown.

Swain, Carol M. 1995. *Black Faces, Black Interests: The Representation of African Americans in Congress* (Enlarged Edition). Cambridge, MA: Harvard University Press.

Swers, Michele L. 2002. *The Difference Women Make: The Policy Impact of Women in Congress.* Chicago: University of Chicago Press.

Tate, Katherine. 2003. *Black Faces in the Mirror: African Americans and Their Representatives in the U.S. Congress.* Princeton, NJ: Princeton University Press.

Tate, Katherine. 2010. "Black Radical Voices and Policy Effectiveness in the U.S. Congress." *The Forum* 8(2): article 5.

Thaler, Richard H., and Cass R. Sunstein. 2008. *Nudge: Improving Decisions about Health, Wealth, and Happiness.* New Haven, CT: Yale University Press.

Thomas, Sue. 1992. "The Effects of Race and Gender on Constituency Service." *The Western Political Quarterly* 45(1): 169–180.

Thomas, Sue. 1994. *How Women Legislate*. New York: Oxford University Press.

Thomas, Sue. 2005. "Cracking the Glass Ceiling." In Sue Tolleson-Rinehart and Jyl J. Josephson (eds.). *Gender and American Politics: Women, Men, and the Political Process*. Armonk, NY: M.E. Sharpe (pp. 242–262).

Thomas, Sue, and Susan Welch. 1991. "The Impact of Gender on Activities and Priorities of State Legislators." *Western Political Quarterly* 44(2): 445–456.

Thomas, Sue, and Susan Welch. 2001. "The Impact of Women in States Legislatures: Numerical and Organizational Strength." In Susan Carroll (ed.). *The Impact of Women in Public Office*. Bloomington: Indiana University Press (pp. 166–183).

Truman, David B. 1951. *The Governmental Process: Political Interests and Public Opinion*. New York: Alfred A. Knopf.

Truman, David B. 1956. "The State Delegations and the Structure of Party Voting in the United States House of Representatives." *American Political Science Review* 50(4): 1023–1045.

Volden, Craig, and Elizabeth Bergman. 2006. "How Strong Should Our Party Be? Party Member Preferences over Party Cohesion." *Legislative Studies Quarterly* 31(7): 71–104.

Volden, Craig, and Alan E. Wiseman. 2011a. "Breaking Gridlock: The Determinants of Health Policy Change in Congress." *Journal of Health Politics, Policy and Law* 36(2): 227–264.

Volden, Craig, and Alan E. Wiseman. 2011b. "Formal Approaches to the Study of Congress." In Eric Schickler and Frances E. Lee (eds.). *Oxford Handbook of Congress*. Oxford: Oxford University Press (pp. 36–65).

Volden, Craig, Alan E. Wiseman, and Dana E. Wittmer. 2013a. "When Are Women More Effective Lawmakers than Men?" *American Journal of Political Science* 57(2): 326–341.

Volden, Craig, Alan E. Wiseman, and Dana E. Wittmer. 2013b. "Women's Issues and Their Fates in Congress." CSDI working paper 07–2013, Vanderbilt University.

Wawro, Gregory. 2001. *Legislative Entrepreneurship in the U.S. House of Representatives*. Ann Arbor: University of Michigan Press.

Wawro, Gregory J., and Eric Schickler. 2004. "Where's the Pivot? Obstruction and Lawmaking in the Pre-Cloture Senate." *American Journal of Political Science* 48(4): 758–774.

Wawro, Gregory J., and Eric Schickler. 2006. *Filibuster: Obstruction and Lawmaking in the U.S. Senate*. Princeton: Princeton University Press.

Waxman, Henry, with Joshua Green. 2009. *The Waxman Report: How Congress Really Works*. New York: Hachette Book Group.

Weingast, Barry R., and William Marshall. 1988. "The Industrial Organization of Congress." *Journal of Political Economy* 91: 765–800.

Weissert, Carol S. 1991a. "Issue Salience and State Legislative Effectiveness." *Legislative Studies Quarterly* 16(4): 509–520.

Weissert, Carol S. 1991b. "Determinants and Outcomes of State Legislative Effectiveness." *Social Science Quarterly* 72(4): 797–806.

Whitby, Kenny J. 2002. "Bill Sponsorship and Intraracial Voting among African American Representatives." *American Politics Research* 30(1): 93–108.

Whitby, Kenny J., and Franklin D. Gilliam, Jr. 1991. "A Longitudinal Analysis of Competing Explanations for the Transformation of Southern Congressional Politics." *Journal of Politics* 53(2): 504–518.

Whitby, Kenny J., and George Krause. 2001. "Race, Issue Heterogeneity, and Public Policy: The Republican Revolution in the 104th U.S. Congress and the Representation of African-American Policy Interests." *British Journal of Political Science* 31(3): 555–572.

White, Joseph. 2011. "Muddling through the Muddled Middle." *Journal of Health Politics, Policy and Law* 36(3): 444–448.

Wilkerson, John, Nick Stramp, and Jeremy Dashiell. 2012. "Tracing the Flow of Policy Ideas in Legislature: A Computational Approach." Conference paper. Annual Meetings of the Midwest Political Science Association, Chicago.

Williams, J. 1983 (January 5). "Reagan Signs Orphan Drug Bill Despite Reservations." *The Washington Post*, p. A1.

Wilson, James Q. 1980. *The Politics of Regulation*. New York: Basic Books.

Wilson, Rick K., and Cheryl D. Young. 1997. "Cosponsorship in the U.S. Congress." *Legislative Studies Quarterly* 22(1): 25–43.

Wiseman, Alan E. 2005. "Partisan Strategy and Support in State Legislative Elections: The Case of Illinois." *American Politics Research* 33(3): 376–403.

Wiseman, Alan E. 2006. "A Theory of Partisan Support and Entry Deterrence in Electoral Competition." *Journal of Theoretical Politics* 18(2): 123–158.

Wiseman, Alan E., and John R. Wright. 2008. "The Legislative Median and Partisan Policy." *Journal of Theoretical Politics* 20(1): 5–30.

Woellert, Lorraine. 2008 (November 21). "Waxman Win Is a Boon for Environmentalists, Bust for Utilities." Retrieved from www.bloomberg.com, accessed May 23, 2014.

Wooden, John. 2005. *Wooden on Leadership: How to Create a Winning Organization*. New York: McGraw-Hill.

Woon, Jonathan. 2008. "Bill Sponsorship in Congress: The Moderating Effect of Agenda Positions on Legislative Proposals." *Journal of Politics* 70(1): 201–216.

Index

Lightning Source UK Ltd.
Milton Keynes UK
UKHW021044190421
382146UK00024B/892